Hermann von Wissmann, Minna J. A Bergmann

My second Journey through Equatorial Africa from the Congo to the Zambesi

In the Years 1886 and 1887

Hermann von Wissmann, Minna J. A Bergmann

My second Journey through Equatorial Africa from the Congo to the Zambesi
In the Years 1886 and 1887

ISBN/EAN: 9783744757232

Printed in Europe, USA, Canada, Australia, Japan

Cover: Foto ©Andreas Hilbeck / pixelio.de

More available books at **www.hansebooks.com**

FROM THE CONGO TO THE ZAMBESI

PRINTED BY
SPOTTISWOODE AND CO., NEW-STREET SQUARE
LONDON

PORTRAIT OF MAJOR VON WISSMANN

MY SECOND JOURNEY

THROUGH

EQUATORIAL AFRICA

from the Congo to the Zambesi

IN THE YEARS 1886 AND 1887

BY

HERMANN VON WISSMANN

TRANSLATED FROM THE GERMAN BY

MINNA J. A. BERGMANN

*WITH A MAP BY F. S. WELLER AND 92 ILLUSTRATIONS AFTER
DRAWINGS BY R. HELLGREWE AND KLEIN-CHEVALIER*

London

CHATTO & WINDUS, PICCADILLY

1891

PREFACE

In accordance with my habit since the year 1880, I am now visiting Germany only that I may recover from the fatigues of my work in Africa, and in order to gather new strength for further exploration of the Dark Continent.

In spite of my having on account of illness as well as of business very little spare time during my four months' stay at home, I resolved to write down as a simple reproduction of my diaries the most noteworthy facts of my second journey through Africa. We can never know whether we may return from those uncivilised regions; and for this reason, and since my last work—the suppression of the East African rebellion—suggests my publishing further accounts at a later period, I have written the following pages, which I beg the reader to accept as a simple narrative of my experiences and observations.

The present publication of my diaries is partly owing to the fact that the terrors incidental to the slave-hunt and to the transport of the unfortunate human chattels are illustrated in the following pages, and I can only hope that I may be enabled to excite the reader's interest in, and sympathy for, those nations which still groan under the yoke of barbarism, and which certainly have a right to our help and protection.

H. VON WISSMANN.

LAUTERBERG : *October* 30, 1890.

CONTENTS

CHAPTER I

FROM THE COAST TO THE BASHILANGE COUNTRY

Return to Africa—My task there—My encountering Kund and Tappenbeck—Why I chose the name of 'Cassai'—Unfavourable beginning Buffalo hunt—A snake-bite- To the mouth of the Cassai—Elephants—Up the Cassai—Waste of waters—Venerable tombs –Abundance of game—Effect of a whistle—Tropical luxuriancy—Mount Pogge— Kund's crossing the Cassai — Nine affluents—Tipsy natives--Picturesque canoe expedition -- The natives' way of life—On the Sankurru—A landslip—Still life of the desert—How I met Dr. Wolf 1

CHAPTER II

DR. LUDWIG WOLF'S EXPLORATION OF THE SANKURRU— RETURN OF THE BASHILANGE TO THEIR NATIVE COUNTRY

Foundation of Luebo station — Luluaburg — Exploration of the Sankurru—The condition of the 'En Avant'—Savage steersmen —Effect of a glaring colour—Brass and copper, African gold—Intimidation of some Bassange for their impudence—'The Sankurru is good, the Lubilash wicked'—Zappu Zapp— Caution ! On the Lubi—The 'En Avant' in danger—A new river—Lomami ?— Average—Ethnography—At the station 37

CHAPTER III

DISCOVERING WISSMANN FALL AND WORK AT THE STATION

Progress of Luebo station—Patrol on the Muicau—Encountering faithful Bugslag—Luluaburg, a centre of civilisation—Plantations—The breeding of cattle—Meteorological observations—With Kalamba—Saturnino de Machado—Hostile Chipulumba—Punishment of some of our soldiers—Up the Cassai with Wolf—An uninhabited wilderness—Tormenting bees—Bars in the river—Wissmann Fall—Wild boars—Falling trees—Missed the 'Stanley'—At the station—Separation from Wolf—Punishment of a chief—Balundu—Ambassadors—Settling political difficulties at Lubuku—Distribution of the Star-Flag—My influence over the Bashilange—Kalamba's visit—Spectacle snake . . . 58

CHAPTER IV

EXPEDITION TO THE UPPER RIVER BASIN OF THE SANKURRU—LUBILASH

Collecting the escort for the journey—A good shot—A terrier trying to attack a hippopotamus—Plundering by my men—Æolian bells—The savage Balungu—Put on the wrong track—The Kanjoka—Dancing women—Boundary of the pure Baluba—Threats—Dense population—On the Bushi Maji—Insolence of the natives—War—Effect of the report of a gun—Treacherous Baluba—Falsehoods of the Balungu—Fruitless negotiations—Warlike expedition to punish our insolent enemies—A hundred prisoners and a large booty—Want of ammunition—My resolve to return—The inhospitable Baluba country—A dangerous retreat—Fair—Bad state of health—At Luluaburg—Conflagration—Le Marinel's dangerous illness 94

CHAPTER V

REGULATION OF POLITICAL AFFAIRS AT LUBUKU—DEPARTURE FOR THE NORTH-EAST—THE JOURNEY TO THE SANKURRU

Meeting of the chiefs of Lubuku—Heavy hail-storm—My fruitless search for Germano—Dr. Sommers—Germano at last—Departure for our long journey to the North-East—Camp building—Robberies and skirmish—Prairies—Villages set on fire—Pacific

welcome—Slave trade of the Bihé people—Primæval forests—
Inhospitable savages—On the Lubi—Simão's gallant swimming
expedition—Punishment of the rapacious Ngongo—A thief
punished by an arrow-shot—On the Sankurru . . . 131

CHAPTER VI

PRIMÆVAL FOREST—HOME OF THE DWARFS—DEPOPULATED COUNTRIES

The Lussambo—Cheating—Beautiful river scenery—First news of
the Arabs—Primæval forest—Batetela—Batua, the so-called
Dwarfs—Negotiations with the Batua—Nothing but primæval
forest—Christmas in the dark—With the Bena Mona—Murder
with poisoned arrows—Critical moment—War—Building of a
bridge—Lukalla—Hunger—Missed an anaconda—Bad reports
about the countries before us—The ravaging slave-hunters—The
exterminating Arab—Duties of the civilised world in protection
of the defenceless Africans—Extermination of a great nation—
With Lupungu and Mona Kakesa—Sale of ammunition—The
large town of the Peshi desolated 156

CHAPTER VII

THE ARABS—FAMINE AND ILLNESS

Camp of a troop of Tibbu Tibb's Zanzibaris—Said, the leader of
the warlike expedition—Said aiming at prisoners in his pistol
practice—Cannibalism in the camp of the Arabs—Sad condition of
my caravan—A man rising from the dead—Many sick people—
On the Lomami—The caravan well-nigh exhausted—The Arabs'
form of government—Hungry people eating poisonous fruits—
Inundations—Everything gloomy—Amputations—Some people
missing—Bridge formed of brushwood—Small-pox—The weakest
part of the army left behind—Losses—Reports about hostilities
between the Arabs and the Congo State—Bad prospects—At
Nyangwe—Hidden threats—Tibbu Tibb's son subjecting me to
an examination—Suspicion against me—Famba's aid—My
Bashilange sent home uninjured—I remain in the Arabs' power
—Separation from Le Marinel and my caravan . . . 196

CHAPTER VIII

AM OBLIGED TO TRAVEL EASTWARD—JOURNEY TO THE TANGANYIKA

Famba's disclosures—Stores of ivory—In the lion's den—'White men are cowards'—Thwarting of my plans—The murderer of a German—The past and present recollections of an old chief—I feel very weak—The places of encampment poisoned by the corpses of slaves—Sad reflections—Apathy of my people—Horrors of the traffic in slaves—On the Tanganyika 230

CHAPTER IX

TO THE NYASSA

Warning against going to the coast—At Ujiji—My going to the south—My exhausted Baluba left with the missionaries—The lake and its discharge—Night journeys—Storm—Mpala—Correct proceeding of the missions—Galula's death—Leopards—Baboons—Progress by land—Water banks—Flight of some carriers—Superstition—Extortions—Wawemba murderers—Scotch mission—Mr. Bain on Ethnology—On the Nyassa—Clouds of insects . . 249

CHAPTER X

TO THE COAST

The Nyassa—The banks abound in game—The Arabs on the lake—Livingstonia—Shiré—Mandala and Blantyre—I am ill—The negroes' deficiency in skill—The journey on the Shiré resumed—Crocodiles and hippopotami—Struggle with a huge heron—Bugslag's true companionship—Portuguese outpost—The Zambesi—Mrs. Livingstone's grave—On the Quaqua—Quilimane—Conclusion 282

APPENDIX I

LETTER OF LE MARINEL ON THE RETURN OF THE BASHILANGE TO THEIR COUNTRY 301

APPENDIX II

THE BASHILANGE COUNTRY 306

INDEX 319

ILLUSTRATIONS

FULL-PAGE

PORTRAIT OF MAJOR VON WISSMANN	*Frontispiece*
STILL LIFE OF THE CASSAI	*To face p.* 14
EFFECT OF THE STEAM-WHISTLE OF THE 'PEACE'	,, 20
WISSMANN POOL	,, 22
STAFF-PHYSICIAN DR. LUDWIG WOLF	,, 38
A RACE WITH THE 'EN AVANT'	,, 42
WOLF'S MEETING WITH ZAPPU ZAPP	,, 46
ARTICLES MANUFACTURED BY THE LUSSAMBO	,, 50
A 'MOHO' AT KALAMBA'S	,, 70
WISSMANN FALL	,, 78
RECEPTION BY THE KANJOKA LADIES	,, 106
DISTURBANCE ON THE BUSHI MAJI	,, 114
A DANCING KASHAMA	,, 126
OUR RECEPTION BY THE BAQUA SEKELAI	,, 114
MARCH THROUGH THE PRIMÆVAL FOREST	,, 162
ETHNOLOGICAL ARTICLES :—IDOL OF THE BALUBA FROM THE LUALABA — BELT OF THE BENECKI—PLUMES OF THE BASSONGO-MINO — PIPE AND TOBACCO OF THE BENA RIAMBA—CALABASHES	,, 172
AT KAFUNGOI	,, 182
THE ARABS AMONG THE BENECKI	,, 186

MONA LUPUNGU BRINGS A PRESENT OF SLAVES	*To face p.*	188
SAID'S PISTOL PRACTICE	,,	202
CROSSING THE CONGO-LUALABA	,,	222
TRANSPORT OF SLAVES	,,	244
FEEDING SLAVES	,,	246
NEAR MTOA, ON THE TANGANYIKA	,,	248
A STIFF BREEZE	,,	256
STORMY NIGHT-QUARTERS	,,	258
LEOPARDS ON THE TANGANYIKA	,,	262
THE MAWEMBA ELECTING A CHIEF	,,	276
BANKS OF THE NYASSA	,,	284
BANKS OF THE SHIRÉ	,,	288
THE SEVENTY-FIFTH CROCODILE	,,	298
TYPES OF THE BASHILANGE	,,	312

ILLUSTRATIONS IN THE TEXT

	PAGE
BANANA, AT THE MOUTH OF THE CONGO	1
A BUFFALO HUNT	9
ELEPHANTS IN THE CONGO	11
TOMBS OF THE WABUMA CHIEFS	16
A JOURNEY ON A HIPPOPOTAMUS	18
MOUNT POGGE	23
KUND AND TAPPENBECK'S PLACE OF ENCAMPMENT ON THE CASSAI	25
MY MEETING WITH DR. WOLF	35
LUEBO STATION	37
ON THE LUBI	48
THE LUKENJA-LOMAMI	50
HUTS OF THE BENA-YEHKA	53
BETWEEN LUEBO AND LULUABURG	58

ILLUSTRATIONS

	PAGE
LULUABURG	68
CHIRILU FALL	72
THE CROSS IN THE CASSAI	76
A WELCOME MEAL	81
A DISAGREEABLE SURPRISE	92
CAPTAIN DE MACAR	95
LULUMBA FALL	96
A HEROIC TERRIER	98
VILLAGE OF THE BENA WITANDA	100
ÆOLIAN HARPS	102
FARMS OF THE KALOSH	108
A KALOSH	110
RETURN FROM THE FIGHT	118
JUNGLES OF PANDANUS	128
BETWEEN LULUA AND MOANSANGOMMA	132
CROSSING THE LUBUDI	140
GRASS SAVANNAH	141
A SMELTING FURNACE OF THE BENA LUKOBA	143
SIMÃO, THE GALLANT SWIMMER	152
CROSSING THE LUKALLA	157
VALLEY OF THE SANKURRU	160
ETHNOLOGICAL ARTICLES: HAMPER, DRUM, AND SHIELD OF THE BASSONGE—HATCHETS AND SPEARS OF THE BALUBA	161
WITH BUGSLAG AND THE DWARFS	166
IN THE VALLEY OF THE LUKASSI	194
ENTRANCE INTO SAID'S CAMP	197
INTERIOR OF SAID'S CAMP	199
PALMS ON THE LOMAMI	206
ELEPHANT ON THE KALUI	211
BUILDING A BRIDGE	215
LIEUTENANT LE MARINEL	228

	PAGE
JUMA BIN SALIM'S IVORY	231
NEIGHBOURHOOD OF KASSONGO	234
PASSING THE ILINDI	237
ON THE TANGANYIKA	249
CAMP ON THE LUKUGA	257
FRIGHTENED BABOONS	263
BETWEEN TANGANYIKA AND NYASSA	266
WATCH-TOWER NEAR BISSISSI	267
OUR PARTY	282
STRUGGLE WITH A GIGANTIC HERON	294
'OUT OF THE WATER CREPT A LARGE CROCODILE'	296
HARBOUR OF QUILIMANE	299
A BASHILANGE CONCERT	307
BASHILAMBOA	309

MAP

WISSMANN'S THREE EXPEDITIONS TO EQUATORIAL AFRICA, 1880-1887 . . *To face p.* 1

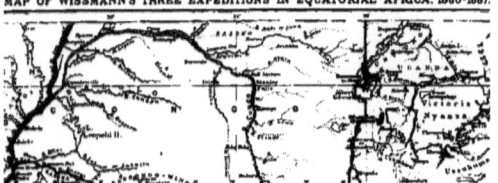
MAP OF WISSMANN'S THREE EXPEDITIONS IN EQUATORIAL AFRICA, 1880-1887.

BANANA, AT THE MOUTH OF THE CONGO

THROUGH EQUATORIAL AFRICA

CHAPTER I

FROM THE COAST TO THE BASHILANGE COUNTRY

Return to Africa—My task there—My encountering Kund and Tappenbeck—Why I chose the name of 'Cassai'—Unfavourable beginning—Buffalo hunt—A snake-bite—To the mouth of the Cassai—Elephants—Up the Cassai—Waste of waters—Venerable tombs—Abundance of game—Effect of a whistle—Tropical luxuriancy—Mount Pogge—Kund's crossing the Cassai—Nine affluents—Tipsy natives—Picturesque canoe expedition—The natives' way of life—On the Sankurru—A landslip—Still life of the desert—How I met Dr. Wolf.

THE fatigues I had undergone during the time of the travels described in my work 'Im Innern Afrikas' had wasted my energy to such an extent that I was obliged, in September 1885, to leave Africa in order to gain new strength in a more congenial climate.

After a nine weeks' sojourn in Madeira, perhaps chiefly owing to my being dosed with arsenic, I felt so much better that I began to think of resuming my work. Through the medium of H.R.H. the Crown Prince of Germany, I had two years previously received a commission from the King of the Belgians, to whom I was under an obligation of another year's service. But, as I was desirous of turning to account my experiences in the newly established German colonies, I applied to his Royal Highness, inquiring whether in any of the German possessions my services might be of value; in which case I begged his Royal Highness, by his gracious intercession, to get me released from further obligations. I was told in reply that, for the present, there would be no work for me in our possessions, and that the King of the Belgians had expressed a special desire that I should return to Africa once more, which desire his Majesty then communicated to me himself. I was given my choice, either to undertake the entire administration of the Inner Congo State, from Stanley Pool upward, or to carry on my work as before, in which latter case I received the following directions.

In taking advantage of the favourable state of political affairs, I was to open the Baluba country to any further undertakings south of the Congo State, and to make the native tribes to the south, the northeast, and eventually to the eastern boundary of the Congo State, acquainted and satisfied with their new political situation.

I was to investigate and, if possible, to counteract the proceedings of the slave-hunters, and report about what I thought of the countries south-east of the Congo State with respect to their cultivation. This was all the more important as I was the only European who had traversed the Congo State by land. It is evident that on such journeys it is far easier to form an estimate of a country than in travelling by water, as one is then able only to judge of the fertile districts on the riverside, besides having naturally much less intercourse with the natives than when one travels in the interior.

In undertaking the administration of the Inner Congo State, I should have been compelled to subordinate myself to the Governor-General of the State. For these reasons I decided upon further investigations of the Inner Congo State, as this would leave me entirely independent and solely responsible.

As mentioned at the end of my work 'Im Innern Afrikas,' I had, when on account of illness obliged to quit the Congo, resigned the command of my expedition to Staff Physician Dr. Ludwig Wolf. Of my former attendants, he was joined only by the shipwright Bugslag and the gunsmith Schneider; Lieutenant von François had left the expedition before, and the 'Forstreferendar' Müller had returned to Europe on sick leave.

I left Madeira on January 8, 1886, and towards the end of the month reached Banana, at the mouth of the Congo, just at the time when the former Administrator-General, Sir Francis de Winton, resigned the government of the Congo State to his successor, Mr. Jansen, a Belgian. From the latter—who had taken the Baluba who had conducted me down to the Congo, while exploring the Cassai, back to their country—I learned that the transport on the river steamer had been accomplished without mishap, and that Wolf had begun to carry out my instructions, to which I shall refer later on.

After a short delay at Banana, Boma, and Vivy, I started for Stanley Pool. The beginning of the journey was by no means promising. The march over rugged mountains between Matadi and Pallaballa during the hottest season brought on a rather serious cough, that obliged me to continue my journey in a hammock. On the first or second day's march I met my German friends, Kund and Tappenbeck, homeward bound. The former was still suffering from the wound he had received on the Cassai, not far from the place where a year ago I had to encounter a severe struggle with the treacherous Bassongo-Mino when investigating the said river.

The report of both these gentlemen, especially with regard to their observations of the southern affluents of the Cassai, and the place where they had crossed the river, hardly agreed with my recollections, which may partly be ascribed to the circumstance that the different tribes know the watercourses by different names, partly to the fact that Lieutenant Kund's instruments of observation had suffered so much during the transport as to disable him from ascertaining astronomically where he crossed the Cassai.

Kund called the Cassai 'Sankurru,' as the natives give it this name at the place where he crossed it. I take this opportunity to mention that I consider it both unjustifiable and unreasonable that several cartographers, from the evidence of these officers, though they had crossed the river only in one place, have given this river the name of 'Sankurru,' whilst I, who have explored it in its full length, have called it 'Cassai.' Nor have I chosen this name without reason. This largest tributary of the Congo, a river to whose volume of water not one European river can possibly be compared, has, in its whole course, a succession of different names. Livingstone, in its upper course, calls it 'Cassabi' and 'Loka;' farther on, in its middle course, it is called 'Cassai,' which name it retains through its longest stretch. After this the names vary continually: first it is called 'Nsaire,' 'Nsadi,' 'Nshale,' 'Loko,' 'Nsali-Monene;' then, after receiving the Sankurru, its largest tributary—which, however, has not half the volume of water the Cassai has—it is called 'Sankurru,' 'Shankolle,' afterwards 'Shari,' 'Nsari,' 'Nshale-Mele,' and 'Qua.'

Later measuring proved that I had always kept in sight that part of the river system that had the greatest mass of water, which in sailing down a river is quite a chance. As for the name of this immense water-artery, it could only either be 'Cassai' or 'Nsaire;' but, the Congo itself being repeatedly called 'Nsaire' by the tribes living near its lower course, and this name also being adopted by the Portuguese, I decided upon that of 'Cassai,' and must, therefore, request the cartographers to put it in their maps.

My two brother-officers, after having given me all those articles they could possibly do without, since they would soon reach civilised parts, left us with their best wishes. And now, while the incidents of this leave-taking are still vividly present to my mind, one of them is no longer among the living. Tappenbeck, after indefatigable toil, at last succumbed to the tropical climate; whilst the other is only now recovering from a tedious illness, the consequence of his fatiguing African work.

My constitution, usually proof against any tropical changes, seemed to disappoint me this time. My cough continued, and the heat, intense even for those parts, and combined with heavy rains, brought on a good deal of fever.

On February 23 I arrived at Leopoldville, on Stanley Pool. I had ordered the 'Peace,' belonging to the English mission, and the only steamer then at liberty, to be detained for a few days, and then made the following arrangement with Mr. Grenfell, who was most obliging in meeting my wishes.

The 'Peace' immediately started for the Equator Station, and thence returned to Quamouth, at the mouth of the Cassai, where I was eventually to go in a rowing barge. Then she was to pick me up and take me up the rivers Cassai and Lulua, into the Baluba country. As I wanted the Germans of my expedition who were staying there to go with me, I requested the Administration of the Congo State to send me some of their officers to take charge of the stations of Luluaburg and Luebo; at the same time they were to bring such provisions as the 'Peace' was not large enough to take in. Besides Lieutenant Bateman, who was in attendance on Dr. Wolf, Captain de Macar and Lieutenant Le Marinel were placed at my disposal.

From my substitute in the Baluba country we learned, meanwhile, that he had formed a station below the rapids of the Lulua, on the mouth of the Luebo, which he had given into the charge of Lieutenant Bateman, an Englishman of the Congo State, while my faithful Bugslag was head of Luluaburg. Wolf himself decided upon taking the steamer 'En Avant,' which had been assigned to him for the investigation of the Sankurru.

At Leopoldville we passed the time in preparations for the journey and in hunting expeditions, with the product of which—a few hippopotami—I prepared several days of feasting for the black garrison.

This reminds me of a buffalo hunt, which I take the opportunity of mentioning as an obvious proof that rules for hunting African game should be given only with caution.

Towards evening I posted myself on the largest island in the middle of Stanley Pool, a spot that, on account of its many puddles, is favourable for, and often frequented by, the buffalo. Shortly before sunset a clumsy old buffalo bull (*Bos euryceros*) came tramping out of the thicket into the clearing where I had posted myself behind an ant-hill. This buffalo was remarkable for its colour. It was of a brownish black, whilst the back and hind legs were speckled white. On inquiring I was told by a native that bulls were often speckled like that, while the females were invariably ruddy-coloured and considerably smaller. The bull was enormously fat and short-legged, and had evidently strayed from his herd. He seemed to be following the scent of a herd, and approached me to within about sixty metres, when, apparently scenting me, he stopped short. Being still very weak, I put my heavy rifle on the shoulder of one of my negroes and aimed at the low-bent brow of the animal. In consequence of an involuntary movement of my attendant I missed my aim, and the buffalo galloped past me towards the right. I had meanwhile seized my small double-barrelled gun (calibre 500) and aimed at the animal's shoulder-blade. He jumped up high, but kept running in the same direction, when my second barrel laid him low. When my attendants noticed that the buffalo tried in vain to get up, they rushed upon him with knives to stab him, notwithstanding my shouts of warning. No sooner were they within a short distance of the bull than he managed to get up again, and instead of rushing upon his assailants he disappeared in the thicket.

I now stopped my attendants and encamped for the night, in order to hit off the scent again next morning, it having already grown quite dark. At daybreak we traced the wounded animal, who had evidently lain down at intervals of about 100 metres. He seemed to have reached the island and tried to swim to the opposite bank. As we could not find any further trace of him, we conjectured that his strength had given way while swimming, and that he had floated down the river. I had certainly very rarely found that a wounded buffalo-bull, and especially a single one, abstained from attacking his assailant when face to face with him.

Before leaving Leopoldville for Madeira I met with a strange accident, which I must not neglect to mention. One evening I had fallen asleep in a travelling chair with a blanket across my knees; I must have stirred in my sleep, as I was awakened by a painful sting in my hand, just in time to see a snake, that had likewise taken up its night-quarters in my blanket, glide from my knees

A BUFFALO HUNT

to the ground and disappear in a hole. My hand began to bleed in the two places where the snake had inserted its fangs, and, as I knew this species to be venomous,

I bound the joints of my fingers, my hand, and elbow with a handkerchief before I sent for the doctor, who cut out the bite and cauterised the wound with hypermanganesiate of potassa. Chiefly owing to my having bound the joints at once, I did not notice any bad effects from the venom. This case is especially worthy of notice because of the singular boldness of the snake, for it is a fact that, as a rule, a venomous snake avoids going near human beings, and only bites when touched, especially while it is asleep and when it feels obliged to defend itself. I have cured a number of snake-bites myself, and know of only one case that ended fatally —one in which the wound was not bound, and where half an hour elapsed before help could be procured. For snake districts I greatly recommend little glass tubes filled with sal-ammoniac, hermetically sealed at either end. One end of the tube has to be broken and pushed into the wound, and after doing this the patient should also be dosed with from eight to ten drops of the same liquid in a glass of water. Strong doses of alcohol, even to intoxication, are also an excellent remedy against the effects of a snake-bite.

On March 9 I left Leopoldville in a small boat that had arrived meanwhile to take me to the mouth of the Cassai, where I was to await the 'Peace.' I was joined by a Mr. Greshoff, of a Dutch firm that was about to establish a factory on the Luebo, and by the then head of Leopoldville station, Herr von Nimptsch, a former Prussian officer. The journey was a miserable one, the boat being no match for the current of the Congo. It was small and bare of every comfort; and we suffered much from the weather, the rainy season having set in with full force, and the boat affording no shelter from rain or sun.

The only pleasant break was the appearance of a herd of elephants on the northern bank, that abounds in game. The attempt to bag one or two was, as usual, thwarted by the negroes, who, being much more light-

ELEPHANTS IN THE CONGO

footed than the Europeans, approach the game more quickly and less cautiously.

Arrived at Quamouth, at the mouth of the Cassai, we learned that the 'Peace' was not due for a week, and we therefore decided to go upon a hunting expedition to a district on the Upper Congo, near the mouth of the Lefini, where game is plentiful. The first moonlight night a herd of elephants was seen wading through the stream above the camp. The huge beasts felt so secure that they had given themselves up to the enjoyment of bathing to their hearts' content. They were playfully racing through the shallow water, chasing each other in their delight, uttering shrieks such as I had never heard before. I crept to the edge of the wood near the bank, but was stopped by a lagoon which emptied itself there. I then rowed up the river in a canoe, making a large curve round the animals; and afterwards drifting up to them, I kept my gun ready to fire. The elephants marked their sense of my nearness by a suspicious snorting, whilst one of them cautiously drove the whole herd out of the water into a thicket. Now the gigantic beasts broke away towards the primæval forest close up to the camp-fires, when, frightened by the glare of the latter, they disappeared into the impenetrable thicket, whither to follow them would have been useless.

In spite of the numbers of elephants, buffaloes, and wild boars, I did not once get the chance of a shot, as it was impossible to creep along either in the primæval forest or in the long grass of the savannahs. I therefore returned without prey to Quamouth, where the 'Peace' arrived on March 20 to take me up the Cassai.

The Cassai, called, as before stated, Nsairi-Qua, both by the people living to the north, the Wayanzi, and the mixed tribes of the Wanfumu and the Bateke, narrowed itself to scarcely 200 metres. We hove the lead, and with a line of thirty-three metres found we were out of soundings. The brown waters were rapidly rolling into Father Congo. For more than a German mile down the river the brown colour of the water was for about a third of the breadth distinctly separated from the yellow. Besides large numbers of crocodiles, the soft-scaled tortoises are frequently met with and seen sailing in straight lines across the stream. At the narrow mouth of the Cassai the gentlemen at Quamouth station had a short time ago noticed traces of a disease among the hippopotami. For about a week large numbers of dead animals had daily been seen floating down the river.

On March 22, the birthday of our late Emperor William I., we started on our journey up the river. Besides the commander of the boat, the missionary Mr. Grenfell, we were accompanied by the above-named Herren Greshoff and von Nimptsch.

We next passed several spots where the water had, in going down, struck me from its frequent and sudden changes of colour. The light brown colour repeatedly alternated with one dark and ruddy, probably caused by strong currents below.

Being amply provided with fuel, we steamed on till dusk, and soon dropped anchor off an island covered with high grass. After dark the island, a pasture ground for hippopotami, was soon alive with them. I took a short moonlight walk with Herr von Nimptsch, and, disturbing them at their supper, we made these pachydermata scamper heavily away to their place of refuge. Only one of them seemed unwilling to be disturbed; he was standing in the deep grass, and warned us off by snorting rapidly. We tried to make him go on by throwing hard clods of earth at him, but as we did not succeed in moving him we decided upon retreating and leaving the irritated animal undisturbed.

Next day we passed into an almost inextricable net of channels separated by long-stretching grass-grown islands and banks. We had to keep carefully in the deep channels towards the right bank, as I remembered to have noticed in those on the left bank large stones that might have damaged the boat. The right bank, as we were told, is inhabited by the Wabuma, the left by the Wanfumu, although the existence of *homo sapiens* could scarcely be credited in the midst of this vast waste of water; nor have I anywhere else got the impression of so undisturbed a desert as in these parts. In this place it was that I with my attendants shot seven elephants and several hippopotami, so that our canoes could scarcely carry the meat which our men were supplied with for several months.

We could almost fancy we were transplanted into an antediluvian period. Fearless, as if man, the most dangerous beast of prey, were unknown in these regions, the huge pachydermata were moving about, while as a rule they only leave their protecting waters and the shadow of the primæval forest at night. Hippopotami were lying basking in the hot sun; elephants were marching along the river-side singly and in herds, occasionally bathing in the shallow places of the river; with buffaloes calmly walking among them. We also noticed an abundance of all sorts of birds—pelicans quietly waiting for their prey, flocks of different kinds of wild ducks which the lagoons were stocked with,

STILL LIFE OF THE CASSAI

beautiful black geese almost resembling swans, and the so-called spur-goose. On some dry branches on the bank were perched lurking cormorants and splendidly dyed kingfishers; the river eagle was seen proudly soaring along the bank; while white-headed vultures were perching on naked branches, and thousands of lesser birds, such as strand-runners, rails, and fish-hawks, were haunting the place. Different kinds of storks were gravely and solemnly stalking across the flooded islands, and on the bank the large heron was visible in the shade of some overhanging branches.

Apparently undisturbed peace is reigning everywhere among those thousands of different creatures, all enticed by the mighty stream, with its cooling floods and its abundance of animal life. Now and again the deep-toned voice of the *behemoth* makes the peaceful stillness resound, involuntarily causing one to start. Here one has to get accustomed to sounds that try one's nerves most painfully by their loudness and strangeness. That reminds me of the above-named elephant hunt in the same neighbourhood. We had killed only female animals and young ones, and were surprised not to have found one male among the lot, when in the dead of night the huge creatures came in search of their families. They stopped close to the camp, where the flesh of their mates was being dried by the bright fires. The scent of the blood must have convinced them of the loss they had sustained, for they raised a wailing sound so deep, so strange and mournful, that I was startled from my sleep and deeply touched with the singularly impressive tones.

At my request we landed in the evening at an island

noted for the interesting tombs of several chiefs of the Wabuma tribe. I conducted the gentlemen who were with me across a small farm, where an old negro who had charge of the tombs lived by himself. Then we passed into the dome-like forest, where the underwood, the ferns and amomum, a kind of jungle, had been cleared, and only the gigantic stems held the beautifully arched leafy roof that cast a deep shadow over the place. It felt almost cold here, and one of our companions most appropriately quoted, 'Und in Poseidons Fichtenhain tritt er mit frommem Schauder ein.' Thirty to forty large elephant-tusks marked the tombs; but the former had suffered much from the atmosphere and were decayed and damaged; nor was it possible to recognise the original shapes of the knives, spears, and arrows, once perhaps the weapons of those buried. The old sexton was evidently relieved when we left this

TOMBS OF THE WABUMA CHIEFS

interesting place without having desecrated the tombs by touching its relics. Next morning early we caught sight of a block of houses at Mushie, where we took in provisions. There was a large supply of manioc flour, maize, dried fish, fowls, and eggs. Close to the village our men found some gigantic trees with low hanging branches, and creeping up their stems some wild vines with immense grapes that were full of small blue berries. Although rather sour, the grapes were not bad; but after eating a good many of them they left a tickling sensation in the throat, so that, not having a botanist amongst us to tell us its proper name, we called them 'Krätzer.'

Just above the villages the Mfini empties its black waters into the brown Cassai. This river, because of the quantity of water near its mouth, may be compared to our river Saale. It shows this black colour after the discharge into it of Leopold Lake—which lake Stanley had discovered two years before my sailing down the Cassai. The Mfini, as stated by Kund and Tappenbeck, is in its upper course called Lukenja. A good distance upward the river is navigable, and if the natives' report may be relied on, it flows farther up through a still unknown lake. Its upper course is supposed to be only a few days' journey north-east from where the Lomami falls into the Sankurru.

We now turned to the left side of the Cassai, along which we intended to keep, and, if possible, to find the mouths of the southern tributaries, whose upper courses I crossed in 1881 and its middle courses in 1884. The best guide for finding the mouths of tributaries in such

C

wild districts is the colour of the water, as it is very rarely the case that tributaries have the same colour as the main stream, which is dyed by waters coming from many different directions.

Scarcely had we passed through the labyrinth of banks and islands, and across the river, at least seven kilometres broad, and reached the left bank, when, following the sudden darkening of the water upwards,

JOURNEY ON A HIPPOPOTAMUS

we entered a meandering watercourse of sixty metres breadth, that was flowing from east-south-east. We could only go up this rivulet for about two hours' journey, because we noticed some stones that would have endangered the comparatively large vessel. The small river Lua, three-and-a-half metres deep, was winding through an endless grass-plain towards its mouth in 3° 10′ south latitude.

Game was very plentiful on the plain. Some elephants were frightened four times at short intervals by the noise of our engine, and on turning I noticed a great number of these animals close to an ant-hill. A leopard was crossing the river immediately before us, but escaped our shots, as we could not get our guns ready before the beautiful beast had disappeared among the high reeds. Most comical it was to watch a hippopotamus that dared not venture to pass in the narrow river: now he kept rushing wildly on in the water, then galloped along the riverside in the hope of getting away from the ever-snorting steam monster that was incessantly pursuing him. I hit the animal at last, for later on, when we were sailing towards the Cassai, it was seen floating on the surface. Herr Greshoff shot a crocodile that was being carried down the river on the dead hippopotamus, and then we encamped to prepare the game for our negroes, who are very fond of the flesh of these animals.

Next day we proceeded along the left bank, and in the course of the forenoon we came upon some light brown water greatly differing from that of the Cassai. Off a large place named Jukissi we dropped anchor on the Quango, near the mouth of the Sali Mbi, which we had discovered when going down. The inhabitants of the village and surrounding farms assembled, and sold us large quantities of fuel and provisions.

Most of our negroes were at the village, when, all of a sudden, a commotion arose among the crowd of natives, and from their shouting and loud quarrelling tones we conjectured that our men were engaged in a dispute.

Mr. Grenfell, who had once seen the effect of the powerful voice of his 'Peace' when investigating the

Mubangi, now sounded the steam-whistle. The impression was again so overpowering that all the natives took to their heels in wild fear, disappearing in the thickets and rushing towards the village. Only one old white-haired Herculean chief, who was standing close to the river, felt ashamed to run, but was terrified to such a degree that he staggered backward, and only kept his footing by catching hold of a tree.

As soon as our crew had got on board we weighed anchor, and steamed up the Quango to find a place that would enable us to take a drawing of the river. About 800 metres above the village, the banks of the river, that on its mouth form a delta, began to rise to such a height that we supposed its waters were all concentrated in this part. We found the breadth to be 650 metres by an average depth of five-and-a-half metres, and a speed of seventy-five metres a minute. The ground was soft and sandy, and the temperature of the water was 81° (Fahrenheit)—scarcely one degree colder than that of the Cassai.

Several miles above the mouth of the Quango we once more passed into that wide lake-like opening to which, in going down, we had given the name of 'Wissmann Pool.'

It is remarkable how continually the scenery near a river changes. On entering Wissmann Pool, the grass islands and the endless prairie-like banks come to an end. Parts of a primæval forest of rattan and palm-trees come in sight, and in straight lines, like the veins in marble, islands lie intersected by deep branches of the river. These islands are covered with palms, of which the oil

EFFECT OF THE STEAM-WHISTLE OF THE 'PEACE'

species thrives particularly well, and covers the ground throughout, so as to make one suppose the islands to have formerly been palm plantations. In order to get a regular plantation of luxuriantly developed oil-palms, all that would be necessary would be to cut down the underwood and ferns, and somewhat clear the thickly-grown palms. Supposing the palm-oil, the product of such a plantation, to be put up in casks and floated straight down to Stanley Pool—where the Congo Railway, shortly to be completed, would undertake the further comparatively short transport—both islands and banks, closely grown with palms as they are, might yield, some day, great profit.

The terrain must be magnificent, the colours being so luxuriant, so deep and soft, as to give one an impression of very rich soil. At present the huge grapes fall off and rot away, unless some native happens to cut the tree to obtain the much-valued palm-wine and take possession of the grapes.

In the mornings and evenings, innumerable grey parrots make an almost deafening noise, and are silent only in the hot sun at noon. Even in moonlight nights this strange bird undertakes long excursions in large flocks, which noisily interrupt the stillness of night.

When next day, the 28th, we proceeded up the river, it struck us how differently the natives were disposed towards us. In some parts they pursued us down the bank with loud invectives and threats, and with bows bent; in others they beckoned to us, eagerly desiring to sell provisions, and altogether showing themselves most friendly. This was very likely owing to the passing of my expedition on its up journey. Wolf and a great number of Europeans who were with me had won over the natives by presents and purchases.

I am not entering into any details about the different tribes, which, though ascertained only by such superficial observation as we could make, have been given in the work 'Im Innern Afrikas,' which enlarges upon our sailing down and exploring the Cassai.

On the 29th we found the Cassai for a long way bare of islands, and took a drawing of the river thirteen knots above Wissmann Pool.[1] With 1,200 metres breadth and nine metres depth, we ascertained a speed of eighty metres a minute. After passing Wissmann Pool, the banks and islands showed thick forests, and with them the hippopotami grew more and more scarce from their now being in want of pasture. The last of them, being startled by our approach, was on the point of plunging into the water, when I fired and hit it when it was within a distance of a hundred metres, so that it fell in quite shallow water. This shot gained me the praise of the Europeans, and above all that of the negroes, who are always greedy for flesh. To produce such an effect is possible only when the shot penetrates the brain, which is of about the size of one's hand.

Henceforward we repeatedly met native islanders on the Cassai, but learned that their sojourn here was only transitory, during the time of the sugar harvest. From the sugar-cane they fabricate a highly intoxicating drink of a very pleasant acid taste. A number of such

[1] For the complete collection of sections *vide* Appendix II.

WISSMANN POOL

manufacturers called out to us one day, and, probably in the blissful mood caused by the consumption of their liquor, saluted us with dancing and singing, and on parting even presented us with a small pig that, having been cooked like a sucking-pig, we greatly enjoyed next day. Once, in order to vary the daily round of dinner, which generally consisted of either fish or fowl, we tried a fricassee of a young crocodile that I had shot, and we could not but own that the tender meat, in

MOUNT POGGE

flavour something between fish and fowl, is by no means to be despised.

As Mr. Grenfell was particularly desirous of terminating the journey as quickly as possible, we generally steamed until evening, and then set to work until it was dark in getting wood ready for next day's fuel. This time-absorbing business will not be necessary much longer, as the natives have taken the measure of the wood required, so as to have it always ready for sale at a cheap price to any passing steamer.

The only elevation amidst the uniform level of the banks of the Cassai—which in our descent we named Mount Pogge—is less conspicuous to those coming up than to those going down the river. It is probable that near this elevation a river from the north empties itself, but the number of channels prevented our making sure of it. One may, however, pretty certainly depend upon its being a branch of the Cassai, and not a separate river, whenever the water does not change colour.

We were now approaching the Bassongo-Mino tribe, whose treacherous attack and hostile fury we had severely punished on going down. Wherever we stopped to collect or purchase wood, the natives fled from their cottages, even if but one of us on some short excursion lighted upon a village. On one of these expeditions I could not resist the temptation of taking some new and interesting weapons and tools from such a deserted village. In place of them I put some bright-coloured handkerchiefs and beads, which amply made up for the value of the things annexed.

On April 2, after passing a bend of the river, we called out simultaneously, 'There is Kund and Tappenbeck's camp!' It was indeed a strange coincidence that the two officers had come upon the river in a spot that could not be passed unnoticed, as it is marked by two immense adansonias that are standing close to the river side, with their stems grown together, a few metres west from the mouth of a small brook. If those adansonias are not the only trees of this species that meet the traveller's eye on the Cassai, they are certainly the most striking. We landed here, and found the camp of our countrymen marked by some small grass sheds, besides a great many remnants of dried fish and the skull of an antelope. In order to mark the place for the future I cut with a hatchet a large and distinct 'K' into the largest adansonia. Astronomical observations made at the request of Kund proved the place to be in 3° 41' S. and 18° 41' E. We could not but acknowledge

KUND AND TAPPENBECK'S PLACE OF ENCAMPMENT ON THE CASSAI

that, considering the savageness of the natives, it was a laudable achievement, with so small and comparatively weak an expedition as Kund's was, to pass the stream in this spot, so immensely broad, intersected with banks and islands covered with reeds. On ascertaining the latitude of this place we proved that Kund's supposition of having passed the Quango and Quilu is right, and that the latter falls into the Quango, as between this passage and the mouth of the Quango we could not have missed the mouth of such an important river as the Quilu in its lower course must be.

When sailing down before Kund's expedition we had been struck with the above-named adansonias, which we accordingly made a note of. The latitude, as we ascertained at this place when last staying there, corresponds with that taken now by Grenfell, while on our map we marked the adansonias farther east in 19° 8'. The vicinity of Mount Pogge, which is conspicuous from a long distance, also confirms our supposition that Kund's expedition had been carried out north of the Cassai to the then quite unknown Lukenja.

After leaving this interesting place we had a very heavy fall of rain without thunder—according to our experience and the assertion of some fishermen, quite a singular circumstance.

Sailing up the left bank for two hours, we found the mouth of a river 200 metres broad, although the channel was only seventy metres in breadth; the excess being due to an overflow. The average speed was sixty metres a minute, the water was almost black, the bottom soft and boggy. We were not able to ascertain the name of this river, and avoided sailing upward, as, on account of the overflow and the dark waters, we could not distinguish whether we were keeping in the channel or moving in the inundated part. The source of this river must be in about 6° N., as south of this latitude the waters are divided between the Quilu and the Loange, which two rivers approach each other to within a short distance.

Next morning we again passed the mouth of a rivulet thirty metres broad. We were now in the Bakutu country, a branch of the savage tribe of the Bassongo-Mino that gave us so much trouble on going down. The numerous villages were emptied wherever the natives caught sight of us. The straight streets of the village were only enlivened by black pigs, which are bred here in large numbers, and by the African pariah dog, which is generally the same everywhere. The fishermen fled in hot haste, pushing their slender canoes ashore, and nothing could induce them to answer our questions; which greatly annoyed me, as I wanted to show some of the tribe that our fighting at the time had only been for the purpose of defending ourselves. The Bakutu seemed to be an exceptionally excitable race, as may be inferred from the following observation, which I made when going down. Nearly all the warriors killed in this battle were wounded not only by our balls but also by one of their own long javelins. This could not possibly be accidental, as on our side we had to record only very slight wounds. I therefore conjectured that the fleeing warriors would not allow any of their companions that they could not take with them to fall alive into our hands, and for this reason gave them the final thrust themselves.

When we reached the Bangodi country the natives gave us, on the whole, a friendly welcome; only in the village a dispute arose among some tipsy Bangodi and our men, whom they had robbed of a newly purchased fowl. The number of natives who, alarmed by the noise, appeared upon the scene with their arms increased, and the women disappeared. I went ashore to settle the dispute, called our men from among the crowd of natives, and sent them on before me to the bank, where the boat was in waiting for us. The Bangodi who had remained behind were mostly drunk; they took up a threatening position, and I, escorting our men, and not wishing to turn so as to show fear, walked backwards towards the boat with my cocked gun directed against the closely following natives. When the men who were watching us from the boat warned me that the excited natives meant violence, firing both the barrels of my gun would have scared them away. They, however, did not venture an attack, but only pursued me with their threats as I was walking in front of them, regardless of their uproar.

In the Bangodi country, instead of the oil palm generally met with on the banks, we found the fan palm, though apparently palms only grew on the islands and on the narrow tracts along the river. Further landward we saw nothing but wood, here and there relieved by places cleared for plantations.

On the 5th we again came upon the mouth of a dark brown river, the Sali-Lebue, sixty metres broad and on an average four metres deep, with a speed of seventy metres a minute. The bottom was soft and boggy, and the water had a temperature of 81° (Fahrenheit), the same as the Cassai had been found to have for some distance. According to the observations of my former expeditions across the upper tributaries of the Cassai, this river must likewise rise north of the sixth degree.

The Lebue forms the boundary between the Bangodi

and the numerous tribe of the Badinga. The latter are the most dexterous river navigators I know; a full-manned canoe, in which twelve men, standing behind each other, were handling oars of two metres' length, managed to keep up with the 'Peace.' Such a full-manned canoe is a beautiful sight, with the stalwart, muscular, dark-brown figures smoothly swinging their oars up and down so as to keep the plumes on their heads in wild motion. Resting one foot on the edge of the vessel, they made the slender canoe glide rapidly along the yellow water, singing in rough tones to the vigorous strokes of their oars. The Badinga always strike me as having particularly muscular thighs and calves. Their gait appears heavy, probably from their almost living on canoes. They have their plantations on islands or close to the river; the palms that furnish them with wine likewise grow near the water, and on their fishing expeditions they have to make use of a canoe.

The everyday life of the Badinga requires, on the whole, very little exercise besides rowing. In the morning the men, after having basked in the first rays of the sun, will inspect their weir-baskets, collect into their calabashes the wine that during the night has been gathering in the palms, and perhaps visit a neighbouring village on the river-side. Then they return home and partake of the meal meanwhile cooked by their wives, consisting of manioc porridge and roasted sweet potatoes, with dried fish, after which they give themselves up to the enjoyment of their palm-wine. Thus, in districts where the palm grows plentifully, you will often find the male part of the population in a state of intoxication. For this reason, therefore, it is not advisable to visit such countries in the afternoon, for the negro, when intoxicated, is easily inclined to quarrel; he will at such times even lose the timidity habitual to him; while, if you arrive in the morning, the people have not had time to get into their daily fit of drunkenness, and have enough to do in discussing the wonderful stranger and in preparing their sales. You will very seldom find tipsy women; they have too much work to do to be able to enjoy their wine undisturbed, as they have to manage the whole farm. Then they have the meals to cook for their lords and masters, to get the fish ready for drying, to keep their cottages clean—which is mostly done with the utmost neatness—and to perform those general duties that also fall to the share of our wives and mothers, though there is not much required of a mother here, the baby negroes being literally left to self-education.

We were struck by the wild rough tones of the Badinga voice, which, in the excitement of transacting business, assumes the most extraordinary modulations.

The Mudinga are inveterate traders. In some places, where probably those Europeans who had gone up with my Baluba had purchased weapons, the people brought everything for sale that they could lay hold of, as the white men will buy everything, down to large pieces of dry wood to line their canoes with.

The banks of the Cassai now begin to ascend to a level height of from thirty to fifty metres, and are covered with wood, unless where manioc and maize plantations, with their bright green foliage, contrast with the dark green tints of the primæval forest. They are densely populated. The stream often decreases in breadth; one may on an average calculate that at 800 metres the currents grow stronger, and in or behind the curves of the banks sand will collect and disappear with incredible rapidity. This sand consists of minute particles of very hard quartz, which if trodden upon produces a singing sound—and this highly amused the negroes of our party. When we landed in the evening close to the forest, which was partly overflowed by the waters of the Cassai, now at their greatest height, we had an opportunity of seeing an interesting hunt. On an ant-hill towering above the inundated ground we saw a lizard about the length of a hand creeping up to a tiny little shrew-mouse. The latter, spying the enemy, tried to escape, and at last jumped into the water, but was seized there by the pursuing lizard and dragged down into the deep.

On the 6th we entered the Sali-Temboa, so called after the junction of the Loange and Lushiko, from a southern direction; three kilometres above the mouth we found by measurement, with an average depth of three metres of water, a breadth of 100 metres, and a speed of 120 metres a minute: which allowed us to proceed but slowly. The bottom was partly sand, partly mud, and the water was so saturated with iron clay as to present a decided orange tint. Close to the mouth —formed by two channels, which together are 230 metres broad—the river, with the same rapidity, is only one-and-a-half to two metres deep.

A short distance above we came upon the huts, the only remnants of my down journey. They were one metre under water, which proves that since then the river had risen about one-and-a-half metre in its shallowest part.

On the 8th we reached the mouth of the Sankurru. On entering the southern branch of its mouth we learned from the natives that a small steamer (Dr. Wolf's 'En Avant') had a short time ago returned from a downward journey on the Sankurru to go up the Cassai. We found the stream to be joined above its delta, and ascertained a breadth of 450 metres by an average depth of five-and-a-half metres and a current of forty-five metres a minute. Sailing down the northern branches round the delta island, we found the current less rapid than during the dry season, when we could even make the iron boat go against the current of this branch.

The islands near the mouth of the Sankurru showed, as is always the case near the junctions of several rivers, a great deal of animal life. The number of hippopotami was as large as at the mouth of the Quango, and of crocodiles as well; one of which hit the boat such a blow as to make us fear that the screws might break. The length of one of these ravenous reptiles we estimated at fully eight metres, with a proportionate breadth and height.

In order to draw a parallel between the water mass of the Sankurru and that of the Cassai, we next day made measurements fifteen sea-miles above the mouth of the Sankurru. The breadth was 750 metres, the average depth seven-and-a-half metres, and the speed sixty-five metres a minute; the result of which is a water mass three times as large as that of the Sankurru.

Having been able to buy a good supply of firewood, we next day proceeded at full speed up stream towards the mouth of the Lulua. We were surprised to find that frequently in the bends of the river the banks had slipped, where they often descend perpendicularly into the water, from a height of twenty-five metres; once, far ahead, we even saw a whole wall of earth slip down, at the same time burying among the deep yellow waves a gigantic tree that had grown on the water's edge. The largest river boat would, if close to such a sliding mass, be dashed to pieces or capsized by the body of water that, after having first been stopped, rushes along with redoubled force.

The primæval forest was everywhere enlivened by numerous parrots and hosts of monkeys, but directly after sunset the deep silence of the desert prevails, which, as a European, you will never experience on your native continent. Be it imagination, be it excitement of the nerves, the slightest sound which at night interrupts the deep quiet seems to startle you. The piercing shrieks of the nocturnal monkey, the splashing of a fish pursued by a crocodile, or the deep thundering of the hippopotamus, causes the auricular nerves to be continually on the alert. On one of those quiet evenings I had encamped with my attendants near our landing-place, when a melodious hymn sung by many voices suddenly interrupted the dead silence. Mr. Grenfell, on board the 'Peace,' was having evening prayers, and I must confess that this solemn music under such circumstances produced the most elevating sensations.

On the 12th, at noon, we saw at a distance the mouth of the Lulua, which I had seen on a former occasion, and soon after I descried some white-robed figures close to the mouth. These latter could only be my people, for the Bakuba, as well as the Mukete and other native traders about here, have no white materials for clothing; their stuffs are only black or brown-red. On approaching, we actually discovered the steamer 'En Avant' immediately above the mouth of the Lulua with my men on board, who, excited at the approach of our vessel, were running to and fro, beckoning to us the while. A boat despatched by the 'En Avant' reached us just when we were casting anchor, and its occupant, the commander of the 'En Avant,' a gentleman from the Congo State under Dr. Wolf's command, informed us that Dr. Wolf, with the gunsmith Schneider, who had now taken the office of engineer on the 'En Avant,' had landed near the steamer. From his report it appeared that Dr. Wolf, after having terminated his expedition on the Sankurru, had been intending to explore that part of the Cassai which is above the mouth of the Lulua, when for the third time in this place the engine had been damaged to such an extent as to forbid every attempt at repair.

I landed at once, that I might find my old friend and comrade Wolf. He was just returning from an expedition; and, in our mutual sincere delight at meeting, we shook hands, and in a rapid discourse, carried on like

MY MEETING DR. WOLF

lightning, we made each other acquainted with the most interesting events since the time of our separation. I now learned that Wolf, after his return from Stanley Pool with the 'Stanley,' had stopped where the Luebo falls into the Lulua. As the Lulua was no longer navigable here, he had, assisted by the returning caravan, cleared the impenetrable primæval forest in a place suitable for the founding of a station, and by building huts and fortifications he had formed what was now the port of Luluaburg. Wolf had then marched up to Luluaburg, and had found the station, under the approved command of our faithful Bugslag, in an excellent condition, and had just been in time to join the joyful entrance of the returning Baluba into Kalamba's capital. After settling his business in Kalamba's country, he had returned to the Luebo, there to make preliminary arrangements for erecting the station; and then he had gone down in the 'En Avant' to the Sankurru to thoroughly explore the latter, with its river system. On his return from this expedition, he had again been at the Luebo; and two days before our meeting him here, on his way to explore the Cassai upward, he had broken down with his steamer.

My friend, alas! in the midst of his work in the Togo country on his march to Dahomey had succumbed to the fever. The contents of his diaries, placed at my disposal by his parents, are added in the next chapter, and give evidence of his valuable and ever-restless activity.

LUEBO STATION

CHAPTER II

DR. LUDWIG WOLF'S EXPLORATION OF THE SANKURRU—
RETURN OF THE BASHILANGE TO THEIR NATIVE COUNTRY

Foundation of Luebo station—Luluaburg—Exploration of the Sankurru
—The condition of the 'En Avant,'—Savage steersmen—Effect of a
glaring colour—Brass and copper, African gold—Intimidation of some
Bassange for their impudence—'The Sankurru is good, the Lubilash
wicked '—Zappu Zapp—Caution! On the Lubi—The 'En Avant' in
danger—A new river—Lomami?—Average—Ethnography—At the
station.

THE description of my second journey 'Im Innern Afrikas' and the exploration of the Cassai concludes with my departure for Madeira, which ill-health had made necessary. Before leaving I had installed Dr. Wolf, the oldest officer of my expedition, as commander.

After my leaving Stanley Pool, Wolf expedited the

construction of the largest Congo steamer, the 'Stanley,' so that he was able to start on October 5, 1885, to conduct our Bashilange, who had accompanied us on our exploration of the Cassai, back to their country. Besides the 'Stanley,' which, after disembarking the Bashilange, was immediately to return to Stanley Pool, the small steamer 'En Avant' was entrusted to Wolf.

The Bashilange had been great sufferers during their several months' stay at Stanley Pool, and many an ardent hemp-smoker had been carried off by inflammation of the lungs. So it was natural that their delight should be great on being embarked for their return to the Lulua, their beloved home. The two steamers took twenty-eight days in sailing up the river to where the Luebo falls into it, and above which the navigation is stopped by rapids. The whole passage was accomplished satisfactorily. The 'Stanley,' with very nearly 250 people on board, besides a great deal of luggage, went along splendidly, in spite of the medium depth of the water. On November 7 the boats cast anchor off a neck of land formed by the confluence of the Luebo and the Lulua, which was at the time covered with impenetrable forests. The first thing Wolf did was to clear a place that he thought suitable for building a station; and, as he had persuaded Kalamba and all his men to stay and assist him, the work was completed in a comparatively short time. In spite of their long absence from home, in spite of their longing to join their wives and children, the honest people, at Wolf's request, consented to stay with him for the present.

The surrounding tribes, by no means relishing the

STAFF-PHYSICIAN DR. LUDWIG WOLF

idea that the white men should settle there, were kept in check by their presence until the day of their departure, when they left the station in so favourable a condition that, with the remaining garrison, it could hold out against any attack of the Bakete or Bakuba.

Lieutenant Bateman, formerly an English officer, was placed under Wolf's command, and, with some of our soldiers and several Bashilange, remained at the Luebo, while Wolf accompanied Kalamba and his men. A five days' march brought him to Luluaburg, where he met Bugslag, who had meanwhile been improving the station in every respect. Wolf then entered Kalamba's residence in state, followed by Kalamba himself, Sangula, Chingenge, and their faithful attendants.[1]

When Wolf had given Bugslag directions for the next few months, he hastened back to the Luebo to hurry on the building of the new station and to start with the steamer 'En Avant,' which was placed at his disposal for the exploration of the tributaries of the Cassai, and, above all, of the Sankurru.

This really very old vessel, without even a deck, was in an extremely bad condition, as Wolf had not been allowed time to have it thoroughly repaired on the Congo, nor had he any spare stores with him. The command of this vessel was entrusted to one Captain Van der Felsen, while the engineering duties were performed by our shrewd gunsmith Schneider, who, in spite of the most difficult circumstances, showed him-

---

[1] Wolf's diaries, which are at my disposal, begin at a much later period. I can, therefore, only repeat these facts as I remember them from his communications.

self perfectly equal to the task, as was proved by events which will be mentioned later.

On January 9, 1886, the preparations for a longer expedition were completed, and Wolf left the Luebo. Although he had twice passed the mouth of the Sankurru, and had entered the Cassai with me in the iron boat, it was yet difficult to find the confluence of the two rivers. This time the colour of the Sankurru, which, as a rule, is darker than that of the Cassai—the rivers are of a different colour in the different seasons, owing to the heavy rain—was not distinguishable. The labyrinth of islands and banks and the delta of the Sankurru have the appearance of a maze. Wolf kept on the right side of the Cassai until he saw by the difference in current that he was on the Sankurru. This tributary flowed from a NNE. direction, and the main river from SSE. The northern bank forms at the mouth of the Sankurru a high and steep wall of red laterite; the shores are covered with savannahs of trees and underwood. The delta island reminds one of our marshy alder groves; even the trees with which the low land is covered resemble our alder, except that they are much thicker.

The Sankurru soon opens into a beautifully majestic river of a breadth of 2,000 to 3,000 metres, and an average depth of three metres. The banks vary more than on the Cassai; sloping hills now and again interrupt the long stretches of wood, and often command a view of apparently endless prairies. Whenever the men were engaged in cutting firewood, Wolf made brief inland expeditions in order to gain an idea of the inner country and to form an opinion of the natives; in short, to find out what it was that the wooded banks, the high reeds, or the rattan jungles were trying to veil from the eyes of the traveller.

They made but slow progress, as the engine of the 'En Avant' was in a very bad condition. After a day or two, worn-out steam-pipes and fire-bars had to be supplied by gun-barrels; and as Wolf had never calculated upon having to use his firearms in this manner, his fighting strength was greatly diminished.

While the water of the Sankurru retained the dark clay colour, the rivulets and brooks flowing from a northern direction were of a deep black. The abundance of fish in this river was marvellous; one kind of eel especially, which was frequently offered for sale by the natives, was of a very good flavour. The number of hippopotami was not much less than on the Cassai, while crocodiles were far more plentiful. One nuisance that we had not to complain of when exploring the Cassai, we were here made sensible of to an unusual extent: the mosquitoes, in spite of their diminutive size, were so bloodthirsty and so numerous, that we seldom succeeded in shutting them out from the protecting curtains. These insects, even more irritating from their loud buzzing than from their sting, were a great drawback to the pleasant evenings; for the sun, when he is declining, loses his scorching power, and a refreshing breeze floats through the valley, while animal life begins to stir everywhere, which gives the European an opportunity for interesting observations.

The left bank is inhabited by the Bakuba, the right by different tribes of the Bassongo-Mino race. The canoes were even larger than those on the Cassai; in one of them Wolf counted eighty warriors. The banks were thickly inhabited, if we may judge from the number of boats that accompanied the 'En Avant.' Sometimes upwards of fifty of these slender vessels, made of some brown or red wood, gathered round the steamer. Off they darted in a grand race past the 'En Avant,' and then waited for her approach, showing their delight at their victory by shouting and beating against the sides of the boat with the palms of their hands; after which, they would begin the race for a second time. They accompanied the strong strokes of their oars with singing.

The territory of the Bassongo-Mino, to which that of the Bashobe and Butoto was joined, extended to about the twenty-third degree of longitude. This same degree was on the left bank the boundary of the Bakuba. As they had treated us on the Cassai, the Bassongo-Mino met Wolf now in a hostile manner, though no fight took place, until Temba, the daughter of a powerful Bankutu chief named Gapetsh, came to negotiate for peace. Fearless, with only few attendants, she came alongside the steamer to sell ivory and articles skilfully woven from palm-fibres. She asked for brass and coloured stuffs in return, and thus gave the first impulse for a peaceful intercourse. This news was quickly spread, and had advantageous consequences.

That reminds me of a very singular occurrence in my bargaining with the Bakuba. I once bought an elephant's tusk, for which the salesmen asked clothing materials. Wishing to make an impression upon

A RACE WITH THE 'EN AVANT'

them, I suddenly unfolded before their eyes a piece of glaring red stuff. The effect was entirely different from what I had expected. With a shriek of terror the Bakuba jumped up, covered their eyes, and fled for a short distance. The effect seemed to me the same as the report of a gun: as this sudden and unknown noise startles the ear, so the eye is surprised by the sudden appearance of a strange colour.

But to return to Wolf. He accepted the invitation of the amiable Princess Temba and accompanied her to her village. They had first to pass through a thick growth of wood joined by undulating savannahs. Then they passed well-cultivated maize and manioc plantations, the luxuriant growth of which is produced by a thick layer of vegetable earth. The village was built after a regular plan, with broad streets, overshadowed by fan-palms. The natives behaved in an exceedingly pacific way. They brought Wolf quantities of palm-wine, and on his return to the river a chief offered to conduct him up the stream.

Wolf was greatly surprised to find ornaments of brass here, which, as we knew, came from the Congo, the precious metal exported from the south being copper. Another proof that these nations are connected with those further north, and that the traders of the Congo, probably the Bayanzi, must go long distances up the Mfini-Lukenja, was the circumstance that here they wore the same massive rings round the neck as there, and that the natives said they had bought these ornaments up to fifteen kilogrammes in weight in exchange for ivory from the Lukenja, a river that was five days' journey further north. They asked Wolf to stay and build a house, offering at the same time to cut down all the trees on the bank so as to allow the large fire-canoe sufficient room for mooring.

Farther up the stream the natives were less peacefully disposed; the followers of a great chief, Jongolata, were most insolent in the camp, where Wolf had established himself for a few days, in consequence of a repair of the engine being necessary. One day, when some goods had been spread for drying, some full-manned canoes approached, from the foremost of which a handsome tall warrior jumped out. He was carrying his bow and arrows, and, supported by his attendants, soon began to perform a wild dance.

The Bassongo, feeling they were strong in numbers, came into the camp, in order by their insolent behaviour to frustrate any amicable intercourse. Guns being unknown to them, they very likely thought Wolf's followers to be without arms. These insolent warriors made sarcastic remarks about Wolf and his men; their especial attention was excited by a rather fat Zanzibari, from which it would appear that *embonpoint* is rare in these parts. The chief, Jongolata, soon became so impudent that Wolf, apprehending an outrage, took out his pistol, which he fired close before the chief's face.

The effect was overpowering; the chief was trembling all over, and the bold warriors took to flight, so that they had gained their canoes before Wolf had overtaken them, when he found them most civil in their manners. Jongolata made him presents of some poultry, and took his leave with vivid protestations of friendship. These Bassongo are generally slim, tall-grown people, not so clumsy and muscular as the Bakuba; they are supposed to be inveterate cannibals.

Farther up the stream no intercourse seemed to be carried on, either towards the north or with the Lower Sankurru. Nothing was found to indicate commerce— no brass, nor beads, nor stuffs, but ivory in abundance, offered at a very low price.

On February 18, Wolf dropped anchor in the very place where Pogge and I, in 1882, discovered and passed the Sankurru. Wolf also learned here from the Bena-Kotto and the Baluba that the river flowed always towards the north. This may be accounted for by the fact that at the confluence of the Lubi and the Sankurru all intercourse of the nations appears to cease altogether. Wolf found out, as I had likewise done three years before, that the river from this point upward is called Lubilash, and a chief of the Kotto, who talked to him much about Pogge and myself, said to him : ' The Sankurru is good, the Lubilash wicked,' meaning that navigation would now prove difficult and dangerous, while in the river flowing downwards and called Sankurru it was good. This prophecy soon came true. The continued soundings, having mostly revealed clayey ground, now suddenly came upon stones. The river, with a strong current, often forced itself between steep rocks of granite and laterite, with only 100 metres breadth and three metres depth. Wolf passed four moderately strong currents, after which he ran aground, and in consequence gave up every attempt to advance any farther.

Up to a village on the river inhabited by the Batondoi, of the Bakuba race, Wolf proceeded by land, and found the river narrowed to twenty-five metres, with an exceptionally strong current.

On his march back, Wolf fell in with the well-known chief Zappu Zapp, of whom he had heard on going up. The chief had sent two of his sons to the river with presents, with the request that he would wait for Zappu Zapp. The messengers told Wolf that he was the first white man that had come to visit their chief; two others—meaning Pogge and myself—not having accepted his invitation. Zappu Zapp was not a slave-hunter, as Wolf had conjectured; but, as I found several months later, he had moved westward as far as the Sankurru, in order to evade Tibbu Tib's roving troops.

To Wolf, Zappu Zapp called himself a friend of the Arabs, as, being misled by Pogge's and my journey to Nyangwe, he supposed the white men to be on friendly terms with them. Wolf found the great chief awaiting him in the appointed place with many warriors. Zappu Zapp had some guns which the Arab Djuma Bin Salim, called Famba, had once sold to him. As Famba had been living with him for nearly a year, Zappu Zapp's warriors had adopted many customs of the Wanyamwesi, who belonged to Famba's party, as well as some scraps of the Suaheli language; so that the Zanzibaris who attended Wolf had been delighted at being reminded of their native country.

As all the chiefs who have once communicated with Arab traders consider the possession of guns and plenty of powder as the only means to power and

WOLF'S MEETING WITH ZAFFE ZAPP

wealth, Zappu Zapp requested Wolf to give him guns in exchange for ivory, which he carried with him in great quantities. On Wolf's decided refusal, Zappu Zapp began to reflect whether it would be possible to possess himself of the guns by force; and, considering Wolf's inferior power, this supposition seemed justified. Both Wolf's caution and respect for his person evidently prevented the attempt, as at their first meeting he had shown a self-possession that greatly intimidated the strangers.

Wolf dropped anchor close to the land, and requested the chief to advance from out of the crowd of warriors to welcome him; Zappu Zapp, however, preferred hiding among the crowd who were begging Wolf to land. When Wolf did so, followed by only one man—the others had remained on board ready with their guns, whilst some Krupp cannon were pointed towards the troops of warriors—and fearlessly approached the people, the chief timidly advanced and saluted him.

It is often the case, as it was in this instance, that such unlooked-for dauntlessness, unaccountable to the negro, makes a marked impression upon him: it has more than once happened to me that the natives, after some such a scene, would ask: 'How is it that the white man has no fear, for all his being so weak and not nearly a match for us? He must possess a charm that makes him invulnerable.'

Zappu Zapp, Wolf says, was, like his sons, clad after the Arab fashion, with a cloth round his hips, over which he wore a long white shirt; whilst a handkerchief was twisted round his head like a turban. The warriors only wore the national costume, consisting of a head-dress of red parrots' plumes, which was held by a band of cowrie shells strung like a diadem. The upper part of the body was naked, with small lines tattooed on the breast and back; the hips were covered with brownish red cloths bordered with yellow, which were arranged in many plaits and ornamented with tassels. In the arm-hole hung a short filagree knife inlaid with copper, and fastened to a cord across the shoulder. Most of them

ON THE LUBI.

carried spears and bows; only some of them had small percussion guns, imported from the East. Zappu Zapp's men, as I stated before, are of the Bassongo tribe, living north and south of the Baluba. The ill-humour caused by their disappointment at not getting any guns was removed by some presents from Wolf, which were returned by Zappu Zapp.

When Wolf reached the mouth of the Lubi he

entered it and sailed up the stream until he first touched the Bena-Ngongo, the same tribe that had robbed us on my first expedition, and then attacked Pogge when returning by himself. The people who came to the bank called out to Wolf to stop or come again, as they wished to atone by a payment for their past offence to the white man. This was evidently the cunning of the insolent and thievish vagabonds, who wished to induce Wolf to land, since his small force seemed more tempting than Pogge's caravan had done: for, when Wolf landed on coming back, the people had nothing ready that Wolf might have accepted as an indemnity; he only met an assembly of armed men, part of whom were trying to hide from him.

The Lubi soon narrowed to sixty metres, and often suddenly changed its course. In one of its bends the 'En Avant' was driven violently ashore, so that overhanging branches caught the thatched awning constructed by Wolf; while the strong current drifted the boat along sideways, and the 'En Avant' would have capsized had not the pillars of the awning been broken and gone overboard. A great deal of water penetrated into the steamer; the hencoop with its occupants, a Winchester gun, and many other things were washed overboard, and the fires were extinguished. This accident shows how necessary it is on such journeys always to carry boats with sufficient room for the crew, and, if possible, not to tow them alongside of the steamer, but fastened to a sufficiently long rope. There ought also to be a man in the boats to throw out the cable in case any mishap should occur.

E

Wolf did not go up the Lubi any farther, but sailed down the stream and stopped in the Sankurru at the landing-place of the Bena-Lussambo. He had proceeded to about fifteen kilometres north of the place where Pogge and I had passed the Lubi, whose waters are reddish-brown. Wolf says much in praise of the luxuriant tropical vegetation of its banks, on which thickets of palm-trees, impenetrable jungles of pine-apples, and sugar plantations alternate with primæval forests.

Wolf made friends with Ilunga, the chief of the Lussambo, and bought a number of valuable objects for a collection, which I found a subsequent opportunity of completing at the same place. Wood-carving may be considered as a special branch of industry of

THE LUKENJA—LOMAMI

ARTICLES MANUFACTURED BY THE LUSSAMBO

this tribe: drinking-horns fashioned after the horn of the buffalo, goblets of great variety of shape, evincing much taste, beautiful spear-handles, and a series of articles variously ornamented, were to be found here. A large milky white pearl was mostly in request.

Keeping along the right bank, which was covered with thickets of the *Raphia vinifera*, or rattan, Wolf on March 9 discovered the mouth of a river whose water was of a more decided yellow than that of the Sankurru, and whose breadth was about 100 metres. The natives called it Lukenja, a word that with the Bassongo tribes evidently means 'river,' as in their country we know several water-courses of that name. The banks rose to a height of 200 metres, and were richly wooded. Natives were nowhere to be seen; only twice were some discovered on trees, but they timidly fled when they were approached. For three days the journey was continued, until some warriors on the right bank, who called themselves Basselle-Kungo, and named the river Laethshu, could be questioned. The left bank, they supposed, was inhabited by the Batetela, the western branch of a large tribe, the eastern members of which I once met near the Middle Lomami. The people, by their stupidity, presented a great contrast to the natives we had hitherto seen; it made a strange impression to hear their 'Yech, yeeh,' as an expression of surprise. The population was scanty, but game was plentiful and very bold. The hippopotami were feeding on the banks in broad daylight.

The river soon expanded to 150 metres in breadth. The banks became flat, now and then boggy, and thickets stretching far into the water made it a daily difficulty for us to land to cut firewood. Not having been able to buy provisions in these dreary parts for five days, we began to feel hungry. Wolf himself had for some days been living on some mouldy beans. The expeditions he undertook on an empty stomach, in order to remedy this want by killing some game, remained without success.

Until now I have passed over Wolf's complaints about the condition of his vessel; some damage and some repair have been mentioned daily, and much has been said in praise of the gunsmith Schneider, who always managed to find out some ingenious remedy. At last, on March 15, Wolf found some natives to communicate with, and it was not any too soon, for the engine and the empty stomachs of the crew were sadly in want of restoratives. The natives called themselves Bena-Yehka, and the name of the river was—'Lomami!' One may imagine how joyfully surprised Wolf felt at this news. He thought he had discovered that the Lomami, which I in 1882 had crossed with Pogge, as Cameron had done before, in taking a turn across the west, fell here into the Sankurru and considerably lengthened the navigable water-line from Stanley Pool to the east.

Since then, further explorations of this Lomami have been undertaken, and have proved that close above the place reached by Wolf the river began rapidly to narrow. At the same time a steamer had gone up another Lomami—which in 1° N. falls into the Lualaba—and proceeded so far that, since then, it has again been a point of dispute whether the Lomami which I crossed in 1882 is the upper course of the latter or of the river navigated by Wolf.

One of my companions on my last journey, Lieutenant Le Marinel, whose acquaintance the reader will be making in the course of this narrative, is just now engaged in endeavouring to clear up this matter.

The Bena-Yehka did not belong to the Batetela, who are notorious everywhere for their fierceness; they were

HUTS OF THE BENA-YEHKA

peaceable and quite inclined to trade. Their huts, shaped like a gable house, and constructed of bark and palm ribs, were neat and cleanly. They had their hair dressed in a band, like a thick black caterpillar, reaching from the forehead down to the back; the sides of the skull were not only shaved, but tattooed in concentric rings reaching very nearly to the cheek-bone and the eye.

The Yehka are great hunters, which is testified by their various weapons, the most striking of which are arrows, used like harpoons.

The river was in possession of the inhabitants of the right bank, the Balunbangando, with their chief Oto; they are cannibals belonging to the Bankuto, and also to the Bassongo-Mino. All the countries I know between the Lomami and Lualaba are inhabited throughout by cannibals; they will, however, rarely confess to being partial to human flesh; generally they deny this, and accuse of this vice the tribe with whom they are at enmity. Wolf gave Oto an old hat; in return he, highly delighted, brought him a kid, fowls, some manioc, and palm-wine.

Until the 19th Wolf remained here. His crew lived on yam, the chief food of the Yehka; then provisions were bought, and the engine was repaired as well as could be under the circumstances. The condition of the 'En Avant' was such as to make it impossible to go up the river any farther. The axle-tree of the wheels was broken, though fortunately in an oblique direction. Schneider now bored through the axle-tree perpendicularly, and put in rivets made of iron gun-barrels. This slight repair only permitted the engine to work slowly, which was not sufficient for sailing against the strong current of the Lomami. Heavy at heart, Wolf began sailing down. He had been in hopes of exploring the Lomami to where Pogge and I had crossed it four years ago. We had arrived at the decision that Lomami, the name which it retains during the greater part of its course, must be the right name for this river.

ON GEOGRAPHY

Once back on the Sankurru, which below the point where it receives the Lomami has a breadth of nearly 2,000 metres, the 'En Avant' had to take shelter under an island, not being equal to coping with the water that, raised by a storm of rain against the current, was moving in high and surging waves.

For several days Wolf remained with a chief named Kole, who was very communicative and made many geographical disclosures which, being noted down in technical words unintelligible to me, I can only repeat incompletely. This 'Fumo'—term for chief—Kole had often been mentioned by our Bashilange. He was commercially connected with the southern Baluba and knew the way to the Lulua well. He was likewise able to give an account of the aborigines, the so-called pigmies, whom he called Babecki, while the Baluba had designated them as Batua. On being questioned by some Bankutu present, he reported about the north as follows: For many days' journey you would meet only the Bassongo-Mino, whose tribes from the south upwards rank as Bajaia, Botecka, Ndongo, Nkole, Bayenga, Dongeufuro, Bondo, Lokoddi, Babenge, Bonshina, Dongosoro, Ikangala Joshomo, Bakundu, Banbangala, and Barumbe. As it is scarcely likely that these Bangala are identical with those north of the Congo, we come upon this name here for the third time. The valley of Kassanga, on the Upper Quango, is inhabited by the Bangala; we find them as part of the Bassongo-Mino, and on the confluence of the Mubangi and the Congo.

On March 22 I found in Wolf's diary, 'Very excellent palm-wine. Long live the Emperor!'

On the 25th Wolf re-entered the Cassai, and now they began to devote themselves to the repair of the engine, if only to be able to sail slowly against the current of the Cassai, which fortunately was not strong. On April 1 they reached the mouth of the Lulua, and on the 4th the Luebo station, where the 'En Avant' was joyfully welcomed after a four months' absence. On this very day provisions had arrived which Bugslag had sent from Luluaburg, such as goats, sheep, salt pork, rice, bananas, peanut-oil, onions, &c., so that the return might be properly celebrated. The exhausted 'En Avant' was unloaded, the collections were arranged, and the boat was repaired as well as could be; so that Wolf, impelled by the spirit of investigation habitual to him, was enabled to leave the station once more. So he sailed down the Lulua and up the Cassai to find out how far up from the mouth of the Lulua the latter was navigable.

On the morning of April 12, when he had scarcely left the Lulua, the axle-tree of the boat broke for the second time, but this was such a hopeless case that Wolf declared himself unable to repair it with the tools he had at hand. Wolf let the boat drift downward, and towed himself ashore close above the mouth of the Lulua. Scarcely had he been lying at anchor for some hours, after having undertaken a short expedition into the primæval forest, when he was entreated by some people who had followed him to come back quickly, as a boat was in sight.

Almost the moment Wolf came to the river side I laid the 'Peace' alongside of the 'En Avant,' and a minute later embraced my friend, who was as much delighted and surprised as I was. He briefly told me how he had carried out my orders given him at parting, and what he had done respecting the exploration of the river system, so promising for the future of these countries.

It is greatly to be regretted that the death of Wolf, which took place at Dahomey, prevented him from detailing his work himself. The diaries at my disposal give a number of short notes, containing a series of meteorological observations which I am unable to decipher.

For all that, I am convinced that the reproduction of the diaries which end here shows more practical knowledge than it would if one uninitiated, who knows neither people nor country as I do, had undertaken the task. My work 'Im Innern Afrikas' and this chapter will give the reader an idea of the energy, the continual exertion, the courage, and intimate knowledge that Dr. Wolf has employed in working for his illustrious employer, the King of the Belgians, for the promotion of science and civilisation in the Dark Continent. There are few who knew as I did the devotion, the noble disposition of the deceased, and who are for this reason able to sympathise with me on his loss. Everyone, from whatever motive it may be, will bear Wolf in kind remembrance.

BETWEEN LUEBO AND LULUABURG

CHAPTER III

DISCOVERING WISSMANN FALL AND WORK AT THE STATION

Progress of Luebo station—Patrol on the Muicau—Encountering faithful Bugslag—Luluaburg, a centre of civilisation—Plantations—The breeding of cattle—Meteorological observations—With Kalamba—Saturnino de Machado—Hostile Chipulumba—Punishment of some of our soldiers—Up the Cassai with Wolf—An uninhabited wilderness—Tormenting bees—Bars in the river—Wissmann Fall—Wild boars—Falling trees—Missed the 'Stanley'—At the station—Separation from Wolf—Punishment of a chief—Baludu—Ambassadors—Settling political difficulties at Lubuku—Distribution of the Star-Flag—My influence over the Bashilange—Kalamba's visit—Spectacle snake.

LET us return to April 12, and to the confluence of the Lulua and the Cassai, where, on returning from the coast, I met my friend and companion Wolf after six months' separation.

We sat discussing our adventures and making plans

for the future till late at night, under the far-overhanging foliage of the huge trees of the shore, on the edge of the slope, where the enormous yellow floods of the Cassai were rolling along at our feet. We were allowed but a short rest; then we took Wolf on board the 'Peace' to steam up the Lulua to Luebo station, while the commander of the 'En Avant,' Captain Van der Felsen, and the gunsmith Schneider, with some of the crew, remained in the boat, which had for the present become unserviceable. In honour of this meeting I had a good many European provisions, especially liquids, in readiness for a grand banquet, the consequences of which not even the fresh breeze on the Lulua could undo.

After sailing round some turns of the Lulua we came in sight of Luebo station.[1]

From the distance we noticed an open space on the water side, which was very striking to the eye after having for five days seen nothing but thick, dark forest, which now during the rainy season reached down to the water's edge and bordered the river all along.

My light artillery, a present of Mr. Friedrich Krupp's, was placed on the shore on a kind of bastion at the extreme end of the clearing, on a neck of land formed by the confluence of the Luebo and the Lulua, to ward off any hostile approach by water. Four structures built of palisades, neatly lined with clay, and with far-overhanging grass-covered roofs, filled up the end of the open space. Towards the land they were protected from any attack by a wall of palisades leading from the

---

[1] *Vide* Illustration.

Luebo to the Lulua. About 100 metres of ground was bare, with a dark wall of primæval forest towering behind.

A great commotion arose at the station on the appearance of our steamer. Soldiers, clad in pure white, came with their arms ready for parade. On our approaching the place, which presented a striking appearance by its agreeable change of scene after so gloomy a surrounding, a European, Lieutenant Bateman, came to salute us at the river side. He had been appointed to my expedition by the Congo State, and was at present commanding officer of the place. Then we landed, and after hearing the favourable report about the state of affairs we assembled in a mushroom-shaped pavilion on the bastion to partake of a refreshing glass of palm-wine.

There was another European present, one Mr. Saturnino, a Portuguese merchant, whom I have mentioned in my book of travels 'Unter deutscher Flagge querdurch Afrika.' Following my expedition to Lubuku, he had tried his fortune with the Bakuba and the Bakete, and was greatly satisfied with his purchases of ivory.

After a close inspection of the station, where the dwelling-house was formed of palings—the planning of which gave evidence of practical knowledge and great diligence—I took drawings of the Lulua and the Luebo to complete my observations of them (*vide* Appendix), and visited the surrounding districts of the Bakete and the Bashilange to convince myself that the station, the provisioning of which for the present depended on purchases, was on a very good footing with the surrounding tribe. A few days afterwards the 'Peace' returned, taking Herr Greshoff and Herr von Nimptsch down to Stanley Pool.

Mr. Grenfell, to whom I was greatly indebted for his kind convoy, obligingly promised to pick up the 'En Avant' at the mouth of the Lulua and take her as far as the Congo. He took with him a member of my expedition, the gunsmith Schneider, who was going home, and who, during the whole time of his engagement, had distinguished himself by untiring activity and great skill and courage.

The 'Peace' running aground some metres below the station made us aware of the fact that some stones in the Cassai made it expedient for us to approach the station with caution. Fortunately the 'Peace' got off again without damage.

On the 22nd, after giving Lieutenant Bateman further directions for his work at the station, I started with Wolf on my return journey to Luluaburg. We had sent messengers before us, who were to inform Bugslag of our coming, and to bring the oxen we rode on to meet us. In every primæval forest that I know of in the African tropical countries there lives a large black gadfly, somewhat like our hornet, but not the tsetse fly, which is fatal to cattle. In 1882 I had lost my last bulls on the Tanganyika through this insect.

After a six hours' fatiguing march in the forest we halted at the village of the Bena Kashia. This name refers to the dispersion of the tribes of our Bashilange; the main body of the Kashia, being the greater part of this tribe, the Baqua Kashia, live in the centre of the whole people, close to Luluaburg, and east of them lives another tribe of Bena Kashia. Jealousy among the chiefs' families was the usual reason for such dispersions.

Part of a large commercial caravan of the Kioque, our old enemies, was present; they were exceedingly civil, for, since we had settled here, the time of their predominancy over our Bashilange was over.

We travelled for several days, each day marching from thirty to forty kilometres, and discovering several districts whose inhabitants had refused to pay tribute to Kalamba on his return from the Congo, and, in order to avoid his wrath, they were forced to leave their country. After leaving the primæval forest we mostly marched through savannahs of trees; sometimes the monotonous, undulating savannah was relieved by deep ravines, which on their slopes showed magnificent dark red-turreted formations of laterite.[1]

On the 28th we approached the river Muieau, where from a distance we were greeted by a pretty clay house, lying amongst gracefully arranged gardens, this being the residence of a permanent patrol that Wolf had meanwhile established on the most important crossing of this river. Three of my old veterans were here, the representatives of our force and commanders of the canoes. I was quite touched by the sincere delight evinced by my old people, companions of my former expedition, on recognising me. On the opposite side three bulls, well saddled and bridled, were awaiting us

---

[1] *Vide* Illustration.

to take us to Luluaburg next day. After crossing the river next morning we mounted our bulls; I took my huge old steed that had carried me to Luluaburg two years before. We were surprised to find a road of nearly eight metres width running in a straight line to the east. It turned out later that Bugslag had caused the footpaths round the station to be broadened, and had in-

LULUABURG

structed those chiefs through whose ground the way led how to build straight roads. He had succeeded, by making those chiefs who did not provide broad paths pay fines, in producing beautifully wide roads in all directions about a day's journey beyond Luluaburg.

Towards noon we came in sight of the summit of the hill, and soon rode up to the station amidst the rejoicings of the crowd assembled from all the villages.

Along the station hill the roads were lined with pleasant avenues. Trees, that soon began to sprout, were planted at three metres distance in the wall of palisades, thus forming a shady circle round the station. It was like coming home when, at the gates of the station, I shook hands with my honest Bugslag. At the station, whose chief buildings had already been finished when we left to explore the Cassai, much had been done to give it a home-like and cheerful appearance. Plantations had been laid out everywhere, an entirely new dwelling-house had been built very prettily and with great care, a nice little garden was in front of it; in short, a pleasant sight met our eyes everywhere.

Messengers hurried away to inform my friend Kalamba and his sister Sangula of my return. This was the third time that I had come to Lubuku unexpectedly, to the country of my loyal Bashilange, to whom I owed so much already. The first time of my coming here was with Pogge in 1881. Being the first white men seen by the Bashilange, our influence was very great. It was with the assistance of these people only that we succeeded in reaching the Lualaba; whence, after separating from Pogge, and supported by the Arabs, I proceeded to the eastern coast. In the year 1884, coming from the west, I returned to the Lubuku country, to my old friends and travelling companions, and, as I had promised them, I brought with me a great many white men. Once more by the help of the Bashilange the exploration of the Cassai was made possible, and this took them into unknown countries for nearly a year. I then sailed down the river towards the sea, and my black friends returned home with Wolf. Now I came back once more, and great were the rejoicings everywhere at Kabassu Babu's return to his friends. I felt quite at home here, recognising each face of the hundreds of negroes who lived at the large village near the station; every one of those crowding around me was delighted at being recognised.

In the evening, when we were sitting in the pretty verandah of the dwelling-house, ornamented with hippopotamus skulls, antelope's horns, and rarities from the desert, I learned that, in spite of the greatest economy, Luluaburg was running short of provisions. With great reluctance conscientious Bugslag had felt obliged to send his treasures down to the Luebo, the building of which station had involved great expense. On the Luebo, want in this respect was also beginning to be felt, and I found myself in the disagreeable position of having to inspect two stations with a large number of people without the means of maintaining them. The fruit of the plantations at Luluaburg was not yet ripe. For this reason, therefore, I resolved to buy the most indispensable provisions from the Portuguese merchant Saturnino, and make these last until the 'Stanley,' with the Belgian officers on board, should bring my new supplies.

Next day we inspected the plantation. After the first harvest Bugslag had sent many loads of rice down to the Luebo. How astonished I was at finding well-cultivated fields in places which I only remembered as a wilderness! The low land between the three brooks winding along the station hill was covered with rice

F

plantations that, in Bugslag's opinion, would easily support Luluaburg and Luebo station for six months —that is, up to the next harvest. Maize, millet, and manioc, covering the gentle slopes of the station hill, were thriving. As it had lately been very wet, there was not much prospect of a good crop of pea-nuts. In the three gardens which were laid out, each according to the purpose it was meant for, on the slopes or in the valley close to the station, a great deal of fruit and vegetables were being cultivated, such as tomatoes, cucumbers, carrots, cabbages, yams, beans, egg-fruits, pine-apples, gimboas (foxtail, a very pleasant vegetable). Bananas and melon trees bordered the roads everywhere, and other fruits, such as limes, &c., imported from the Congo and Angola, were being grown, besides tobacco.

The stock of cattle had greatly increased under Bugslag's care, and they were in good condition considering the season. In countries where, after the rainy season, the grass shoots up to a great height and thickness, and thus becomes useless as food, circumstances, in spite of the greatest care, are not favourable. They manage to improve the grass by burning it, after which the blades begin to sprout everywhere. The whole of Africa is adapted for the breeding of cattle, except perhaps in the districts haunted by the black hornet. In the eastern part of the continent, where the rainy season is shorter than in the western, the grass is more soft and tender. In the west, great care should be taken to obtain soft grass, which can only be managed by burning; this is done by lighting several fires while the grass is proportionably tender, after which the young grass begins to shoot up everywhere. On those pastures where large herds of cattle graze, the grass is kept the right length, but the cattle should be put in places where it has reached the length they prefer. They should never be kept where a certain plant most dangerous for cattle is found, as many travellers have experienced, amongst them Pogge, who at very short intervals lost nine bulls in consequence. It is well to change the water frequently, unless some larger water-course is near. During the night the cattle should be put into high places, where a fresh breeze will decrease the number of mosquitoes. It is therefore advisable not to use a stable during the night, but a pent-house, open at the sides, so that in exposed places the draught may keep off the said insects. The cattle will always feed most in the morning and evening; they should therefore be put into shady places during the hottest time of the day. Our attempt at keeping bulls at the Luebo station had been an entire failure; we had lost several in their fights and through other causes, so that we had only three left.

The cows had increased with unfailing regularity, but had not as yet been trained for being milked; ninety-eight sheep and thirty goats were running wild in the vicinity of the station during the day, and were driven home in the evening after working hours. It is strange that the negroes do not keep cattle in droves as we do; but, for want of shepherds' dogs, it would be necessary to have as many people as head of cattle to keep them together. The station was stocked with numerous ducks, fowls, pigeons, parrots, and guineafowls; nor do I doubt that every other kind of poultry would thrive here. For convenience' sake we had given over a considerable breed of pigs to one of the neighbouring chiefs.

Our little dogs had suffered most; of the fifteen imported, chiefly terriers and one fox terrier, only five were alive. Some had been hunting in the long grass or in the heat, or had fallen victims to snake-bite; two had been killed by leopards, one of the latter having jumped over the palisades of the station. Strangely enough, only the male dogs had succumbed to diseases, while we had lost the females by accidents. The survivors—one of which had been rescued from the claws of the leopard, though with several wounds; another, with a broken leg, had escaped from the clutches of a wounded wild boar—had repeatedly mingled with native dogs, and the result of this breed was regarded as a very valuable present by the chiefs in all Lubuku.

The meteorological observations, I am sorry to say, were, through the wrong setting of some instruments, not so complete as might be desired. The most surprising result of these observations, and one which accounts for the luxuriance of growth in the countries of Central Africa, was, that there was not one month of the year without rain. This is especially striking in the three months, June, July, and August. There had been rain three times in June, twice in July, and frequently in August; though of course, in the two first-named months, this was not sufficient to keep the plants from scorching during the intense heat; there was a heavy dew at the time which made up for it. In this way it is possible to reap maize three times, in some parts even four times, millet twice or thrice, and rice twice.

After one day of rest we set out on a visit to Kalamba. At the entrance of the village thousands of people were assembled and posted on each side of the road, and everywhere I was greeted with 'Moiio Kabassu Babu!' On both sides of the 'Kiota,' the market and meeting-place, the men were sitting in long rows; the hemp-pipe was solemnly passing round amidst boisterous coughing and the deafening noise of the whistles and big drums. Twenty of my newly recruited soldiers fired three salutes, which were greeted with vigorous shooting by the surrounding natives. Then the dense crowd of about 5,000 people opened, and amidst cheering and clapping of hands old Kalamba, towering above the multitude, approached with his sister Sangula. I need not be ashamed of my deep emotion on greeting with a hearty shake of the hand those tried friends, to whom I owed so much. Endless inquiries were made, and the cheering all round was literally deafening. I jumped on my saddle in order to be better seen, and on my repeatedly crying 'Bantue' with the utmost exertion of my voice, so as to enforce silence, I soon stopped the noise. I then gave a 'Moiio,' telling them that the sea had restored my health, and that, led by a strong impulse, I had now returned to my friends. Kalamba in reply said how delighted he was to see his Kabassu Babu back once more. His far-sounding 'To wola' ('I have spoken') was followed by firing of guns, beating of drums, and cheering. After having thus celebrated the day, they got ready for a grand dance. Accompanied by Kalamba, his sister Sangula, and Kalamba-Moana, the successor to the throne, I entered the chief's neat and pretty house, which had been erected during my absence. I talked over with Kalamba all I purposed doing at present, and he readily promised that, wherever I desired to go, he would send his sons (subjects) with me, even if he, being an old man, should be prevented from undertaking long journeys.

Before riding back to the station I met Katende, the chief of the Bashi Lamboa, whom a year ago I had defeated and taken prisoner, together with Kalamba. He had come to pay tribute to the latter, and was complaining of the extortionate demand. After a short interview with Kalamba I arranged about the remaining amount, and got leave for him to return home. Refreshed by a cup of millet beer, I started on my homeward journey before dark with some fattened sheep, and a goat born with three legs—all presents of Kalamba's.

On May 5 I started on a visit to the merchant Saturnino, who was at the time living with Kapussu Jimbundu, north of the Lulua, to buy provisions for the station, and thence to march to Luebo station. Wolf was to go from there straight to Luluaburg and make preparations, as I proposed going with him in the well-tested iron boat 'Paul Pogge' to explore the Cassai above the mouth of the Lulua. I crossed the Lulua close to the station where, as on the Muieau, a permanent patrol was stationed who only cultivated rice and sugar for the station, the soil being exactly suitable for these products. I passed many large villages as in a triumphal procession, and spent the night at the village of Kapussu, a chief who was a half-blood albino. His skin was

A 'MOITO' AT KALAMBA'S

copper-coloured, though his hair was not light as is the case with the real albinos, while his hazel eyes shunned the light as theirs do. Next day I got on the wrong track, and lost my way so completely that, until evening, I marched across the fields. Only those who know the wild growth of those countries, with the long stretches of primæval forests bordering each of the frequent watercourses, can have an idea of the fatiguing toil of such a march. It was night when we reached a small village, whose occupants conducted us next day to the Moansangomma. This river I crossed on a float made of the ribs of the *Raphia vinifera*, sometimes ten metres in length, and soon after reached the camp occupied by Saturnino and his assistant Carvalho. In a short time I had concluded the disagreeable negotiations with the two gentlemen, who wanted to profit by my situation as much as possible, and started on the 7th after a day's delay in order to meet Wolf on the Luebo. For several days I marched along the same road that Wolf had travelled when I had sent him to the Bakuba Prince Luquengo. The Bashilange of these parts, with whom we had scarcely come in contact, were mostly Chipulumba—that is, people who refused to smoke hemp or to reform their wild martial habits. I also repeatedly met trading Bakuba, who wanted to buy slaves and salt.

When I wished to cross the Lulua at the Bena-Mbala's, and therefore called across to the island where the people lived who were to ferry me over, they, Chipulumba to the backbone, would not let me pass. Threats and promises were of no avail, and I was forced to reascend the slope, difficult as it was for the bull to pass, and try to cross the river farther up. Scarcely had I left the shore when I heard the report of a gun, and found that one of the five soldiers who had accompanied me

CHIRILU FALL

had fired a shot amongst the insulting Chipulumba, which gained him my serious disapproval.

On the 9th I crossed the river from the Baqua-Kash country, at a place where a small tributary, the Chirilu, rushes as a waterfall of six metres height into the Lulua. In the middle of the stream my bull, whose head was held by a man at the stern, came pushing against the canoe so that it was not possible to steer. The bull succeeded in putting one foot over the edge of the canoe and made it capsize. As the two negroes who were with me could swim, we gained the shore, swimming some distance behind the bull. I did not much relish such swimming expeditions, since in the same Lulua, at a place where I used to bathe every day, a negro had been seized by a crocodile five years before. This time it seemed more risky than ever, as, just before, we had observed several of these terrible reptiles. I may mention here that the crocodile seems to assume its exterior from its surroundings, which by Darwin has been called 'mimicry.' On light sands I used to see animals of a yellowish green, while on dark and boggy ground they looked dark brown, and even crocodiles lying on stones resemble the colour of their resting-place.

I followed the Lulua downward, and, in order to get to know the way, I always kept close to the river side, though this obliged me to pass through uninterrupted primæval forests. These forests are inhabited by Bashilange, who are short and thin, and remind one of the dwarf-like Batua. As is mostly the case with the inhabitants of primæval forests, they are marked by shyness and reserve.

At eleven o'clock in the evening, in complete darkness, I traversed the last forest and reached Luebo station, where I found Wolf. Next day preparations for the journey had to be made, sentences passed, and punishments inflicted. One of our soldiers, known throughout the country by their becoming uniform, had been availing himself of our influence to make extortions. It appeared that our people, when sent on messages, had been carrying off goats, fowls, nay, even slaves, which they had possessed themselves of either by threats or by force. As nothing would be more likely to injure our influence than such proceedings, I adopted the severest punishments. I despatched some natives with a hippopotamus whip, who were to carry out the punishment, a sound thrashing, and to impart the reason for it to the offended chiefs, who were to receive an indemnification for their loss, which was to be deducted from the offenders' pay.

After giving Mr. Bateman instructions in case the 'Stanley' should arrive during our absence, or our return should be delayed longer than expected, we went on board the iron boat 'Paul Pogge,' fitted out for a month's journey, and took with us six Zanzibaris, three Angola negroes, and one native, with whom we sailed down the Lulua. On the morning of the 14th, after an undisturbed night on sandbanks, we again found ourselves on the slowly flowing Lulua, whose mouth we reached by noon. We then sailed up the Cassai, 1,000 metres wide, intersected by islands and sandbanks, on one of which we encamped. While our men were pitching the tent, I found a large nest of eggs resembling those of a plover, which, not being hatched, improved our meal. Wolf, who had gone ashore in a boat to fetch wood, also tried to get provisions, and fired at a flock of geese, but, missing them, he might have laid us low instead of the geese, as the grains of shot were buzzing about our ears.

On the 15th we proceeded up stream. The banks were high, and covered with primæval forests; in the background we noticed closely wooded mountains, up to a height of 100 metres. We had been informed by Pogge that between the Lulua and the Cassai we should for days see nothing but huge forests. The Cassai was in the middle distinctly divided by a long row of sands. On one of those stretches, about 2,000 metres long, we found a deserted dog howling most piteously; he had evidently been left behind by a native who had fled from us. On our approaching and attempting to rescue him, he fled and suddenly plunged into the water, but had floated so far down that we did not notice whether he reached the shore or not.

The banks appeared to be uninhabited, as throughout the day we saw no canoe, no human beings, no fish-hooks, nor a road leading to the river; nothing but traces of buffaloes and elephants.

A most tormenting nuisance were some small stingless bees, that came with such persistency into our eyes, ears, and nostrils as to keep us in incessant conflict with them. It was literally impossible to eat, as they settled in such numbers on each morsel which we were about to put into our mouths, that we had soon to give up the attempt.

On the left bank we noticed, on the morning of the 16th, four large canoes—those beautifully slender vessels of the Lower Cassai which at first sight show they were meant for longer expeditions than simply to cross

THE CROSS IN THE CASSAI

the river. We made a landing-place, from which we found three branching roads, on two of which we sent patrols with goods, and injunctions to approach the natives cautiously and try to buy provisions. They soon returned, accompanied by relatives of the tribe of the Bashi-Bombo, bringing manioc flour, fowls, and palm-wine. The Bombo—Bashi means the same as Baqua, Bena, and Ba, i.e. people—with their muscular, heavy bodies, the tattooed cuts on their stomachs and backs, resembled the Bakuba of the opposite shore.

On continuing our journey, one of our Zanzibaris turned out to have disappeared. He had been enjoying too much palm-wine and had fallen asleep in the forest. I had just got ready with five men to search for him, when he came reeling along, but was soon sobered by a well-deserved thrashing.

The river widened up to 200 metres, and was on each side mantled with primæval forests, without any signs of human beings, besides a good many sands, and not till evening did we come upon a thickly wooded island. No pastures being near, we did not see any hippopotami. The only living creatures were hosts of parrots, small herds of monkeys, and a night-heron scared from out of the shade of the trees. The Bashi-Bombo had told us that we should soon make a large fall, above which there would be the mouth of a river, most likely of the Luvo.

On the 17th we saw oil-palm groves ever and anon on the slopes of the high banks, now and then canoes, and towards evening rubble-stones in the bends of the river; an unmistakable sign that we were nearing difficulties as regards the navigation of the river. In the evening, just before encamping, we halted near a gigantic rock towering in the middle of the stream like a huge sugar loaf. Our attempts to cut some mark into it were thwarted by the brittleness of the granite. On the surface of it there was the sign of a cross, formed by two veins of quartz projecting from the rock.

We then pitched our camp in a place trodden down by hippopotami and elephants, in a prettily-shaded bay, from which a brook was rushing down in small cascades.

We refreshed ourselves with a sweet caoutchouc liana, the size of a large ball, and then began to prepare our meal.

On the morning of the 18th, after rounding a bend, we suddenly saw before us a bar of rock stretching across the whole breadth of the river. It was so low that the water overleaped it or forced its way through gaps. Close below the right bank we succeeded in inciting our six rowers to the utmost exertion in pressing through a channel. After rounding the next bend of the river a strange picture presented itself to our eyes, for which we had been prepared for the last twenty minutes by a loudly roaring sound. The whole of the huge river was rushing down eight metres deep into a kind of wide-spreading lake.

The wall of rocks that forced the river to take such a leap was crowned by four islands luxuriantly covered with palms and pandanus, and dividing it into five channels and five waterfalls. The one on the right side, the father, as it were, was the largest, about sixty metres broad; while the others, the four children, measured from ten to fifteen metres.[1]

This clear bright lake, surrounded by banks of dark forests, the foaming wall of roaring falls towering in the background, together with islands rich in growth—all this formed a very striking picture.

This, then, was the boundary of communication by water: a channel system extending over many thousands of sea miles, crossing Equatorial Africa from here to the Falls of Father Congo below Stanley Pool; up the Congo to below Stanley Falls; on the Sankurru and

[1] The two waterfalls of the Cassai—about two days' journey farther up—which I discovered in 1884 and called Pogge Falls, are Mbimbi-Mukash and Mbimbi-Mulume—i.e. Mbimbi, *fall*; Mukash, *woman*; Mulume, *man*.

WISSMAN FALL.

Lomami in due easterly direction close to Nyangwe; from the Congo to the Mubangi and Welle of Schweinfurth and Junker, and on the numerous little tributaries.

We sailed up the right bank, as I wished to take the boat across the fall in order to go up to Kikassa and Pogge Fall, if possible, and thus to form a connection between my former and my present travels. Arrived at the top, however, we noticed some more rapids and small cascades above the fall, and I therefore gave up my plan. Wolf and I cut two large W's into the huge stem of a gigantic tree of the primæval forest that grew off the fall close to the shore, which will easily catch the traveller's eye. The neighbourhood of the fall was enveloped in a cloud of foam, and everything was shiny, damp, and covered with moss.

We now crossed over to the left bank, where we kept in smooth water to close below the fall. A great many remnants of smashed canoes were buried among the sands in the shallow water. The shape of these canoes was different from those we had seen before, not slender and pointed on each side, but with rounded stern. The inhabitants above the fall did not, it seems, use their canoes for travelling, but simply for crossing the river and for fishing purposes.

A number of women whom we found engaged in fishing took flight before us. Contrary to the habit of the tribes we had seen before, they had dyed their skin with a mixture of oil and red wood. A few minutes after, five men armed with their bows and arrows were seen approaching us cautiously. We at once saw they belonged to a new tribe, judging from their strange head-dress, painted skin, and figures much slighter than those of the people we had seen on the Cassai before. We succeeded in banishing the distrust of the people, so that they came near us when their number had increased to twenty. They called themselves Tupende, and belonged to the same tribe in whose territory I had crossed the Cassai twice before. They pretended not to know anything of the mouth of the Luvo, which I supposed to be near; and they appeared to be greatly astonished at my being acquainted with the state of affairs up the stream, when talking of the Chikapa and of Kikassa. They spoke of Pogge Falls, and said that above the fall where our camp was pitched the river was impassable for a long distance. They sold us palm-wine and fish, and then we re-embarked and made the 'Pogge' carry us down the river. Before parting with the beautiful sight of the falls, I accepted Wolf's proposal to give them the name of 'Wissmann Fall.' These two successive cataracts, formed by the largest tributary of the Congo, are an emblem, as it were, of my working together with my late friend, the highly respected traveller, Paul Pogge.

Some kilometres down the stream we were enticed to land by a sort of crashing sound in the wood. Undefinable short and grunting sounds keep even the connoisseur of African game in doubt as to whether the animals breaking through the thicket in a boggy place are elephants, buffaloes, or boars. These three inhabitants of the primæval forest have voices of great similarity. We crept along, and I succeeded in killing by a single shot a boar which was covering the retreat of a whole herd; this was very welcome to us, since we had been in want of meat for several days. Even our Zanzibaris, who always pretended to be strict

A WELCOME MEAL

Mahometans, were by no means averse to eating the prohibited meat. They thought that, when travelling, such transgressions might be permitted.

The nocturnal repose of our camp was interrupted by the tremendous noise of a falling tree. This is preceded by a repeated crashing sound, resembling that of a badly fired salute: the falling giant either tears the lianas that hold him up, or breaks through the surrounding lower trees. Then follows a heavy groaning fall, making the ground all round about vibrate; the huge trunk has broken down, its strong branches shattered.

Having heard that there was an abundance of game in the neighbourhood, we went on a shooting expedition; but we were only able to ascertain that the district abounded in elephants.

In the evening of the 19th we pitched our camp close to the mouth of the Lulua, and next morning sailed up this river.

Some fishermen told us that, an hour before, the same iron canoe that had taken back the Baluba had sailed up the stream. The news greatly vexed us, for this hour's loss of time compelled us to sail all the way to the station against the current; while in this boat, evidently the 'Stanley,' we might have easily reached the Luebo the same day, if only a dense fog had not prevented our seeing the steamer. Our journey from the mouth of the Lulua up to Wissmann Fall had taken us twenty-two and a half hours' fatiguing rowing, and the down journey only eight hours. We estimated the distance at about fifty-eight sea miles.

Wolf was suffering from very painful ulcers, hence the narrow and uncomfortable seats in the boat made him exceedingly tired. The lancing of them, which I did by making a cruciform incision with a sharp pocket-knife, was naturally most painful.

The current of the Lulua had unfortunately greatly increased, and so we did not reach the station till the 22nd. The 'Stanley' was moored alongside of the bank, and the station was swarming with Europeans. Among those who had arrived were Captain De Macar and Lieutenant Le Marinel, two officers sent from the Congo State to take charge of Luluaburg station; a Swedish Professor (Von Schwerin); Mr. Anderson, the captain of the 'Stanley,' also a Swede; his mate, De Latte, a Frenchman; the engineer, a Scotchman of the name of Walker; and Herr Stehlmann, from Luxemburg.

The 'Stanley' had brought my goods, which enabled me to return to Mr. Saturnino some of the articles that I had bought at much too high a price. The assistant of Saturnino, Mr. Carvalho, had settled near Luebo station, and was engaged in building canoes in order to sail down the Cassai with Saturnino and the remainder of his goods, and also, encouraged by our statements, to buy ivory on the way.

As the 'Stanley' was only staying for a few days, and would then take Wolf down to the coast, I charged him to prepare an account of our last journeys, since, as I was on the point of going towards the East, this would perhaps for some years be my last opportunity for communication with Europe.

Wolf's furlough had nearly expired, and, although his strong constitution had successfully resisted the influence of malaria, he had been suffering much lately from nervous headaches, toothache, and continual ulcers, for which reason a change would be of great benefit to him.

Since Wolf knew that Germany was on the point of taking her place among the colonial powers, he proposed to remain in Germany only for the time that he needed for the arrangement of our mutual work, and then to place his experience 'in Africanis' at the disposal of his country. How he eventually carried out his plan is well known.

On May 28 the day of separation had come, and in parting I pressed the hand of my friend, the partner of so many dangers and fatigues. I felt almost deserted when I saw the 'Stanley' turn the last wooded corner. Wolf was the last of my officers with whom I had three years ago set foot on this continent.

My next care was to take my goods and the articles belonging to the gentlemen under my command to Luluaburg. I therefore sent messengers to Kalamba to ask for 200 men for this purpose. Kalamba sent the people as soon as possible, so that on June 6 the loads, accompanied by the officers, were able to follow. We had only to walk through the girdle of the primæval forest, then we met the bulls sent by Bugslag, whose efficiency I had formerly had occasion to test—an efficiency which greatly satisfied and surprised the Belgians.

I received a very tedious wound in my right hand when teaching my bull to leap. A deep, narrow chasm which I could not leap, the animal not being broken in, induced me to drive him before me by a rope to which a carbine hook was fastened. As the bull refused to leap, I urged him on, but I was careless enough not to let go my hold of the rope when he leapt. The carbine hook opened in my hand and inflicted a deep wound. Fortunately, the sharp end of the hook did not touch a nerve.

The patrol on the Muieau reported that the neighbouring chief Kassange had lately ill-treated one of my soldiers when at his village on a commission of Bugslag's. I despatched three men to the village to fetch the chief, who at first refused to come, but was afterwards brought to me in fetters. I sentenced Kassange to the payment of a strong beautiful bull, which he had lately bought from a Kioque caravan, and which, together with those that Kalamba gave us later, completed the number necessary for my journey.

At Luluaburg, which we reached in the evening, Bugslag was awaiting us with a grand meal in the verandah. Roast ducks, pickled pork, cucumber salad, and other dainties rare in Central Africa, greatly astonished our new comrades.

During my last stay at Luluaburg a Balungu caravan had arrived from the well-known chief Kassongo Chiniama, who lived north of the Muata-Jamvo of Lunda. The Balungu knew of a white man who, coming from the north, had years ago passed near their village. This could have been no other than Lieutenant Cameron.

My prospect for the future depended upon the arrival of my old interpreter, Germano, whom, before starting to explore the Cassai, I had sent to the coast to buy provisions at Malange for the remaining balance of my credit. Unless something had happened, he ought to have been back long ago. What provisions the 'Stanley' had brought from the Congo would just suffice to keep the station for six months, probably until communication with the Congo should be opened again. No tidings having arrived from Germano, whom I had directed to send messengers on before to report his starting from Malange, I presumed that months would elapse before his return. I therefore resolved to visit Kassongo Chiniama in the Balungu country, to get certain information about the upper river system of the Lubilash Sankurru, of which the most contradictory statements existed. At the same time I wanted to find out the tribes between the Bashilange and the Lunda.

Immediately after the arrival of Germano I proposed to leave Luluaburg and, according to orders, go towards the east to explore the upper course of the Lualaba. Meanwhile, I intended to initiate the two Belgian officers into the affairs of the country, so as to give Luluaburg and Luebo station definitely into their charge. I hoped to have, by that time, so arranged political affairs that the new commanders would in future only have to negotiate with Kalamba, the upper chief dependent on them.

In Lubuku, the country of the hemp-smoking Bashilange, my tactics had always been to keep the natives separated into two parties, so as in case of need to lead one against the other. I had made Kalamba and Chingenge chiefs of the two parties. Experience had taught me that these tactics, which always made the management of the natives difficult, were necessary no longer. This had been made evident to me during the two long journeys with the chief of the Lubuku Bashilange, so that I resolved upon a single control of the natives. There could naturally be no doubt as to who was to be the chief dependent on me or my successor. Kalamba was the mightiest, the most respected, and, above all, the most devoted of all the princes of Lubuku. His sister, Sangula Meta, the highpriestess of the Riamba worship, who had great influence over her brother, was even more devoted to me and to us all than he was. Both brother and sister had given so many proofs of their trustworthiness and affection—virtues so rarely found among negroes—that I could not but banish all scruples about Kalamba's faithfulness. Added to this, Kalamba's eldest son, his successor, Kalamba Moana, who was much more intelligent than his father, seemed to be equally trustworthy. During his father's absence he had in every respect behaved in a most praiseworthy manner to Bugslag.

As I considered Luluaburg and its surrounding Bashilange as the centre whence the Congo State should undertake the further exploration and civilisation of its southern countries, and as the easiest and cheapest way to this object was to have one agent only—to superintend and direct from one station—I now began, in the immediate circuit of the station, in the friendly country—i.e. Lubuku—to make the greater chiefs, the eldest members of a family called Baqua or Bena, responsible masters of the districts allotted to them, so that the numerous would-be independent seniors of the villages might easily be managed. So I made the chiefs of the Baqua Chirimba, Baqua Kambulu, Bena Kussu, Bena Chitari, &c.—to each of which belonged from five to fifteen villages—real masters of their district. I intended to extend my authority over fifty of such families. Each of the chiefs was to have a star flag, and all these flags were to be placed under the large union flag of Kalamba's. The latter, to whom a certain, not too large, tribute (*mulambo*) was to be paid by the chiefs only, was to engage himself always to supply warriors for any chance campaign, conductors for a journey, labourers for keeping the roads clear, &c. He was to provide sufficient means for passing to and fro on the river crossings, to induce the population to grow rice, and to carry out different other projects to which I shall refer later.

In order to inform the fifty family chiefs, as I am now going to call them, a number of patrols set out, with the intention of branching off in all directions. Escorting each was one of my veterans from the coast, accompanied by four or five of the more important of Kalamba's warriors. The chiefs were summoned to the station, and, in African fashion, they were to bring presents according to the wealth of their tribe, whilst at Luluaburg they were to receive flags and a proper chieftain's suit. One may imagine what excitement this message caused among the active and talkative Bashilange.

Two days after the departure of the patrol the summoned chiefs appeared, mostly without grand suites. One brought four sheep or goats, another a small elephant's tusk, a third a small boar, that with the greatest difficulty was led by twelve men, &c. Each of them had scruples that were to be removed, petitions, if possible, to be listened to, grievances about under-chiefs to be redressed, and, finally, requests of various kinds. Each one returned proudly with unfurled star flag (the new ensign of the Congo State), dressed in glaring garments, quite ready to be a staff in the alliance of lictors that Kalamba was now to command as a life-guardsman of the new state.

Only three chiefs refused to come, and they were written on the blackboard, in order to be forced into submission as soon as time permitted : this had to be done, for the sake of example.

During this time the station was like a beehive. Troops of natives came and went uninterruptedly; messengers were despatched with threats or promises; the chiefs gloried in appearing with as many village seniors as possible. Whenever any irregularities happened near the station I went myself to the places in question, as, for instance, when I went to Kongolo Mosh, who owned large villages north of the station beyond the Lulua.

This indolent chief, a most inveterate hemp-smoker, possessed no authority over his village seniors, and difficulties had arisen in the station when it was necessary to procure labourers or carriers ; in consequence, I had ordered all the seniors of the villages belonging to Kongolo to come to the chief place, had listened to their complaints, and then compelled them to make the sign of submission to their upper chief, which is to rub their heads and chests with sand, and, as a mark of pardon and peace, to give him Pemba, a ceremony in which the elder (called father in African) has to make a white mark with chalk on the forehead and chest of the younger (son).

One single old Chipulumba, who would not hear of any peaceful proceedings on the part of the younger generation, firmly refused to submit, and I had no choice but to make him prisoner and take him back to the station. I declared war at once against one of the chiefs who would not obey the summons to Luluaburg, as he could be reached in a day's march. This sufficed; he first sent ten goats as a present, and then came himself. Other subjects of one of the greatest princes, Chilunga Messo, were brought captive to the station, and kept confined till they submitted. These days, so exciting for Lubuku, made it evident to us how ambitious were these Bashilange, and how jealously they demanded the respect due to them.

The reader will be astonished to learn with what forces we undertook the subjugation of a people numbering many thousands. The strength of my troops at Luluaburg was from twenty to thirty men. They were mostly inhabitants of the coast, and almost exclusively men who had accompanied me on long journeys—the most distinguished of the many hundreds of carriers in my service. The soldiers wore a red fez, a white blouse, a white band round their hips, a sword, a belt with a cartridge-box, and a carbine. By summoning about sixty coasters living with the natives round the station, especially people of the warlike tribe of the Ginga, I was able to raise the troops to nearly 100, and should have had, of course, part of the natives on my side. My greatest help was nevertheless the trust which the Bashilange placed in me after a four years' acquaintance, a trust that will seem extraordinary even to those best acquainted with the negro, and which can be accounted for only by the unusual intelligence of the Bashilange. I am not now entering upon a close examination of this advantage, as I have already done this in my former works.

On June 21 Kalamba arrived at the station with his sister, his son, all his grandees, and a suite of about 500 warriors. He brought a present of fourteen sheep, and resigned to me some people who were guilty of crimes and offences, whose punishment he thought I should claim as my right. I sent the criminals in fetters to the Luebo to work, but asked Kalamba to punish the offences himself, after explaining to him the way in which white men deal with transgressions.

I made an agreement with Kalamba that I should give the chiefs of Lubuku time to arrange matters within their sphere, while I would visit Kassongo Chiniama on the Lubilash; and that at a great meeting I should place all the chiefs under his command; and that if Germano, as I hoped, should have arrived meanwhile, I should set out for my long journey. Some days before, a letter had come from Germano, through some Kioques, in which he reported that on the way to the coast he had lost thirty men, a third of his caravan, from small-pox, which had made him prolong his journey to four months. From fear of small-pox, which was known to rage in the interior, on the way to the Lulua, few carriers were to be had at Angola, and he would not be able to start before May. So I could not expect him till August.

Kalamba Moana was to accompany me on my journey to the Balungu; and while he was making preparations and collecting followers, my officers and I prepared ourselves for our future business at the now quiet station. Captain De Macar, who was to accompany me to the Balungu, was to take charge of the station

A DISAGREEABLE SURPRISE

later on, after my final departure; while Le Marinel was to go with me on the long journey to the East, whither I was taking the Bashilange, in order that he might eventually take them back to their country.

The two gentlemen were engaged in preparing for their future duties; they studied languages and made meteorological observations at the station, which I had taken pains to make possible again by repairing several instruments.

Besides the usual work at the station, we were much engaged in the building of bridges, which presented many difficulties on account of the frequently swollen water-courses. We could soon pass every stream in the course of a day's journey on bridges, and even when in the saddle; only on the Lulua was intercourse carried on in a number of large canoes. In building a bridge we made use of palm-stems as stretchers, as they were so long and firm, and could easily be cut near the rivers.

One day I came upon some labourers who were in the act of cutting the top off a felled palm-tree. I wanted to teach one of them, who showed himself clumsy in handling his axe, how to use it, by taking it myself and striking several blows. At the third blow the bystanders uttered a cry of warning, and at the same moment two large dark snakes came darting out of the top of the tree, but fortunately rushed past me into the thicket. I had, it appeared, cut off the extreme end of the tail of one, and part of the back of the other, to which may be ascribed the lucky cirumstance that the reptiles did not bite me. As far as I could make out, they were spectacle-snakes (Haja-Haje). These and the puff adder are doubtless the most venomous and dangerous of all African snakes.

CHAPTER IV

EXPEDITION TO THE UPPER RIVER BASIN OF THE SANKURRU—LUBILASH

Collecting the escort for the journey—A good shot—A terrier trying to attack a hippopotamus—Plundering by my men—Æolian bells—The savage Balungu—Put on the wrong track—The Kanjoka—Dancing women—Boundary of the pure Baluba—Threats—Dense population—On the Bushi Maji—Insolence of the natives—War—Effect of the report of a gun—Treacherous Baluba—Falsehoods of the Balungu—Resultless negotiations—Warlike expedition to punish our insolent enemies—A hundred prisoners and a large booty—Want of ammunition—My resolve to return—The inhospitable Baluba country—A dangerous retreat—Fair—Bad state of health—At Luluaburg—Conflagration—Le Marinel's dangerous illness.

On June 26 I marched from our village with Captain De Macar, twenty coasters, and fifteen Bashilange, in order to pick up natives, who were to accompany us to the Balungu at Kalamba's and farther on the road. The first day we stayed with Kalamba, where we were joined by Kalamba Moana, with about 100 men. The notorious Kioque chief, Mona Ngana Mukanjanga, who before Pogge's and my coming had brought the first firearms to Lubuku, had arrived with a caravan. After our first journey this chief had justly apprehended that we should lessen his influence, and had accordingly sworn hostility to us. He had repeatedly tried to influence Kalamba against us, and threatened to drive us back with Kioques as plentiful as 'grass' in the savannah. Now Kalamba told me smilingly that the great Mukanjanga had, for fear of me, fled to the primæval forest.

In our march we stopped at every village, to pick up five men at one, ten or more at another, and so on. Our

CAPTAIN DE MACAR

reception was a pacific one throughout, and we had so many presents given us at every place that we were able to live in princely style. Chingenge, twenty-five of whose warriors joined us, brought four sheep, a goat, a pig, a duck, a parrot, pine-apples, bananas, tomatoes, onions, and millet beer. He, being my oldest friend, was ready as usual; in many respects he would have been

LULUMBA FALL

more qualified to be the upper chief of Lubuku, but his election might have been objected to by too many chiefs; for, being more energetic than Kalamba, he had had many disputes and many a fight with most of the grandees of Lubuku. For this reason, therefore, much as I regretted it, he had to subject himself to Kalamba. I, however, purposely ranked him as Kalamba's first vassal.

From this point I turned to the south to visit Prince Katende, of the Bashilamboa. Here also we were most kindly welcomed: they had forgotten that a year before, in a war with the Bashilamboa, I had been obliged to burn their villages. The Bashilamboa, who with their chief Katende had refused to acknowledge Kalamba as their superior, had gone to the Lulua and had settled in obscure Chipulumba villages. I was made aware of their obstinacy the evening after my arrival at Katende's. I had gone down to the river with De Macar to hunt hippopotami, when I met a canoe, which I hailed and requested its occupants to take me to an island from whence the hunt would be facilitated. They, however, whom Katende's men called Chipulumba, refused to oblige me, and rowed to the opposite shore, from whence they mocked me with the name of Toka-Toka,[1] requesting me to come over to them to fetch the canoe, or to show them how far my fire-arms would carry. In compliance with this request, I aimed at the bow of the canoe, which they had tied to a tree, and my shot cut the palm rope by which it was fastened, so that, caught by the current, it floated downward. Believing that I had intended this result, they fled, amazed at the sure aim of my weapon. At this place the Lulua was 200 metres broad. I then visited the magnificent Lulumba Fall, which Pogge had discovered four years before and had erroneously called Kangonde Fall. Before crossing the Cassai I had here once shot a hippopotamus that, roaring and tossing, had approached my canoe. At the time I had one of our terriers with me; after the shot the little creature jumped overboard and swam to the place where the hippopotamus had appeared. The mortally wounded monster came twice to the surface; the last time, the

[1] Albino.

terrier, on the point of attacking, was so near him that the water, splashed by the foot of the hippopotamus, dashed over his assailant. The terrier, however, did not give in, and when his prey was no longer visible he swam round and round, barking with excitement; nay, he even tried to reach the hippopotamus by putting his head under water.

Although European dogs easily lose their inclination to hunt in Equato-

A HEROIC TERRIER

rial Africa, my experience has taught me that the terrier belongs to the race that can best resist the climate. There is no game that a good terrier will not attack. I am sorry to say that it was just the dauntlessness of the little heroes that made us lose them.

On July 2 we passed the Lulua and pitched our camp with the chief of the Bena Lokassu, named Chimboa. I had now nearly 200 men, about 150 of whom were armed with guns, and so I terminated my recruiting business.

From the extensive, well-cultivated fields intersected with broad roads which we saw when on the march, we soon found that we were not about to encamp with Chipulumbas, but with well-civilised Bashilange, the Bena Jionga. We were kindly welcomed, and, as everywhere in this country, my people were allowed the free use of the fields. Only meat—meaning in Bashilangish fowls, locusts, dried caterpillars, goats, &c.—had to be bought. For this reason, therefore, the allowance that I gave the people—which for a week, perhaps, did not exceed the value of a yard of stuff—sufficed. Travelling with the Bashilange is very cheap; they find something to eat everywhere, while the coasters would soon be at a loss. When they feel strong enough, I must own, it is difficult to keep them from taking what they find, and, in spite of warning, I had to put some of Kalamba Moana's men into chains for having stolen fowls. I had not taken many provisions with me, nor could I give out many; for, as I had calculated pretty nearly what Germano would bring from the coast, I had arrived at the conclusion that I should not be able to make my long journey to the east. Knowing the general circumstances in Inner Africa, I should have made what provisions I had or expected to have suffice; but the stay of my expedition at Stanley Pool had made a large hole in my resources. Everything was exorbitantly dear there, though I had sold to the Congo State the ivory that I bought whilst exploring the

VILLAGE OF THE BENA WITANDA

Cassai, in exchange for provisions; and though I had made my Bashilange work for wages at Leopoldville. Added to this, Wolf had been persuaded during my absence to pay our coasters higher wages, in order to satisfy them, since they had seen that the soldiers on the Lower Congo received much higher pay. Though I had succeeded in somewhat reducing the wages, yet my money difficulties continued. From my first journey I had been accustomed simply to give what was most necessary, and only when absolutely obliged to do so had I granted the after-claims of the negroes, who were always increasing their demands.

It is very difficult to accustom oneself to African thriftiness, especially if one is a new-comer. A young European is easily inclined, in order to make the negro more peaceably disposed, or to be relieved of long haggling, to allow an increase of salary. The disadvantage of such a proceeding lies not in having to increase once, or even more than once; it lies in the negro's becoming aware of how he will gain his end by begging, which accomplishment he will make use of in a very dexterous way. I was told by Wolf that Lieutenant Bateman had a knack of easily making friends with the natives. My first journey with Dr. Pogge, who knew how to travel very economically, was a good lesson to me.

Since we crossed the Lulua we had entered a beautifully fertile and picturesque district. Nearly all the summits of the hills were covered with groves of oil-palms, the remains of former villages. On the slopes extended rich fields; the long-stretched ridges between numbers of watercourses showed grass savannahs, and the banks of the brooks, often thirty metres deep, were covered with primæval forests.

On the 4th we entered the territory of the Bena Witanda, covered with numerous villages. The Moiio, a rivulet of twenty metres breadth and two or three metres depth, was crossed on a suspension bridge, which in consequence of a very ingenious arrangement was quite safe. The houses were gable-shaped, as all the Bena Riamba were compelled to have them.

At the Bena Witanda we found an Æolian bell, which was as simple as it was melodious. The bell-shaped cup of a dried pumpkin peel was suspended from a tall pole bent at the top. Round about the bell, pieces of well-dried grass a span long were fastened to thin ends of bast, which, when shaken by the wind, produced a melodious noise. These villages were also without

ÆOLIAN HARPS

shade; in the centre the Kiota, with long-stretched piles of firewood, was kept scrupulously clean. Round each house a little garden was laid out, planted with wild hemp, tobacco, onions, pumpkins, tomatoes, and capsicum, which latter is abundantly used for the dishes of the Bashilange.

The conductors of our Balungu, the messengers sent me by Kassongo Chiniama, often gave cause for disputes.

The Balungu were hot-headed to such an extent that on the slightest occasion they fell into a towering rage, in which state they did not satisfy themselves with words only, as do the Bashilange, but at once made energetic use of their sticks. Being on an average greatly superior to the Bashilange as regards strength and dexterity, the consequences of such a dispute were mostly serious for the latter.

I began now to greatly distrust the information of our guides. They often contradicted themselves about stating distances. At first it was said to be only a seven short days' journey from the station to their chief. But since crossing the Lulua, the number of days' journeys, though we kept on marching, instead of decreasing, daily increased. I often had scruples as to whether I had made proper preparations for the expedition. The Balungu appeased my doubts by swearing that Chiniama would surely take it upon himself to maintain the caravan for nothing, and also to give the men provisions for the return journey. Neither would they listen to my scruples about the small quantity of ammunition, for, they said, along the road lived only 'goats,' a term for cowardly, un-martial people.

It seemed to be pretty certain that after crossing the Lubi we should have to pass two larger tributaries of the Lubilash, before finding on the banks of the third the village residence of Kassongo. In the Balungu language, river is Lubilashi, Lubilanshi, or Lubiranzi.

South of our route the Balungu knew of another road, through the Bakete countries. The territory of these natives, contemptuously called Tubindi or Tubintsh, lay two or four days' journey south of our road; part of the Bakete is said to be called Akauanda and to border upon Lunda.

On the 6th we reached the district of the Baqua Kanjoka, one of the most populous in the Bashilange country. Here, to the east of the Bashilange tribe, the transition to the pure Baluba shows more distinctly than anywhere else. The clever tattooings are seldom seen, as is the case with the pure Baluba; these tattooings were here and there replaced by coloured ornaments. The appearance of the men was taller and stronger, and they were also more clumsy in figure, than the almost gracefully-built Bashilange.

The reader will be astonished to learn that we were received here not only kindly but even submissively, while Lieutenant von François, who had been sent here more than a year before, complained of the savageness of these tribes, and often found himself and his followers hard pressed by them. Most likely this gentleman, who was then a stranger in the country, was mistaken, as many others have been: he considered the noisy reception, and the boisterous, restlessly wild behaviour of the people as a mark of hostility, while, most likely, it was caused only by surprise and delight. The people accompanying Von François, whom I questioned about it, with the view of eventually resenting the behaviour of the chiefs, were likewise of opinion that the chiefs, in perhaps rather a savage manner, had been contending about whom the white man was to live with, and that the traveller had misinterpreted the means they had used to gain their end into hostilities, whereas the carriers had never been apprehensive of danger.

The principal chief of the Kanjoka—Tenda, or Tenda Mata—a man with pleasant features and a gentle voice, who, in consequence of his marked indecision and indolence, sometimes gave one the impression of his being an idiot, but who, in reality, was very cunning, brought a small herd of goats in honour of our arrival. I, however, gave him a very sharp reproof when he offered Kalamba Moana his 'mutullu,' i.e. present, which made the Kanjoka, who were screaming with delight, suddenly very quiet and subdued. Tenda, expecting that great demands of tribute would be made upon him, was somewhat excited; but I should have been wrong to calm him, for a great chief must request great presents, and consequently those who do not are not much thought of.

The Kanjoka country is particularly rich in iron, and there are some excellent smiths there. Salt also is produced, so that the Kanjoka, with the products of their country and their iron manufacture, undertake commercial expeditions to the south as far as the Lunda country. Within an hour I bought 125 very beautiful hatchets, for each of which I exchanged coloured handkerchiefs. Tenda had, for the last year, sent nearly every month hatchets and axes to Luluaburg.

Kalamba Moana asked me to let him go, with the assistance of 100 men, to the chief Kassongo Luaba, who was at war, one or two days' journey from here, with the Baluba and hard pressed, to which, however, I did not consent, as close investigation proved that he was completely master of the situation. Kassongo Luaba was the most enterprising chief of the Bashilange, and their greatest traveller. He was reported to have been far beyond Lunda, as far as the lakes, to buy copper (Bangueolo in the Katanga country). He also knew Muata Jamwo, and was said to have seen a white man with him, perhaps Dr. Pogge.

After the settling of the tribute and of the presents to be made in return, I ordered a three days' rest, so that my men might supply themselves with provisions for the districts farther east, which were said to be poor. Tenda, at his own request, received permission to accompany me with twenty men. He also brought me a guide, the chief Kasairi Pambu, who lived two days' journey eastward.

Kasairi was a tall, handsomely-built man of about sixty, with grey hair, a heavy moustache, and an imposing carriage and bearing. The chief carried a spear eight feet long, and a heavy club a metre in length. A bunch of parrot's feathers was fastened in his hair at the back, and two skins of civet-cats, held by a belt in front and behind, constituted his dress.

On the evening before we set out on our march a long row of women approached my tent, accompanying their monotonous singing with slight movements of the hips. Each woman carried a calabash filled with palm wine or millet beer, and these they put down before me one by one—a goodly array of pumpkin bottles; then they formed a circle round me, and the dancing continued until I delighted the fair ones, some of whom belonged to Tenda's harem, whilst others were female relatives of his, by giving them some beads. The present they

RECEPTION BY THE KANJOKA LADIES

brought induced me to arrange a party, to which I invited the whole gentry of the village and of my caravan.

Next day we passed the last Bashilange, a small village of the Bena Kashia, and in crossing the Lukalla, which falls into the Lubi, we entered the eastern boundary of the country of the Baqua Kalosh, a large family of the Baluba tribe. The Baluba represent the largest tribe of Equatorial Africa. They extend south of the Bashilange, who also call themselves Baluba—though evidently largely mixed with other tribes—from the Cassai to far beyond the Lualaba, and even as far eastwards as the Tanganyika. Their northern boundary lies about six degrees south latitude. The south of the Bangueolo is still inhabited by Baluba. A large part of Muata Jamwo's country is occupied by Baluba; and though the Baqua Lunda cannot be called Baluba, they are, at any rate, a tribe nearly related to them—perhaps a mixture of Baluba and Kaffirs who have immigrated from the south. This supposition was caused by observations of Pogge's on his journey to Muata Jamwo.

The villages now ceased; the Kalosh lived dispersed in farms. Their huts were built on a square understructure of pounded clay. Strong rods driven in in the square were bent together at a height of two or three metres, intertwined by parallel-running rods and covered with grass. The door, fastened with shutters of bark or palm ribs, was so low that one had to bend when entering.

The difference between two nations is seldom so strongly marked as is seen to be the case on crossing the Lukalla, the most easterly point reached by Europeans (Von François). The Kalosh are a heavy, muscular, one may say a gigantic people; among them giants of six feet in height are frequently found. Their broad, strongly developed jaws give the face somewhat the appearance of a bull-dog.

The manners of the Kalosh are noisy and savage, their voices, like the Bakuba's, are deep, their gait is heavy and ponderous; the hair is held together in thick masses by palm-oil mixed with clay, thus affording a

FARMS OF THE KALOSH

good protection against the club, the favourite weapon of the Kalosh. I never saw bows, only long spears with iron points, of which a warrior mostly carries two or three. High shields constructed of willows form a rude protection. Now and then I saw Lunda knives carried in the arm-hole, or small Bashilange knives in their belts.

The sign of a chief consisted in a short-handled hatchet with a very large and broad blade. Instead of tattooing they sometimes painted themselves with red, yellow, or white colours. The women anointed their whole bodies with oil and red clay, the richer ones with oil and pounded red-wood, which they were said to buy from the north.

We halted at one of the largest farms belonging to the chief Kashama. This chief, a handsomely-built and heavy man, whose thick beard was intertwined with small beads, and whose arms were almost covered with iron and copper rings, brought me a fat sheep as a present.

On our march next day we were astonished at finding a dense population. The country, as far as one could see across the prairie, was covered with farms. Hundreds of people accompanied us screaming, and the warriors running alongside the caravan beat the ground with their clubs, or exhibited their dexterity in throwing spears.

We were stopped by messengers who were sent to tell us not to march on before sending presents to the neighbouring chiefs; and that, if we did not conform to this custom, we should be delayed by force. I sent back word that we did not wish for war, but that we should march on as long as it pleased us. I warned them to be cautious with their threats lest I should lose my temper and lessen the presents. The behaviour of the Baluba messengers was such as to require an energetic answer, and the Kalosh evidently calculated upon intimidating my Bashilange.

Kasairi Pambu, who next day wanted to introduce us into his territory, took great pains to prevent a serious

A KALOSH

encounter, which the behaviour of the natives might bring on at any moment. He drove those back who insolently approached our bulls; nay, several times when an uproar arose between his tribe and my people, in which the former at once assumed a threatening position, he broke the spears of the offenders. As was to be expected, his behaviour, after he gained his end and after we were encamped near his farm, became just as insolent as that of the surrounding crowd, which numbered thousands. In this bare, shadeless country, only showing undulating prairies with few trees, everything seemed bent on annoying us, even the flies that chose to settle on our eyelids. Kasairi Pambu, contrary to African custom, did not bring any present, but expected one from me first; he, however, expected in vain.

The attitude of the natives became more and more threatening. One chief accused Mona Tenda, of my party, of an old debt, and sent word to me that he would not let us go before Tenda had paid it. Kasairi came with a large suite in the evening, requesting me to stay where I was instead of starting the next day, as was my intention; and he even threatened me with war when I curtly refused to do so. I then told him that if he dared to threaten me in my camp I should have him punished. My Bashilange were rather depressed, but the behaviour of my few veterans from the coast, who, after a few years' experience, always took their cue from me, somewhat raised their courage. In order to prevent any misunderstanding I gave a 'moiio' at dusk, telling them that we should start to-morrow. I concluded with scornful laughter at the boldness of the Kalosh who dared to hinder our starting. The laughter was responded to by the caravan, and as a result Kasairi Pambu sent two goats and promised to serve us as guide the next day. Our departure eventually took place without any disturbance.

We marched on and on between hundreds of farms.

through the undulating prairie, whose slopes differed in height 100 metres at the utmost. The soil was so bad that not even the water's edge was bordered with trees.

We now entered the district of the Baqua Disho, who in no wise differed in their appearance from the Kalosh. A large potato field gave us room for our camp, and at the same time food for our people.

South of the Disho lived the Baqua Tembo, likewise Baluba.

Another day's march led us for about two hours through a savannah of brushwood that was uninhabited. Then we descended into a valley that was only prairie, and which was populated even more thickly than the district we had traversed during the previous days. Dense crowds repeatedly tried to delay us, requesting us to stay. The three soldiers marching before me halted on such occasions, and my quiet bull, regardless of the uproar, led the way and made the crowd disperse before his broad horns.

We approached the bottom of the valley, where the first of the three tributaries of the Lubilash forced us to halt. The Bushi-Maji, or Kishi-Maji, was at this time, in the dry season, about 100 metres in width and 1·25 in depth; but the canoes we saw showed that a great part of the year it was too deep to be waded through. I rode through the river, and after calling out to De Macar to superintend the further progress, I walked up the bank to find out a place suitable for the camp. Scarcely had I left the river for ten minutes, when the guide of my coast soldiers, the bold and cunning Humba, came running to tell me that a disturbance had commenced on the crossing, and that the natives showed themselves hostile. I hastened back to the river, and found the greater part of the caravan, mostly men and all the soldiers, on this side, while on the opposite side only women and some sick people were waiting to cross. On the slope of the bank, in an amphitheatre round them, stood many hundreds of natives, who, perhaps disgusted that we did not stay in their district, were ill-treating my people and trying to take part of the loads from them.

Just at the moment when I reached the river a canoe stopped on this side. I jumped in; my manservant, Sankurru, followed with three of my best men, Humba, Simão, and Kataraija. The native guides of the canoe in their fright jumped overboard and fled down stream; as they had thrown away the oars, I seized a short stick and pushed the canoe towards the opposite shore. My stick, however, proved too short for the depth of water; we floated down, and were jeered at by the Baluba in front of us. We now jumped into the water and waded across. The greater number of Baluba, only men, pushed towards the point where we wanted to land, and when we had approached the shore to within about thirty-five metres they threw large stones at us. The delight of the Kalosh became greater and greater. Then suddenly a stone nearly hit my face, some spears followed, and even a shot from one of the few guns in the possession of the Baluba, which showed us that now we had to act. I took my rifle and shot the foremost of the stone-throwers between the eyes through his head, so that he fell down on his face.

I

With the second barrel I laid another man low, when he was just about to throw his spear at me. My companions as well as those from the opposite bank, who were watching the proceedings, began to fire at the Baluba. The dense crowd retreated from the river, and my three companions and I made use of that moment to climb the bank, under cover of the precipice. The whole number of Baluba fled, and my people tore after them shouting with delight at the surprising result.

A strange effect of my first shot was seen in the case of a native lying close to the shore. The ball had entered his head between the eyes, and caused the skull to split all round quite evenly. The crowd—which, according to the calculation of the women, numbered at least 500—had fled in all directions, leaving five dead behind.

On returning to our caravan some natives appeared up the river, calling out to us that we must, during the hostilities, consider a small brook falling into the river opposite as the boundary between us; those living south of it, not being engaged in the contest, were accordingly assured of neutrality.

Close to the edge of the Bushi-Maji I chose as a place of encampment a small neck of land, formed by the river and a lagoon, and accessible from the land only, with a breadth of ten metres. The connection with the mainland was quickly cut off by a barricade of trees. All the canoes that were found near were fastened to the bank; then we posted sentinels, as some patrols reported the approach of a large number of Baluba. Towards evening a gigantic chief, accompanied by only

DISTURBANCE ON THE BUSHI MAJI

a few people and without arms, came to our camp, intimating his peaceable intentions by clapping his hands. I called him near; and after he had expressed his surprise at the first white man he had seen, he proved his pacific disposition by offering to ask natives from the opposite side to come close to the shore, under the pretence of negotiating with them, in order to give me the opportunity of shooting at them from behind a tree. The disgust with which I refused his treacherous proposal greatly astonished him. His manner showed that caution was necessary with the Baluba.

Kashawalla learnt that by starting at sunrise we should reach the Luilu, the central tributary of the Lubilash, in the afternoon, and that from thence it would be only a long day's journey to the Lubiranzi. Both these rivers were said to be of the same size and depth as the Bushi-Maji. Between the latter and the Luilu lived the Baqua Mukendi, beyond the Luilu again Baluba. In order to get to Kassongo Chiniama, I had, I was told, to go three days' march towards the south between the Luilu and Lubiranzi. This was corroborated by my Bashilange guides; but such a statement only proved that their former assertions had been incorrect. My cunning Humba told me that after his inquiries he was convinced that our Balungu were not sent by Kassongo, but were part of a caravan of traders, who in conducting us to their chief wanted to gain his favour and be rewarded by him. Kassongo Chiniama was said to possess many guns from the south, from Lunda, and to be subject to Mona Kanjika, who lived only a day's journey from him; Mona Kanjika, again, was subject to

Muata Jamwo of Lunda. The Balungu, being now sharply questioned, and convinced that they could no longer deceive us, gave us many interesting reports. They spoke of a European who had come from the east, and who had passed through their country many years before accompanied by a Mukalanga (an Arab). This had evidently been Lieutenant Cameron. Then they told us that another white man with Kangombe carriers (Bihé people) had been with them, who had come from the south, and had gone round the east of Lunda; he had presented Kassongo with a revolver, and was probably a Portuguese trader who later was at war with the Arab Famba, and had had to flee with the loss of the greater part of his goods. I was the first white man, they said, who had come from the west.

Here, then, we had approached a point where the journeys of the three first Europeans, from the east, from the south, and from the west, met. The people also knew that Pogge and I had formerly passed farther north. They were evidently acquainted, too, with the western tributary of the Lualaba, the Komorondo; for they said that, in going to Katanga to fetch copper, they were obliged to pass the Lomami and another large river, which flowed through a series of lakes. Later, when unfavourable circumstances prevented my exploring the Lualaba, I reproached myself for not having tried to advance into the Balungu district.

When night had set in, an uninterrupted noise of drums and shouts began in the territory of the punished Kalosh. Under cover of the darkness they came to the edge of the river and jeered at us. I sent them word by the Balungu that I wished them next day to surrender the two warriors who had begun the fight by throwing stones, and that if they did so I should keep the peace; if they did not do so I should come over and burn their farms. They answered scornfully, that I might come if I liked; they would to-morrow morning oppose me with a force innumerable as the grass of the savannah (a favourite African comparison), that would annihilate me and my party. The Baqua Mukendi before us were likewise alarmed, and they just waited to see where I was going, since, now I was here, they did not mean me to leave the Baluba country any more. My Bashilange slept little during the night, for the incessant screaming from the opposite bank—an exulting, piercing sound which, uttered through the hollow hand, resembles the bark of a hyena—kept them in constant excitement.

Next morning I had to distribute cartridges, for, to my surprise, I found that the Bashilange, firing across the river the day before, had used up nearly all their ammunition. Our departure was certainly not to be thought of, as it was possible the Kalosh might follow, and we did not know how the tribes in front might be disposed towards us. Considering the insolence of the Kalosh, the only means to get rid of them would be to attack them in their hamlets, and to scatter them in such a way that they would not be able to assemble again before our departure; this would at the same time intimidate the other tribes. At daybreak I crossed the river with 100 men, leaving De Macar in defence of the fortified camp, for the Kalosh were descending in endless swarms to the bank.

The natives living opposite the brook called out to me to request that I would wait; they would try once more to restore peace by surrendering the enemies demanded, or by a payment on the part of the Kalosh. I gave them time, which I indicated by pointing with my hand to the height of the sun, and waited on the shore.

RETURN FROM THE FIGHT

Nothing, however, was to be seen of the Kalosh, and when the sun reached the height I had fixed upon, I marched straight through their hundreds of farms, of which those in the immediate neighbourhood were even then deserted. Troops of enemies followed us beyond reach of a shot, with their long spears, beating their shields and mocking us. I forbade shooting and marched briskly on. I was soon amongst farms that were still inhabited, and everywhere the people began to flee in the utmost haste. Everyone ran to and fro with his belongings, but I marched steadily forward to the summit of a hill that commanded a view into the far distance.

I now sent out companies, each consisting of ten men, in all directions to make prisoners and to report about any warlike gatherings. I showed the patrols the boundary of their advance, and gave orders that if they saw smoke ascending from the farm where I stopped they were to return to me, after having set on fire such farms as they could reach.

I soon knew by the bright fires that the troops had here and there encountered the enemy; only from one quarter we got the message that the force of the Kalosh was too strong to be attacked by the patrol. A reinforcement was sent at full speed to the spot, and rapid shooting from the same direction, which seemed to get more and more distant, announced the defeat of the enemy.

When the firing had ceased on all sides I set the farm on fire, and pillars of smoke rising everywhere in a half-circle told me that my signal had been noticed. My troops now approached, literally loaded with fowls, and driving goats before them like prisoners. I marched slowly back, and did not reach the Bushi-Maji till late in the afternoon, and from the cheering shouts in the camps I concluded that everything was all right there. When we reached the camp, the booty, some thirty goats, several hundreds of fowls, and the corn, was distributed, and the prisoners, numbering over a hundred, were fenced in, so as to be better watched. According to my guides' account, about ten Baluba, who had fled in every direction after a short resistance, were killed. One of our party, however, was missing, and by the evening we saw his head, which they had fastened to a long pole, displayed by the Kalosh.

The natives on our right bank, who had assembled in great numbers near the camp, were at first thoroughly intimidated by the surprising result; but that this mood would not last long was proved by the behaviour of the Kalosh, who began to jeer at us from the opposite bank as soon as it was dark. I had now to decide upon the next steps to be taken.

For six more days we had to pass through territory quite as populous as before, and on one of those days we must again come upon part of the Kalosh tribe, who, as the Mukendi thought, would certainly make war. By that time we should have reached Kassongo Chiniama, of whose disposition we were by no means sure, and of whose hot-headed, warlike people our guides were an example. Provisions were getting scarce, as we had been deceived about the distance; but, what was more serious, our ammunition was so much reduced that I had not more than five cartridges at the utmost left for each man. It was impossible to deter the Bashilange from shooting, even at ridiculously long distances.

Our way to Kassongo Chiniama had led us far beyond the southern boundary of the Congo State, so that I could take upon me no further risk, if only for the reason that Kassongo Chiniama no longer belonged to the Congo State. Thus I was left no choice but to decide upon a retreat, though the idea of having to go back for the first time in Africa was exceedingly painful to me; however, I had to think of my Bashilange and avoid the loss of human life in prospect of my intended long journey. Though I had not seen the Luilu and Lubiranzi, as I should have desired, the reports about these two rivers so agreed with each other that an error about the situation was not probable. I had seen enough of the country and its people, and the scenery was said always to remain the same—grass-savannah everywhere. The population as far as the boundary of Balungu consisted of Baluba, with whom I did not wish to have anything to do.

The Baluba have remarkably little inclination to improve their arms and utensils. Their spears are simply long pointed rods of hard wood; their shields are made of coarse wickerwork, their clubs are without any carving, and their kitchen pots and pans are of the same shape as those used farther west; indeed, everything showed rudeness and an entire want of a sense of beauty. The huts, in the shape already described, were slovenly; anything there was of iron, weapons or utensils, was Lunda work or imported from the Bashilange. The country itself is miserably monotonous. They have nothing that would be suitable for commerce with neighbouring people, except human beings, and everything imported is paid for with slaves. Even firewood is wanting. Nor is there any game, in consequence of the dense population scattered everywhere. Goats are not often found, while sheep and pigs are not met with anywhere. Next to Ugogo, in the far east of Africa, this country is the most inhospitable that I know of and the most unsuitable for any attempts at civilization. But what disgusted us most was the childish insolence of the people; in the case of great numbers, this may prove dangerous for a traveller.

I did not impart my resolution to turn back to my party, though Kalamba Moana, Tenda, and the other chiefs were intensely anxious to know what I should do. Kalamba Moana gave a 'Moiio' in the evening, proposing that I should restore the prisoners, which, he said, would allay the hostility of the tribes, so that we might proceed without disturbance. How little a negro knows his own race! The Kalosh would certainly have considered our surrendering the prisoners as a sign of fear. I refused such proposals, and told Kalamba that the prisoners were mine, and not one man should be restored, nay, more, that on the morrow I should again attack the Kalosh and make more prisoners. I made this 'Moiio,' convinced that some Baluba were near the camp and would overhear Kalamba Moana's and my speeches, by which I hoped to intimidate the Baluba.

Next day I gave the customary signal for departure, and commanded the van of the caravan, which always consisted of my veterans, to cross the river and march the same way back that we had come. This command, the true reasons for which no one knew, caused a great commotion among the Bashilange, and the greater part of them sincerely regretted that I would not continue the journey. They of course joined their guides without disputing, and the caravan was so arranged that those with arms who had no loads to carry were distributed on every side, in order to protect and guard the carriers, women, and prisoners. Though everybody fled from us, as they had done yesterday, my caravan behaved badly, and taught me that a retreat with negroes, even under the most favourable circumstances, is always a critical affair. Small troops of natives kept running at a safe distance alongside of our caravan, now taking a threatening position in front of us, now collecting behind, without seeming to be able to venture on an attack. The caravan might have been compared to a flock of sheep surrounded by wolves. Our people pressed together, rushing on in such a hurry that I lost much of the trust I had put in the Bashilange.

Only once did the Baluba come so near that one of my men fired at them. The chief task of the soldiers who marched in front was to prevent the others from pushing forward. My veterans could only effect this by driving back those that pressed forward too quickly; thus we were able to make a retreat which, at least from a distance, appeared to be a quiet one. In this confusion a number of the prisoners managed to escape. If the Baluba could have assured themselves of our real condition, they certainly would have made an attack. In order that it should not have the appearance of a retreat, I halted several times to rearrange the caravan.

The pursuit, or rather the disturbance on the part of our enemy, did not cease till we ascended the ridge of the hill and left the populous valley of the Bushi-Maji. As I said before, I felt richer by this very important experience. If I had my choice again I should prefer a rash and apparently hazardous attack to a retreat under seemingly favourable circumstances with undisciplined negroes. The moral superiority of an attack makes such an impression on him that he does not notice the strength of the enemy; on the other hand, it tells on those attacked so overwhelmingly that they do not recognise the weakness of the assailant. This observation was of particular advantage to me in 1889, during the first encounters which I had to engage in with young troops, when suppressing the East African rebellion.

We encamped in the same place that we had occupied when coming, and noticed that the Baqua Disho, who were no doubt well acquainted with the events of the last few days, were less timid than might have been expected. When the people came into our camp to trade, several prisoners disappeared, evidently with their assistance; even one of our dogs was stolen, but was restored again when I made it plain to the chief, who was present in the camp, that he would not be allowed to leave before I got the dog back. They even wanted, obviously urged by the Kalosh, to induce us to stay.

The summit of a hill that commanded a view for miles of the densely populated country afforded a suitable camp next day. The number of invalids increased alarmingly; inflammation of the lungs especially began to show itself, caused by the cold nights and the strong winds that were continually blowing across the open prairie of the Baluba.

My quinine was used up, and the mustard plasters had been spoilt; these latter I tried to replace by poultices of hot flour mixed with red pepper.

As we went on, our old guide, Kasairi Pambu, with

some other chiefs, made his appearance, and, marching in front of us, they dispersed any gathering of armed people. We halted on the Lukalla, the boundary of the Baluba country, still the territory of the Kalosh. We found them holding one of the fairs, as is customary with all Baluba and most nations of Equatorial Africa, in celebration of which about 4,000 people were assembled in a large square. Besides the usual provisions offered for sale, there were articles of earthenware, and articles made from the palm, *uruku* (a dark red dye), and *pemba* (a white dye). Our appearance did not in the least disturb the assembly. A very stringent law had made this fair neutral ground, and we learned that even people of hostile tribes might appear without danger. The chief in whose territory the fair was held kept watch in his greatest pomp with half a dozen guards, in order that no dispute might disturb its peace. His companions were known by the broad axe which they carried on their shoulders, and whenever a somewhat loud dispute arose they were immediately at their posts. The chief Kashama, the controller of this fair, wore a beautifully arranged ornament of the plumes of the corythaix and parrot on his head. Round his throat and neck he wore a garment trimmed with strips of long-haired goat's skin, and round the hips a crinoline-shaped band of white skins. In his right hand he held a large fetish horn, in his left a far-sounding rattle (an ornamented calabash filled with stones). Round his ankles were twisted many cords with iron bells, so that each step of the giant made a tinkling sound. Behind him crouched one of his guards with the large judge's hatchet, and beside him a man who now and then beat a large wooden drum.

At intervals, Kashama performed his dances, accompanied by the screaming of the multitude, in the large space kept open for him. These dances consisted of grotesque leaps alternating with indecent rolling of the hips. After each dance a woman, likewise dancing, approached, placing her fairing before the chief. Each parish whose representatives are present on trading business has to give a present to the chief of the fair.

During the night the thermometer fell below 8° Celsius, so that De Macar and I took all the clothes out of our boxes to put them over the blankets.

Even next morning till about nine o'clock my hands were stiff with cold, rendering writing very difficult.

On the 17th we again reached Mona Tenda's village, and indeed it was high time to give my people rest, for disease had alarmingly increased. Inflammation of the lungs and fever were raging, and I was greatly alarmed at the complaints of back-aches and flashings before the eyes, as small-pox often begins with those symptoms, and there were ten cases of small-pox in the village even then.

The chiefs of my party, to whom I had made known that I should only await the arrival of provisions and ammunition before proceeding to Kassongo Chiniama, came to me requesting me to abandon the journey. They thought the Kalosh had revenged themselves by bewitching us, this being the only reason of our having so many invalids. Knowing that Germano was soon expected from the coast, I resolved upon marching back

A DANCING KASHAMA

to the station. First, however, I ordered three days of rest, and sent back some Baluba of our party with the message that I was ready to ransom the prisoners who were their relatives, asking, on the average, four goats for each prisoner—of which concession they soon availed themselves. In the end, we took a number of prisoners with us to the station, intending to send them back later on. I allowed some Baluba, relatives of Kasairi and Kashama, to accompany me to Luluaburg, thinking it might assist us in getting on a better footing with the Kalosh.

The merchant Saturnino, who had again followed me, and who was now on his way to the above-mentioned Kassongo Luaba, came to visit me; he also had been invited by the Balungu. From his guides I learnt that my suppositions about the tributaries of the Sankurru were quite right. The people added that the most eastern tributary, the Lubilasha, sprang from a lake twenty days' journey farther south.

Two of the Baluba who had fought against us on the Bushi-Maji presented a remarkable appearance. Both of them had a number of grains of shot in the back and chest. They requested me to remove them, saying that only a white man could heal wounds made by fire-arms. They thought a great many people had been wounded without daring to come to me. I of course helped them as well as I could, and in order to reward their confidence I dismissed them with a small present.

Three Bashilange had succumbed to their illness; before starting for Luluaburg a number that were unable to march I entrusted to Mona Tenda's care, leaving a

JUNGLES OF PANDANUS.

few of my soldiers behind to take them home after their recovery. The Balungu took their way home south through the Bakete country.

The appearance of the country was the same as on coming. Marching through Baqua Mulenda and Baqua Chia we met a small caravan of Mukenge, at the head of which the star flag was displayed. We had chosen the same way as Von François had done at the time, and, like him, we had great difficulty in passing the boggy pandanus jungles bordering the brooks. The principal chief of the Baqua Kassassu, one of the opponents, paid a fine for his non-appearance, and had to accompany me to Luluaburg.

We passed the source of the Moansangomma, which falls into the Lubudi, whose mouth Wolf had found on the Sankurru. The number of the weak and sick was so large that we had frequently to make a day's halt.

A few hours before reaching Luluaburg I learnt that there had been a great conflagration at the station. I saw on arriving there on the 25th that the large barracks, containing twenty-one rooms, had been entirely destroyed by fire. The walls, consisting of strong trees plastered with clay, had been burning for three days. Nothing else had happened; Germano had not arrived; but letters had come from Angola, which reported about the provisions to be expected.

The time now approached when I had to place under command of Kalamba the chiefs who had received the flag of the Congo State. I agreed with him that this should take place at the station. Only the villages in the nearest vicinity of the station, under their chief Chiniama, were to become immediately subject to it; while Kalamba was responsible for all the other chiefs of Lubuku. September 10 was fixed as the day of meeting of the princes of Lubuku, and once more patrols were sent in all directions to deliver the invitations.

News had arrived from Lieutenant Bateman on the Luebo of his having had an encounter with the Bakuba, who had retreated with the loss of five men. I therefore sent down orders to communicate this to the great chief Luquengo, and to request that he, according to his promise to Wolf, should place himself on a good footing with us, unless he wanted us to visit him with a few thousand Bashilange.

At the beginning of the rainy season the Europeans had, as usual, much to suffer from fever. Lieutenant Le Marinel was visited by a dangerous fever, which so exhausted him that we began to fear for his life. As he could not swallow quinine I gave him injections, experiencing great difficulties from the want of proper medicines. I had only sulphuric quinine, which I dissolved in acetic acid for the injection. The consequence was that the injection caused large and deep wounds. The quinine took effect in spite of all, and after the intense irritation was removed by injections of morphia, I had the great satisfaction of finding him free from fever, after a nearly two days' sleep, which was so profound as only to be interrupted by the painful injections. A so-called cock-tail, a beverage compounded of brandy, sugar, eggs, bitters, and nutmeg, proved a very salutary nourishment and stimulant. It was a long time before the weakened constitution of the originally strong young officer was restored to perfect health.

CHAPTER V

REGULATION OF POLITICAL AFFAIRS AT LUBUKU— DEPARTURE FOR THE NORTH-EAST—THE JOURNEY TO THE SANKURRU

Meeting of the chiefs of Lubuku—Heavy hail storm—My fruitless search for Germano—Dr. Sommers—Germano at last—Departure for our long journey to the North-East—Camp building—Robberies and skirmish—Prairies—Villages set on fire—Pacific welcome—Slave trade of the Bihé people—Primæval forests—Inhospitable savages—On the Lubi—Simão's gallant swimming expedition—Punishment of the rapacious Ngongo—A thief punished by an arrow-shot—On the Sankurru.

Now followed, as it were, a Sisyphus-work, which did not lead to the aim desired for two months, viz. to make Kalamba head chief of Lubuku, though he had to be subject to us. It had not required much trouble to force the seniors of the villages to submit to their upper chiefs, but to unite the different opinions of the latter, each of whom considered himself greatest, proved more difficult than I had counted upon.

The returning patrols, who had given the chiefs notice of the appointed meeting, brought some of them back with them. Others had reported themselves ill, some were from home, and others again plainly refused to come. The most obstinate was Kilunga Messo, who, whenever I went to him, promised everything, paid his fine, and declared himself ready to obey, but would not subordinate himself to the command of Kalamba. As I had advisedly arrived at the result that the Bashilange could only be ruled by one of their own party, I did not give way, but resolved eventually to carry out my intention by force. Thirty-six chiefs met at last at Luluaburg, among them Kilunga Messo; but

BETWEEN LULUA AND MOANSANGOMMA

Kalamba, who was at times very obstinate, played me the trick of not coming, because, as he sent me word, he was afraid of being fetished by Kilunga Messo, whom he durst not look in the face before he (Kilunga) had smoked hemp in his kiota. So I was compelled to induce the last opposing chief, Kilunga Messo, to submit at Kalamba's village, or rather town, for the place contained at least 10,000 inhabitants.

The reception at Kalamba's, when I brought him the last of the opposing chiefs, was a grand one. My 'Moiio' was repeated by at least 5,000 voices. In the centre of the kiota, round which the innumerable mass of people had crowded, Kilunga Messo had to walk three times round the sacred fire of hemp, saying the while that he did not entertain any evil thoughts against Kalamba; then, sitting between Kalamba Moana and another chief, he had to smoke hemp; after which he was led into Kalamba's house, where the reconciliation of the two old enemies and the personal subordination of Kilunga Messo to Kalamba took place. Great was the delight all round that peace now reigned at Lubuku, and that they had no longer to fear the nations beyond the boundary of the hemp-smoking Bashilange; nations weak in comparison to the now united Lubuku. Playing at war, shooting, hemp-smoking, dancing and singing terminated the festivities of the alliance of Lubuku.

Before I rode back to the station Kalamba gave me a beautiful bull, which he had bought of the Kioques, and promised to observe all that I had asked of him as the condition of retaining his supremacy.

The chief requirements were the following: All the old hostilities were to be forgotten. The chiefs alone were to retain power over their inferiors. The tribute was to be paid regularly, once a year, and it was not to be excessive. The chiefs were to be at liberty to complain of Kalamba to the head of the station. No wars were to be carried on without the consent of the head of Luluaburg. Convicts under sentence of death were to be surrendered to the station. The drinking of *juramento*—a poison which was used, in a contest between two, to decide as to the judgment of God—was prohibited. For journeys, wars, or particularly important work, Kalamba had to furnish men; for those used for work or for an escort a regular tax had to be paid, and those for warlike purposes he had to furnish gratis. The market price was to be the same throughout Lubuku.

I was engaged till the end of September in regulating these political affairs, whose stability will of course always be dependent on the controlling power of the station.

The meteorological phenomena of the months of August and September had been exceedingly strange. The rainy season had set in, but not in earnest; for although the sky was always overcast, we had only occasional drizzling rain or short showers without thunder, a very rare occurrence in these regions. Cold winds often developing into whirlwinds were frequent, and on August 14 a curious phenomenon occurred. Black clouds, which moved with extraordinary speed, were visible in the north-east. A wind, that seemed to us icy, came in storm-like gusts from the same quarter across the savannah, scorched by the meridian sun. The thermometer sank from 33° to 19° C., bananas were broken down, and many houses were unroofed in the next village. After the threatening dark clouds had drawn near across the Lulua, there was a shower of hail, rattling down in transparent icy crystals—mostly in cubes whose sides were of from one to two centimetres long—on men and beasts, causing them to scream with pain, and look out for shelter. This lasted for seven minutes, then the hail became gradually smaller, then rounded, and at length turned white, resembling the hailstones of our country. The Bashilange were quite as astonished at this incident as we were. Not before the beginning of October did the regular rainy season set in, with its one or two storms daily, mostly taking place between 5 P.M. and midnight.

At the same time I learnt that caravans were advancing, and with them the longed-for Germano. Reports of a war between the Bangala and the Kioques, through whose countries Germano had to pass, had made me very anxious.

On October 1 I started with Le Marinel to meet Germano on the Cassai, where difficulties for the caravan were to be apprehended. In crossing the Luebo we entered the territory of the Chipulumba. These tribes, to whom Pogge and I had given the name of 'the thieves' on our first journey to Lubuku, were even more hateful to us now than before, on account of thefts, punishments, threats, and a thousand and one troubles.

The eastern Bashilange have adopted the plural 'Tu' instead of 'Ba' of the Tupende.

It is singular what a difference there is between the hemp-smoking Bashilange of Lubuku and this thievishly insolent and lying mob.

Not one hour passed in the camp without my intervention being necessary for settling or punishing robberies, thefts, or some other acts of violence.

On crossing the Luebo we met a caravan who had seen nothing of Germano, though they had marched exceedingly slowly, besides stopping on the Cassai for some time. I now began to conjecture that Germano, on account of the above-named war, had been forced to retreat to the coast, or that he had been deprived of his provisions; and, greatly disappointed and depressed, I returned to Luluaburg. As without new provisions a further prosecution of my task was not to be thought of, I resolved to go down the Congo in the iron boat with a choice crew, and thence to return by steamer to procure provisions. No sooner had I selected the best of my veterans, among them Humba and Simão of course, and some Zanzibaris of Luebo station, and made the most necessary preparations for the rather long and hazardous journey, than suddenly, on October 17, the news arrived that Germano and a white man were within three days' journey.

I started next morning, and as early as eight o'clock met a small caravan headed by a European unknown to me. Dr. Sommers, having separated from the expedition of the missionary Bishop Taylor in Angola, had come here with Germano, intent upon independent missionary work. He had left Germano three days before, and had marched on in order to announce his coming. Next day I actually met Germano on the Muveau, with a thousand excuses for his unheard-of delay. With him were 200 carriers and 100 head of cattle. A large part of the caravan belonged to some black traders who had joined Germano. A great many of the provisions I had ordered had been spent in presents to chiefs, who had made difficulties on account of the war. My intended journey was at all events made possible now. The stock of cattle at the station was pleasantly increased, and by my desire Germano had brought turkeys and domestic cats, which I wanted to try to introduce in these parts. As I had apprehended, the expedition had had to encounter difficulties on the Cassai. Dr. Sommers and Germano had been compelled to oppose the insolent demands of some Kioque chiefs by a warlike demonstration.

Now commenced the organising with all our might of the expedition to the east. We were fully occupied in hiring carriers, packing loads, superintending the soldiers' exercises, shooting at targets, and other preparations. Kalamba requested a further delay of a month, which I refused, and we succeeded in completing the arrangements for our departure within ten days.

A several days' fever, however, again forced me to delay. At last the stations were placed under Captain de Macar, Dr. Sommers, and Lieutenant Bateman; the latter, as head of Luebo station, remained with him, and on November 16 I left Luluaburg with Lieutenant Le Marinel, Bugslag, Humba, Simão, besides 15 soldiers, 42 coasters, 38 ransomed Baluba slaves, and 250 Bashilange carriers. Sangula Meta, Kalamba Moana, and Chingenge joined us with 600 followers, among whom were 100 women. The caravan was accordingly 900 and odd strong, armed with 500 guns, mostly muzzle-loading.

Luluaburg, where I had worked so long, felt almost like home to me. Especially when, riding at the rear out of the gates, I called out a farewell to some of my old veterans, who remained behind, I could scarcely master my emotion, all the more when the oldest, an ancient with white hair and beard, strewing ashes before me as a fetish for the journey, exclaimed at parting: 'Deus guarda vossa excellentia!'

At Chingenge we passed the Lulua and marched N.N.E.; this was a more northerly direction than I had formerly taken with Pogge. The country at first remained the same as near Luluaburg; palm groves alternated with dense growth of primæval forest, and in the valleys were savannahs of thick trees. The clearings of the wood showed thickets of pine-apples; the narrow bottoms of the steeply-cut brooks and their slopes were mantled with primæval forest. The ridges of the rounded parts of the plateau between two slopes were covered with laterite. The humus was washed away and floated to deeper places, where it lay rather thickly. The water currents had penetrated through the layer of laterite, and thence through a layer of about thirty metres of sandstone, down to the hard bottom of Plutonic rocks. It was only upon our approaching the Moansangomma that the layer of sandstone failed, and the valleys of the brooks grew more shallow, wide, and boggy.

The continual rainy season did not much disturb us, since the regular thunderstorms did not set in till evening, or even night; my people were so far compelled only to cover their huts more carefully than usual. At first I took great care to arrange the huts myself, in order to accustom the Bashilange to build the Kilombo (camp) in a circle. The country abounded in guinea fowls, savannah fowls, and especially pigeons. Of the four species of the latter, I mention the beautiful golden green parrot-dove, living in flocks of ten or fifteen.

Without any remarkable change we passed through the villages of Bena Riamba, the people of which were devoted to us. Everywhere we received the customary presents and lived sumptuously, as our people were allowed free use of the fields, and they had only to purchase the ingredients for their meals of vegetables.

As soon as we had passed the boundary of Lubuku on the 26th, and come to the Chipulumba tribes, first among them the Bena Moanga, quarrels and acts of violence commenced. Any trading that they could not agree about turned into a fight, the consequences of which obliged us to apply our surgical knowledge to the wounds inflicted. The fault did not lie with the Chipulumba alone, for our Bashilange were repeatedly hurried into acts of violence by their sense of superiority and hatred. Bugslag, who invariably wound up the caravan with part of the soldiers, had been obliged in the Baqua Lussabi country to drive away the obstinately pursuing Chipulumba with a harmless shot; the people wanted to repay themselves by plunder for objects that they pretended had been stolen from them.

It turned out that one of our men, who had remained behind, was seized and retained by the Lussabi, so that I had to send back twenty men in search of him. The natives received my soldiers with firing, but as soon as the fire was returned they deserted the village, leaving a boy and girl in the hands of my people.

CROSSING THE LUBUDI

In the evening my man was restored, together with a present of a few goats, after which I likewise sent back the captive children. I had two Bashilange, one of my ransomed slaves and a coast-carrier, punished with fifty lashes for having taken fowls from the natives by force and thus caused disputes.

We waded through the very strong current of the Lubudi, where it was twenty metres in breadth and one metre in depth. At the urgent request of my people I distributed two charges of powder each to the Bashilange, and five cartridges each to the soldiers and carriers. North of the Lubudi we lighted upon a vast grass savannah, similar to the one we had met with at Baluba. These undulating prairies seem to extend west of the

Lubilash district along the seventh and fifth degree, as far as the Kalunda countries.

As in all grass savannahs, with their dark red porous laterite, we found an abundance of iron here, and near the extensive village of the Bena Lukoba, situated on a large pond resembling Mukamba Lake, we came upon a number of beautifully constructed furnaces.

GRASS SAVANNAH

An immense cylinder of hard-baked clay of nearly two metres diameter served as a receptacle for hard dry wood, amidst which layers of the iron clay were packed. The burning of the logs could be slackened by lessening the draught. The heavy particles of iron, melted out of the iron ore, fell to the bottom of the cylinder, and as the strongly heated structure prevented their cooling, they passed into a reservoir purified by a tube which conducted the draught from below. The houses gradually assumed the shape of the eastern Baluba houses, and the tattooing ceased: instead of it we found painting with black, white, and red colours—the only ones known here. The pond near the village, about 500 metres long and 150 metres broad, with an average depth of 1·6 metre and a boggy bottom, had a temperature of 26° C., and was stocked with large wild ducks; round its flat grassy banks crouched the night raven, which is always found on large plains or near the water. The bustard, finding a congenial locality, was also frequently met with.

On the 30th we approached several villages, whose inhabitants, Baqua Kajinga, had a month ago attacked and robbed a caravan of Chingenge's. Two of Chingenge's men had been struck by poisoned arrows, and they were afterwards killed and buried. The Kajinga, in fear of punishment, had taken flight, and Chingenge asked permission to burn their villages as a requital, to which, his account proving true, I consented. When the site of the three small villages of the rapacious Kajinga was only a heap of smoking ruins, Chingenge with his warriors went to the place where the members of his tribe were buried and, after the fashion he had learned from us, fired three salutes.

On inspecting the village before the conflagration, poisoned arrows were found; the poison, however, seemed to be very old, for an experiment tried on a fowl had but small result.

A very narrow track of primæval forest, extending

OUR RECEPTION BY THE BAQUA SELEKAI

for miles, separated the country of the robbers from the Baqua Sekelai, from whose villages a deputation came to meet us, beckoning to us with palm-branches. The chief, marching at the van, assured us that he had not been engaged in the before-mentioned attack, but that he was commissioned by the Kajinga to pay a fine as an

A MELTING FURNACE OF THE BENA LUKOBA

atonement for their crime. After assuring him that we had no hostile design, we pitched our camp in the centre of his numerous villages, whose inhabitants owned many guns. The customary presents having been exchanged, the chief reappeared, carrying thirty Baluba slaves, three goats, and a leopard's skin, as an atonement for the crime committed and in payment for the ivory stolen from

Chingenge. I decided that, considering the punishment they had sustained in having their villages burnt down, I would make this payment do, which, according to African custom, I divided between myself, the judge, those who were robbed, and their chiefs.

I repeatedly accepted presents and payments, even if consisting in slaves : in the first place, because this is African custom, and secondly, because the refusal of a present would be considered an insult; moreover, the slaves would have a much better lot with me or with the Lubuku than with the savage natives. There were a large number of such captives at Luluaburg, who had to work a certain time for the station, for which they received clothes and maintenance. After a time, which depended on the work they had done, they received full wages and were naturally free. After being ransomed, they mostly built their villages near the protecting station, and seldom made use of their permission to return home.

In the very populous district of the Baqua Chameta I allowed my caravan a day's halt, and, yielding to the wishes of the natives, I distributed brass wire and small beads for the purchase of provisions. Our old Sangula found a man here whom she had, years before, chosen for her husband, but who had abandoned his rather domineering consort by running away before the end of the honeymoon. The old lady pardoned her former lover, announcing to me her intention of taking him as a travelling companion. At first he seemed greatly rejoiced at this prospect; but when we started two days after, he was nowhere to be found. Sangula was most

SLAVE TRADING AMONG THE BIHÉ CARRIERS

indignant at his ingratitude, as she had dressed him up and supplied him with all her treasures.

Part of a caravan of Bihé people were present here, and I had a great mind to make them prisoners for their slave-trading. I had to abandon the idea, however, not knowing what to do with them. They carry on the most shameful slave trade imaginable. Black traders from Angola or Benguela turn Bihé carriers or attendants, who, though thievish, are comparatively bold and warlike, and who undertake longer journeys than any other negroes of the west coast. They go in quest of countries where a gun is unknown; they make arrangements with the chiefs about supplies of slaves, and they will even join slave-hunters. They then take their prisoners to the Bakuba tribes, where they exchange them for ivory, which they take home by the nearest route, mostly by Kabao and the Lulua.

The Bakuba buy male slaves for the sole purpose of killing them at funerals. The higher the rank of the deceased, the more slaves have to follow him to the grave.[1]

The head of Luebo station had been informed of his wicked proceeding, and he had repeatedly succeeded in depriving the Bihé caravans of their slaves or their ivory in order to prevent their coming again. I also sent a message to Luluaburg, informing Captain De Macar of the presence of such a caravan in these parts.

My instruments of observation caused many difficulties. In using the prismatic circle, the artificial sky refused to act; the quicksilver, through some carelessness, had become impure, and apparently begun to

[1] Vide *Im Innern Afrikas*.

decompose, so that to purify it was almost impossible. My aneroid barometers (Wolf had given them into my care on my departure) also showed great deviations.

After leaving the open prairie we again entered thickly wooded savannahs, with many stretches of primæval forests. Brooks became frequent, and were so deeply indented that the roads, winding round them, passed along across saddles and ridges which made it very difficult to keep the track. The inhabitants began to resemble the Baluba as regards the arrangement of their dwellings. A number of small villages with from ten to thirty huts crowned the saddles or summits. The inhabitants were seldom found to have guns, and since a European had never been in these parts, and the news of the war with Katende had perhaps made our name formidable, fear was spread wherever we appeared. But the roving and savage Baluba, who quickly take up impressions, soon lose all fear.

As the inhabitants desperately opposed the quartering of my people, i.e. the permission to use their houses, I had a camp pitched outside the villages.

On entering the territory of the large tribe of the Baqua Putt, the north-east Bashilange, the larger continuous primæval forest commenced, containing many elephants and wild boars. It must be by error that Stanley in his work 'In Darkest Africa' has stated that traces of buffaloes were found in the huge primæval forest mentioned by him; and that his men, after many days' journeys, had in their excitement shown him the first bunch of grass as a mark of the near termination of the forest. Where no grass grows the buffalo cannot live, and, considering the slowness of these animals, they could not rapidly change their abodes.

The small stingless bee, incessantly flying into one's eyes and nose, was the same nuisance here as in the forests on the Cassai. One should take care not to squeeze one of these little insects on one's skin, as the very aromatic honey that the bee carries will immediately prove a bait for a hundred more bees.

The cool brooks, whose crystal waters were rippling over pure white sand, daily afforded us a refreshing bath in the deep shadow of the forest dome; this is most conducive to health, if taken before the evening meal.

For some days we passed villages which seemed to have been deserted some time before; this we could not account for, until at one of them we ascertained by the cadaverous smell of those who had died of small-pox that this epidemic had been the cause of the deserted dwellings.

On December 5 we again met people who, with their arrows strung, were aiming at the van of our caravan; but who were pacified by the gift of some beads and afterwards served us as guides. They were savage and beggarly fellows, and, like all the people of primæval forests, timid and unsettled. As our guides stopped every ten minutes, and always where the roads crossed, so as to make greater demands if they were to guide us farther, I at length sent them away, and, keeping on the broadest road, we soon made a large village, whose inhabitants met us, ready for battle. Cheering demonstrations soon opened the phalanx, and, making use of an old camp of a Bihé caravan, we found comfortable shelter and food. The excited Bena Luwulla soon took off their bows and their huge bundles of arrows and became accessible and trustful. On our approach these natives had shown themselves like fierce dogs, obliging us to the utmost patience; but they quickly became confiding and even friendly, which soon made us forget our disagreeable reception.

We pitched our next camp near the Lubi, in the same place where, in 1881, I had crossed the river with Pogge; this time, however, I chose the left bank, which I wanted to follow down to where the river falls into the Sankurru. From the opposite shore some Bassonge approached, who from their appearance showed that they belonged to a different tribe. I here ascertained that Wolf, on sailing up the river, must have mistaken the distance: he had not passed this point, and the Bassonge said that the white man, whom on account of his large beard they had taken for Pogge, had turned back farther down. Excepting the sharp turns, which are known to have nearly caused the loss of Wolf's vessel, the river is navigable forty sea miles above. Near Bena Chikulla there is said to be a fall, up which the Bena Lussambo, inhabitants of the Sankurru, go on commercial expeditions.

I here found the home of the swimming lettuce, a small plant, met with in great quantities in the high seas many miles off the mouth of the Congo. These vegetables, resembling miniature heads of lettuce, sprout in the boggy source of a small brook; by the loosening of the roots, which hang in the water, they are severed from their birthplace, and, following the current, they reach the sea after a journey of months.

Our path took us to the north, to the edge of the left Lubi valley. From time to time there opened a lovely view of the narrow river valley, 150 metres deep.

Through its luxuriantly rich ground, the Lubi was meandering between thickets of palms and fields. Inviting as the tropical vegetation of the river may appear, those who know the maze growing from out of the dense, richly watered layer of humus, are glad that they may admire it from a distance, for 'da unten ists fürchterlich,' pathless, damp, and swarming with thousands of insects.

We stopped with the chief Mukeba, whom we had known before, and found that here the Baqua Putt had adopted many customs from their neighbours, the Bassonge. Such was, contrary to the habit of the Bashilange, the tilling of the fields by the men, while the women only did the house-work.

Here I saw for the first time glazed vessels of earthenware, which are made in the following manner. The dark red bark of a tree is pounded and mixed with hot water; with this compound, whilst still hot, the ready-baked pot is covered. By the time it is cold it is turned into a brown-red glaze, which it retains even after it is used on the fire.

On December 8 we pitched our camp in an open place, close to the Lubi, opposite the villages of the treacherous Bena Ngongo. This tribe, whose insolent theft Pogge and I had to complain of in 1881, had attacked and robbed Pogge on his return. In the fight Pogge had lost four of his men, but defeated the robbers. They had, undoubtedly with a bad design, also tried to induce Wolf to land when passing in the 'En Avant.'

A few Ngongo soon appeared at the ferry opposite, calling across to ask how much they were to pay for their former offence, as they were convinced that I had come to punish them. I mentioned my demand of two elephant's tusks and ten goats, which they promised to bring next morning. But first of all I asked for the restoration of one of my Bashilange women whom they had kept confined ever since.

Next morning a chief made his appearance on the shore, and showed us two young slaves whom he offered as pay in default of ivory, saying that the stolen woman was no longer with his tribe, nor did they own any ivory; both were lies, as the natives on our side assured me. I consequently refused the offered payment, and threatened to make war next day, unless they brought the woman before night. The Bena Ngongo, however, seemed to feel quite secure, as our search for canoes on this side had proved fruitless.

Discovering distinct traces of canoes among the reeds of the opposite shore, I asked my men which of them would be ready, covered by our guns, to swim over and first of all secure one canoe. This was a very hazardous undertaking, the closely wooded water's edge opposite being lined by Ngongo archers, and the river abounding with crocodiles. In accordance with their habit on most similar occasions, Humba and Simão advanced, declaring that they would undertake this dangerous expedition. I chose Simão, as he was the better swimmer, and directed him to go up the bank, then to swim over and drift along the edge of the reeds up to an opening, into which he was to swim and search for a canoe. Le Marinel, Bugslag, and myself would meanwhile be ready with our rifles, so as to cover Simão by our shots, should anything show in the opposite thicket.

Simão did as he was bidden, and, unnoticed by the Bena Ngongo, he reached the opening. With a knife between his teeth he so worked himself into the reeds as to re-appear soon with a 'canoe which, though far below, he safely brought to shore. The hostile natives had not noticed our design before the canoe was in the middle of the stream, beyond the reach of their arrows; the reeds had intercepted their view.

Complete darkness having set in, we explored the opposite shore with the canoe, bringing two more over with us.

Next morning, before daylight, I crossed over, accompanied by Le Marinel and 200 men, marching through deserted villages to the largest among them, situated on a hill 300 metres high. The head of our caravan hit upon a troop of Ngongo, two of whom had been killed and one wounded. The village being burnt down, we walked in several divisions through the mountainous, closely wooded territory of the Ngongo along the river. I heard reports in several places, but whenever we saw a village set on fire we took it as a sign that the enemy had been defeated. Towards evening all the troops, according to orders, assembled at the ferry. Six prisoners, several goats, and many weapons were taken, among the latter the large state-axe of the chief, and the big drum whose sound could be heard for

SIMÃO, THE GALLANT SWIMMER

miles. The Bena Ngongo had collected in a large camp, which was discovered by two of my troops, but, induced by our superior force, they had taken flight into the gigantic Mukubu forest which we remembered from former times.

I considered this expedition expedient, since we heard everywhere on the way that the Bena Ngongo had boasted of the attack on Pogge, and had interpreted as cowardice Pogge's kindness in surrendering the prisoners.

The march to the Bena Jileta was exceedingly exhausting for our carriers. The deep slopes, thickly covered with primæval forests, so dispersed the caravan during the uninterrupted march from the early morning till about 4 P.M., that the last of my people, with their strength nearly wasted, did not reach the camp till dark. The Bena Jileta were, on the north, bounded by the Bakuba, the Bena Ikongo tribe, with their chief Fumo Nkolle, whom Wolf had visited on the Sankurru.

Our sleep next night was interrupted by a disturbance in the camp. One of my men was brought in wounded. An arrow had pierced his breast with such force that the point was bent on one of his ribs. With great exertion, they had withdrawn the barbed arrow, thus causing the deep wound to bleed profusely, which, the arrow being poisoned, was very beneficial. I nevertheless took the precaution to apply ammonia both internally and externally. The wounded man had left the camp and gone into a potato-field on robbery intent, when, without seeing anyone, he had been pierced with an arrow and taken flight. The thieving propensity of the Mushilange having caused the act of violence, I did not make the natives responsible for it. They thought one of the Bena Ngongo, on whom we had made war the day before, had followed us to take his opportunity to revenge himself.

Next day we descended the wooded hills into the valley, pitching our camp in a large opening close to the confluence of the Lubi and the Sankurru. The dark brown Lubi, here of a breadth of 100 metres, joins the tawny waters of the Sankurru-Lubilash at this place, presenting a tranquilly majestic aspect and opening a distant view downward; very pleasant to the eye after the monotonous march during the last few days in the primaeval forest. We soon saw the large beautiful canoes of the Bena Lussambo coming, strongly manned, from the opposite side towards us.

The brother of the chief Ilunga, named Mutomba, who had made friends with Wolf, brought us presents, promising to be ready next day with all his canoes to let us cross. To make sure, I kept one of them on this side, leaving a sentinel on the shore.

During the night several canoes approached, coming from the Lubi, and filled with armed warriors, probably the Bena Ngongo, bent on revenge. They, however, took flight as soon as the sentinels began to fire.

We had now reached an interesting point. The mouth of the Lubi marks the north-eastern boundary of the Bashilange, the north-western of the Ngongo, whom we could not number among any of the larger tribes, as their language differs from all the tongues spoken round about. North of the mouth of the Lubi lived the Bakuba, who were, as on the Lulua, mixed with Bakete; east of the Sankurru the Lussambo, who perhaps may be numbered among the Bassongo-Mino. It was most interesting here to meet again with Bakete. These people must have been settled where the Bashilange live to-day, and been dispossessed by the latter, who, according to universal tradition, are said to have come from the south. Part of the Bakete live in the south-east, a little south of Katende, on the right bank of the Lulua; others live north-west of the Bashilange, north of the confluence of the Lulua and the Cassai; and here, close to the Sankurru, we again met Bakete.

The commerce with the Lussambo, on account of the unheard-of prices they charged, presented difficulties which caused many disputes in the camp.

During the next night the Bena Ngongo again attempted to approach our camp with a hostile intent, but were betrayed to my sentinel by the friendly natives, and, finding themselves discovered, they took to flight.

CHAPTER VI

PRIMÆVAL FOREST—THE HOME OF THE DWARFS—
DEPOPULATED COUNTRIES

The Lussambo—Cheating—Beautiful river scenery—First news of the Arabs—Primæval forest—Batetela—Batua, the so-called dwarfs—Negotiations with the Batua—Nothing but primæval forest—Christmas in the dark—With the Bena Mona—Murder with poisoned arrows—Critical moment—War—Building of a bridge—Lukalla—Hunger—Missed an anaconda—Bad reports about the countries before us—The ravaging slave-hunters—The exterminating Arab—Duties of the civilised world in protection of the defenceless Africans—Extermination of a great nation—With Lupungu and Mona Kakesa—Sale of ammunition—The large town of the Peshi desolated.

ACCORDING to promise, Mutomba appeared at six o'clock with canoes of twenty metres in length by one metre two centimetres in width and four centimetres in depth, which are very dexterously pushed standing with the long oars that we found in use on the Cassai. The end of the tongue of land between the confluence of the Lubi and the Sankurru was a suitable place for a station which might soon become important. From this point both rivers and the apparently much-frequented ferry may be superintended.

I had the next camp pitched behind a belt of wood fifty metres deep, stretching along the shore. While we were crossing the river some Bassonge had appeared,

CROSSING THE LUKALLA

commissioned by the Bena Ngongo to ransom their prisoners in exchange for goats and salt.

We ascertained here—as Wolf had already informed us—that the mouth of the Lomami was north of the territory of the Lussambo, who only lived along the river, while the country farther inland was said to be nothing but uninhabited primæval forests. Beyond the Lomami lived the Bassongo-Mino, and to the east the savage Batetela, behind the forests which extend through many days' journeys and are peopled by roaming Batua. Everything corroborated Wolf's observations. I bought a number of articles beautifully carved in wood, which were intended to complete Wolf's collection at Berlin. Mutomba engaged himself henceforward to guide us as far as the Batetela country, furnishing us with a number of names with such confident assurance that my interpreter Kashawalla asked me to pay his fee beforehand.

It struck me forcibly that when we started along the Sankurru we took a N.N.E. direction, which proves that the river between here and Katchich, where I discovered it in 1881, must make a strong curve. We passed through the dreadful labyrinth of the primæval forest—the guide pretending that there was no better road—and, in spite of the people in front constantly working with axe and knife, we proceeded but slowly. After a short distance Mutomba refused to go on, but offered to supply two of his men as guides. With astonishing impudence he denied his having promised to accompany us; nor did the presents he had received, and which greatly exceeded what was reasonable, at all come up to his expectation. Le Marinel was so indignant at this that he almost knocked the man down. The latter would have well deserved this punishment, but we had to keep in mind that the Bashilange had to return the same way, and I had to do my utmost to keep their road free from obstacles. Le Marinel's indignation vividly reminded me of my years of apprenticeship to African travelling; I had by this time begun to resemble my then instructor, the experienced old Pogge.

We halted, much fatigued, in the middle of the forest close to the river, and now it became obvious to us why the cunning Mutomba had brought us this way, for soon the canoes of the Lussambo appeared. Once more they found an opportunity to sell provisions for lovely beads. The chief himself soon put in an appearance, saluting us in a pacific way as if nothing had happened, which exceedingly amused me and again greatly provoked Le Marinel.

After two days' fatiguing march through primæval forests we reached the first Bassongo or Bassonje, a large tribe extending to the Lulua, and apparently related to the Wassonga or Wasongora, so that north of the Baluba people we were again able to ascertain the existence of a widely scattered tribe. It is certainly more difficult to ascertain the relationship of these people than of the Baluba, because the latter seem to have everywhere turned out and extirpated the aborigines, the Batua; while among the Bassongo and Wasongora a great many dwarfs are still found, who in many places have mixed with the latter.

From the highly situated village of the Bena Wapambue we had an open view into the wide valley of the Sankurru, which just here forms a curve at an angle of above 90°. The wide, splendid river flows past a sandstone wall, nearly 100 metres high, whose magnificent and brilliant colouring is relieved by the surrounding dark tints of the primæval forest, which, with the evening sun shining upon it, seems steeped in deep purple. This beautiful scenery, seen in such a light, might be the subject of a magnificent painting. When I saw it I greatly regretted, as I had often done in this continent, not having an artist with me who might give people at home an idea of the splendour of colour that may be produced here by the evening lights.

A lively movement of canoes, most likely caused by our presence, took place on the smooth surface of the river, which flowed about 200 metres below us. The kind old chief Soka Kalonda, who had visited Pogge and me in 1881 when staying with his upper chief Katchich, as well as the dense population, who were wholly unarmed, behaved exceedingly well. We once more felt quite comfortable and without need to take measures for our safety, which always depresses the mood of a caravan. Our people carried on peaceable intercourse

VALLEY OF THE SANKURRU

with the neighbouring villages, buying provisions at a cheap rate. Numbers of people were swarming in and out of the camp to see us, and all the chiefs from the environs who visited us left us content; as, being so well-disposed, we were easily induced to exchange presents. Our former deportment and the recent punishment of the Bena Ngongo had greatly conduced to our being so kindly received.

The soil here is very rich; the manioc plants attain

ETHNOLOGICAL ARTICLES. HAMPER, DRUM, SHIELD OF THE BASSONGE; HATCHETS AND SPEARS OF THE BALUBA

the size of trees—indeed, we saw manioc roots of the thickness of a man's arm. Everything that grew in the primæval forest showed a similar luxuriance. The river also adds to the variety of food of the Wapambue, who offered a great number of different kinds of fish for sale.

We here learned that the Bassonge chief Zappu Zapp, whom Wolf had met on the Sankurru, was not slave-hunting, as the latter had supposed, but had been settled in this neighbourhood since 1882, having been turned out of his old home by the rapacious expeditions of Tibbu Tibb's slave-hunters. We were also told that Mona Kakesa and Mona Lupungu had emigrated from the south-east, and that only the Bassonge chief Zappu stood his ground. This was the first report of inroads of the Arabs west of the Lomami, whose extended ravaging expeditions we were soon to experience.

On resuming our march we were first of all conducted in a north-westerly direction, until, dismissing the apparently idiotic guide, I turned farther east, following a broad path. Soon we were met by natives with provisions, who led us to their village, surrounded by thick palm groves and impenetrable hedges. They were people of the tribe of the Batempa, who are likewise Bassonge. The remainder of the caravan did not arrive till late in the evening, having been delayed by a brook thirty metres broad and three metres deep that could be crossed only on the trunk of a tree. As was formerly the case among the Bassonge, we frequently met here with albinos, who with their red and white complexion, so different from the negro type, are frightfully ugly.

MARCH THROUGH THE PRIMEVAL FOREST

Our way led across undulating prairie, bordered on the left by immeasurable primæval forest, which, as our guides said, extended without interruption to the Lomami. Behind us we could still distinguish the course of the Sankurru by a streak of fog which, as far as the eye could reach, covered the ground like a gigantic snake, stretching from south to north. The deeply indented brooks were bordered by white sandstone; the crystal water was cool and of pleasant taste.

On passing some miserable villages of the lean little Badingo, we found the population to be evidently a mixture of Batua. The Batua are said to live in the large primæval forest, which we were warned not to enter; the roads, which mostly consist of elephant paths, being very much grown over, and leading through many ravines, which are very difficult to pass. But as I did not want to turn too far to the south towards the route of my former travels, I took on the 21st a more northerly direction, which led us into dark primæval forests abounding with lianas, where, before coming upon some villages, we had to cut roads which were entirely blocked up by felled trees. Close behind these barricades, some natives, painted black and red, and ready with their bows, stopped our passage. As it was of consequence to me to open peaceable intercourse with the timid savages and to acquire guides, I halted before we reached the villages and pitched a camp. The people called themselves Quitundu, also Betundu, and the village was called Backashocko. They belonged to the Batetela, mixed with Bassonge who had fled into the forests. The shape of the huts was like the Batetela's:

small stems, rudely shaped to a point, were roughly joined by trellis-work and covered with grass. Hides and stuffs made from bark covered the hips of the Betundu, whose hair, plaited in two or more stiff tails, stood off their heads like horns.

I was greatly pleased to see in the afternoon some Batua of pure quality, real beauties. The people were short, of a brown-yellowish colour, or rather light yellow, with a brown shadowing. They were long-limbed and thin, though not angular, and wore neither ornaments, paintings, nor head-dresses. I was chiefly struck with their beautiful and clever eyes, lighter than those of the Batetela, and their delicate rosy lips, by no means pouting like those of the negro. The demeanour of our new friends, whom I treated with particular kindness, was not savage like that of the Batetela, but rather timidly modest, I may say maidenly shy. The little men on the whole reminded me of portraits of the Bushmen of the south of this continent. Their arms consisted of small bows and delicate arrows, which, before using, they dip into a small calabash filled with poison which they carry fastened in their belts.

By means of great patience and a continual encouraging smile, and by forcing my voice to the most gentle intonation I could manage, I succeeded in communicating with them, and catching some of their idiomatic expressions, which entirely differed from those of the other tribes. Amongst others it struck me that here, in the midst of the Batetela, who for the word 'fire' have the term 'kalo,' they had the expression 'Kapia,' the same as our Bashilange, with whom they have a certain softness of language in common, something of the singing modulation of our Saxons. Does not this circumstance also correspond with my supposition, that the Bashilange, the most northern of the Baluba people, must be largely mixed with Batua? In the same way I felt justified in the above-named supposition by the similarity of the chief pigment, their delicate frame, their rather long limbs, &c.

For each word the Batua told me I gave them a bead, in giving them which I had to be careful not to touch them, for my coming near them made them start with fear. Bugslag approached them, kindly talking the while, armed with a long pole which he raised behind one of the dwarfs; then he suddenly made his hand glide down until he touched the dwarf's head. As if struck by lightning, the little savage took to his heels; but we succeeded later on in taking the measurements of some Batua who came to visit us, all varying from 1.45 to 1.40 metre. I never saw any women among them. The difference between the young and the old men was very striking. While the young people, with their rounded figures, their fresh complexions, and above all their graceful, easy, quiet movements, made an agreeable impression, the old might literally be called painfully ugly. The reason of which seems to be the poor food and the savage and roving life in the primæval forest. In consequence of their extreme leanness, the deeply wrinkled skin of the body assumed the colour of parchment. The long limbs were perfectly withered, and the head appeared disproportionately large on account of the thinness of the neck. The people conversed rapidly and with much emphasis: the young greatly respecting the word of the old.

WITH BUGSLAG AND THE DWARFS

Here, as I had everywhere occasion to observe, the Batua were, on the whole, not so much despised by the Bassonge tribes as by the Baluba; they were very much feared on account of the poison of their arrows, which was said to be very fatal in its consequences. We were told that the Batua were soon going to kill the powerful chief Zappu Zapp, who had made himself master throughout this neighbourhood.

The real home of the Batua is the vast dark primæval forest, which in all seasons yields a variety of fruits— perhaps only known to and eaten by them—roots, fungi or herbs, and especially meat, the latter chiefly of lesser and lower animals, as rats, nocturnal monkeys, bats, a number of rodentia, many of which may be unknown, now and then a wild boar, a monkey, and by chance even an elephant. Other game is not found in the primæval forest, but of smaller animals there is all the more abundance. Caterpillars, cicadas, white ants, and chrysalises also offer an abundant change to the Mutua (singular form).

Henceforward we frequently met Batua, without, however, being able to make any observations, the little folks being too much reserved to come forward at all. On the morning of our departure, some Batua approached me with a trifling present of manioc roots, and when I smilingly refused it, they pursued me, imploring me to accept it; upon my granting their wish, they went away contented. On the previous day I had given these Batua some small presents in the hope of augmenting my stock of words; they evidently acted in this way under the impression that my presents, if they did not return them, would give me some power over them. Such mistrust is quite a mark of the genuine savage.

The deep quiet of the primæval forest, which continually put obstacles in our way, thus causing much work and trouble, was scarcely interrupted by the note of a bird. I rarely remember to have heard the piercing cry of the helmet-bird of an evening, or the noise produced by the rustling wings of the rhinoceros-bird. Only the white ants were incessantly making a rustling sound at their work. Any attempt at astronomical work had to be abandoned under this never-opening leafy roof.

In the place where the Lomami and the Sankurru separate, we found that, though they still called themselves Betundu, the natives' huts differed in shape. They were of the same shape as we had formerly seen among the Bassonge, which indicated that the latter, who had fled from the south, were predominant here. During the night, apprehending an attack on our part, the Betundu left the villages in our vicinity. The brutal savageness of these forest people induced me to command that each man of the caravan should carry his own gun, and not, as the Bashilange frequently did, fasten it to the baggage or give it to the women to carry. Our good sons of the hemp did not present a very warlike appearance. They chiefly preferred to proceed on their way in continual chatter, the large hemp-pipe on their backs, sticks in their hands, and entertaining the idea, very flattering to me, that Kabassu Babu would take care of them, and that under his guidance they would come to no harm.

First among the more important brooks which fall into the Lomami was the Luidi, which I had crossed near its source with Pogge. Want of food began to be felt by my large caravan, the scanty population of this forest only cultivating their own necessary food in the small clearings, which were, with great difficulty, denuded of roots. The purchase of provisions was likewise made difficult by the savageness of the Betundu. They took an endless time to decide whether or not they would give anything for the price offered. A piece of cloth went from hand to hand. It almost irritated us to watch the intercourse of these savages amongst each other. Like wolves, they contended for some article that attracted their fancy. Their every movement was passionate, their glance shy; their demeanour resembled that of a wild beast in its cage. In truth, these people had grown up as it were in a cage, for this vast primæval forest, which never permits a glimpse of the sky, can be compared to nothing else; the horizon is narrowed to very short distances. A chief, who during the sale was on the point of darting his spear at one of my people, was thrown down by the ever-ready Simão, the gallant swimmer of the Lubi; he (Simão) broke his spear, and did not let him go until he had given him a sound thrashing. I am sorry to say that this did not tend to induce them to bring more provisions; they even threatened to bring the Batetela down upon us.

We plodded on and on in the dark through the villages of the Bena Piari Kai, the Balonda and Bakialo, where, after the flight of the natives, we were forced to take what provisions we could find in the huts and fields.

But even this, added to the many roots and fruits which the Bashilange fetched from the forest, provided us only with the barest necessaries.

Now, following the only road, we turned farther south, and on the 25th we kept Christmas, the festival of the light of Christianity, in the midst of the dark primæval forest and dark paganism.

The natives' manner soon became timid and savage, to such a degree that there was no possibility of getting hold of any name. Those we questioned were contending about some present, quarrelling and fighting like ravenous dogs, and we could get nothing out of them. Here we found the most wonderful articles used as headdresses. One of them was quite consonant with cannibalism, being withered fingers cut off at the second joint; these, fastened to wooden pins, pointed upwards from out of the thick mass of hair. As I had formerly repeatedly found among many tribes of anthropophagi, they cut off and throw away the fingers as well as the toes before beginning their loathsome feast.

At length, on the 26th, the dense forest was ever and anon interrupted by clearings. In the evening, after a thirteen days' march through the primæval forest, we joyfully greeted an open space. We encamped at the boundary of the Bena Mona tribe, close to the village Kiagongo on the river Lobbo, with its great volume of water. It was long since we had last heard the leopard's voice during the night; it was a week since we had last seen goats, as the inhabitants of the wood rear the fowl as their only domestic animal. We had done now with always being caught by straggling plants or roots, with incessantly creeping and squeezing between trees and trunks, with climbing steep slopes, and stopping to cut our way with the axe. Our clothes and those of our people were nothing but rags; many of our Bashilange had even been compelled to procure skins, the bits of cloth on their hips not even affording the most necessary covering. The fugitive natives did not return, though they kept near.

According to one of my Bashilange who had climbed a palm to gather nuts, some natives were shooting at a target, and were only scared away by the appearance of my people in search of food. We had to possess ourselves of victuals, as there was no one there to sell them, and my people were quite exhausted by their starvation in the forest. In the night we were wakened by screaming and vigorous shooting, and on my arriving on the spot to prohibit useless firing in the dark, two wounded Bashilange were brought to me. One had been struck by an arrow, which had entered the joint of his knee; the other, a woman, had only her arm grazed. After applying ammonia, the wound of the latter was dressed and effectually cured. The man, however, after Le Marinel had succeeded in withdrawing the barbed arrow, which was quite bent, died in dreadful convulsions five minutes after being wounded. We thus learned the powerful effects of the native poison. On the same night we buried him and a Mushilange who had died of inflammation of the lungs in the middle of the camp, in the hope that the natives might not find a trace of the grave and have the triumph of having killed one of our party; and, on the other hand, we wished to prevent the corpses providing them with a welcome meal.

Early in the morning we started, and soon met twenty armed men who stopped our passage, ready to throw spears or shoot. In spite of last night's treachery I began to negotiate with them, since I wanted to learn at last where we were, and what direction we had to take in order to avoid the large primæval forest which was looming round about us. The Bena Mona were induced to walk on before us, and I succeeded, though with great difficulty, in preventing my indignant soldiers and Bashilange from firing at them. Armed men meeting us incessantly, the leading troop increased more and more.

The outward appearance of the Bena Mona reminded us of the Bassongo-Mino; they were tall, slight, and yet muscular, and, like the latter, chiefly wore clothes made from the palm, dyed black,[1] with the same little handkerchiefs as a head-dress. They were mostly armed with strong bows and large bundles of long arrows, very rarely with a spear, and they frequently carried beautiful knives and the war-axes known to us from the Bassonge. The people were savages without a fixed abode, and were evidently feared as warriors, for I remember that the savage Bena Mona were often mentioned with great awe.

We soon saw that our guides were moving on towards one of the largest villages on the summit of a hill in front of us, a place that seemed suitable for

---

[1] A beautiful black colour is given to all materials, including wood, by burying the article in question for a certain time in the boggy ground at the source of certain brooks.

ETHNOLOGICAL ARTICLES: IDOL OF THE BALUBA FROM THE LUALABA BELT OF THE BENECKI—PLUMES OF THE BASSONGO-MINO—PIPE AND TOBACCO OF THE BENA RIAMBA - CALABASHES

action, as from the behaviour of the savage Bena Mona and the excitement of my people it had become obvious to me that we should not get off without being compelled to use force. Before reaching the village, shots were actually fired at the rear of the caravan, which did not keep me from proceeding onwards and upwards until the report was brought from behind that Bugslag had been cut off with the rear. I made Le Marinel halt, let the caravan close in, and with a few of the soldiers turned back; but presently I met Humba, who informed me that the difficulty at the back was settled, and that Bugslag was marching on. At the same time I saw from the dark clouds of smoke that my soldiers, after repulsing the pursuing enemy, had set the farms on fire. Bugslag, as I learned later, had been in the act of buying a fowl from a native whom he met on the road, and while he was bargaining, an approaching troop had shot an arrow at him. My party had at once returned the attack, and the natives, leaving eight of their people mortally wounded behind them, had retreated to their village, whither they were pursued by my people.

In spite of the enemy's having increased in the van to above 100 men, I gave the signal to march on. The guides, who had not learnt what had occurred behind, were continually running before us, evidently delaying a further attack until their numbers should be a match for our forces, which they could now survey. About 200 warriors lay in wait at the entrance of the village, and when our guides had come to an agreement with them, negotiations, unintelligible to us, were carried on without our being able to move forwards.

Naturally the caravan gradually collected, forming a crowd, at the van of which Le Marinel and I were halting on our bulls, ready for battle, while Bugslag was in the rear. The women, according to their nature, had crouched together in the midst of the crowd like a scared flock of sheep, while those who carried arms had put down their loads and stood ready towards the outside. Armed people incessantly drew near from all sides, and in a short time we were closely hemmed in. The natives, ready with their bows and arrows, and their spears, were yet undecided as to what they had better do, while my people were waiting for the word to fire. Whichever party were to use their arms first must be successful; neither spear nor arrow could miss our dense crowd at two metres distance. A shot from our guns would likewise be sure to hit one of the savages, closely surrounding us as they did, and, so as not to miss the advantage of being the first, I was on the point of giving the command to fire, when the circle in front of me opened a little, and an elderly man, who, like the formerly-mentioned Bassonge chief, called himself Zappu Zapp, walked up to me.

I told him that I intended to encamp farther on, and that, if his people were to bring fowls or victuals generally, the Bena Mona might earn many a fine piece of cloth and many a bead before the day was over. I was in hopes that the chief, with the object of waiting for a larger number of his party, would give us this respite, which was necessary to me that I might prepare for battle, and particularly that I might distribute the dwindling ammunition. My haughty tone, and especially my repeated laughter while conversing with Le Marinel, may have conveyed to the natives the impression that I did not regard them as so very formidable. During the conversation I had my gun ready before me on the saddle, the muzzle directed to the chief and my finger on the trigger, so that at the least sign of their using a weapon, my *vis-à-vis* would have fallen.

The whole crowd now began to move, and on different roads to the right and left messengers were despatched, probably only to call the neighbours for the impending good catch. I had arrived close to the place where I wanted to halt when again violent shooting was heard at the end of the rather lengthened caravan where Bugslag was riding. It was now all over with our pacific intrigues, for those running in front and at our side seized arms, and arrows shot past, so that I even laid low some of those who were in front. The rest I left to Le Marinel at the van, hurrying backward myself, since the full force of the Bena Mona seemed to be attacking us. The firing ceased once more before I reached the rear, and, finding a load of cartridges in the caravan, I opened it and sent ammunition to Le Marinel and Bugslag. Only at intervals shots were fired at the Bena Mona, who were fleeing in all directions. Then clouds of smoke were seen ascending everywhere—a sign of the presence of the Bashilange.

I now gave the signal to close in, and, in order to get out of the reach of the hostile villages scattered round about us, I marched on unassailed. Still reinforcements of savages advanced in crowds, who, on our approach, turned and fled. On the way we passed a village nearly 2,000 metres long, deeply shaded by oil palms, where our people, to their great delight, found corn.

On account of the intense heat I encamped near the edge of a brook in a place which could easily be surveyed. According to rumour about twenty natives had been killed, while on our side only wounds were reported. I had the camp closed entirely, placing concealed outposts round about, so as to protect ourselves during the night from a treachery similar to that of the preceding day. Towards evening troops of natives were seen everywhere near, but, taught by Le Marinel and Bugslag's rifles, they kept at a safe distance. In a large circle round the outposts I had fires of dry wood kindled, which lighted the foreground within fifty feet throughout the night. Consequently our night's rest was only disturbed through the noise I made in waking some sleeping outposts when visiting the sentinels.

At the first dawn we started, and turned our backs on the country of the unfriendly Bena Mona. We soon reached a labyrinth of villages again, which, however, were deserted; but, the way leading too much to the south, we turned and found another open road to the east, which messengers whom we had sent out for the purpose on the previous day had not found. One never can rely on Bantu negroes, even the best of them, and a European, travelling with such people, has to be always at hand himself, if he wants to feel convinced that important work is being properly carried out. In spite of yesterday's excitement, I had found many an outpost asleep at night, and even my best men had overlooked the large open road to the east. The beautiful broad path on the open ridge of hills made marching a real enjoyment after our experiences in the primæval forest.

After fatiguing labour we succeeded in building a bridge across the Lukulla, which, in a succession of falls, rushed along over rubble stones. As the trunk thrown across made great caution necessary, the crossing lasted until evening. Twice some of the people tumbled off the bridge; they were rescued, but lost their guns and our provision box, containing our whole stock of crockery and our last bottle of brandy. I myself ran down stream, and diving, searched for the hamper, but in vain; only by chance I recovered one of the guns. The Bena Mona had been shrewd enough to consider the crossing of the river as a favourable moment for an assault; but as on their march they lighted upon a barricade of trees, by which as a fortification I had joined two jungles, where I had placed a sentinel, they turned before they were fired at.

We Europeans, having been without rest day and night lately, with very scanty food, felt great bodily weakness, though excitement kept us alive. Our caravan began to suffer very much, the famine having lasted too long already. A great deal of illness prevailed in consequence of the poor nourishment. Some of the men staggered with hunger and weakness while marching; and unless we came upon inhabited districts, the open savannah would be more ominous than the primæval forest, where our people had after all found many fruits and fungi to satisfy their craving hunger. In such districts it is by no means easy to maintain a body of nearly 900 people. On setting out I had calculated upon the same state of affairs which I had formerly experienced with Pogge scarcely one degree farther south, and which would have made it possible even to travel with 10,000 men. The marrow of palms was now nearly our exclusive food, but even this was obtained only with the greatest difficulty. In the first place the strong tough tree had to be felled, after which with great trouble the heart of the tree, which is under the crown, had to be cut out with an axe.

The Bena Mona, who inhabit this barren country, are by nature a very wicked tribe; I may say they were the first nation which, still unmolested by slave-hunters, opposed us in so decidedly hostile a manner. The Bena Mona had, it is true, already experienced the ravages of white men, in the shape of the Arabs, who were in possession of guns; and it is possible that they put the same construction upon our motives, and that this gave birth to their hostile disposition towards us.

On account of the number of cross roads and the dark primæval forest looming before us to the east and north, I marched southward up the Lubefu river. We hoped soon to make a camp in a place where we might get food, for the spectre of hunger was seriously menacing my gradually weakening caravan. On the 29th we reached some villages of the Bassange, which we well remembered to have passed before. Since the rumour of our skirmish with the Bena Mona had preceded us, the natives fled before us, taking everything with them; and only a few of my people succeeded in possessing themselves of trifling quantities of food, which, in the

hurry, had been left behind. Our attempts to supply our wants by the chase remained without success, the country being bare of game. My men discovered a huge python snake which they found coiled up in a bush, and fetched me to shoot it, the Bashilange being fond of its flesh. I pointed the muzzle of my gun at the head of the anaconda at a distance of one metre, before, awaking from her apathy, she noticed me. I aimed and missed the head of the gigantic reptile, which, after the report, disappeared in the thicket like lightning. The Bashilange, who knew the sure aim of my gun, regarded my bad shot as a fetish of the Bena Mona.

We could not be far off my route of 1881 when we reached some provisionally built villages of the Bassonge under their chief Mona Kassongo. Kassongo had fled here from some hordes of Tibbu Tibb's, and rambling patrols, making use of the dark night, were returning to their former homes, to fetch what food they could from their fields. At any rate, we got a few provisions, which gave us hope and courage for the future. Kassongo came to see me with about sixty gun-carriers, complaining of the dreadful visitation of the southern districts by Tibbu Tibb's hordes. He told me that the powerful tribe of the Benecki was entirely annihilated, and that Mona Lupungu, my former old friend, had turned to the south, where, with the other greatest chief of the Kassonge, Mona Kakesa, he had taken refuge in the Baluba country from the murdering and devastating expedition of the Arabs. Kassongo had been here for two months, hoping for the departure of the slave-hunters, and always ready to flee to the north, towards the primæval forests of the Batetela. We got so many contradictory reports from all directions about the war which—as I well knew—was raging in the southern countries, that we did not know what to believe. We no longer found regular villages, but only scattered troops of different Bassonge tribes, who, partly knowing me, supplied us with provisions as well as they could under their straitened circumstances.

Chiefs visited me, bringing presents of slaves, requesting that later on I would exchange them for goats, they not being able to provide me with a goat, nor even a fowl.

I learned, as a matter of great anxiety, that many of my people had sold powder and percussion-caps in order to obtain provisions. This was almost the only article of exchange demanded by the poor hunted natives, as being their only means to defend themselves against their formidable enemies.

The New Year's Eve of 1886 found us three Europeans of the caravan thinking of the future with great apprehension. Le Marinel, in honour of the day, and in order to divert our grave anxiety, brought forth a bottle of rum—which, however, in our present weakened state of health agreed with us very badly. Full of care, we saw the sun rise on the first day of the year of 1887. To the north and east loomed the dark primæval forest, whose terrors were still fresh in our memories; to the south and west everything was said to be depopulated for a long distance. Round about us were encamped 900 people, weak with starvation and fatigue. Our goods were of no avail, nor even our numbers, for eatables were nowhere to be found or bought. In low spirits, therefore, we continued our journey to the east-south-east, as far as Kafungoi, where we found Pogge's and my route. But how much altered! Where formerly thousands of Benecki, the inhabitants of the strikingly beautiful and rich town, had joyfully welcomed us; where we had revelled in enjoyments such as an African country, inhabited by industrious natives, has to offer; where in peace and amity we had been conducted from village to village—we now found a waste, depopulated by murder and conflagration. The same huge groves of palm trees, which formerly had marked the town of the happy Benecki, welcomed us to their shadow. Only dismal silence, here and there interrupted by the chirping of the ploceïdæ, had given way to the welcoming sounds of the former harmless inhabitants. The niches in the palm thicket on both sides of the straight roads, which three years ago had been filled with the tidy farms of the Benecki, were now overgrown with grass of a man's height, whilst here and there a burnt pole, a bleached skull, and broken crockery were reminiscences of the existence of our former friends. Where were the thousands and thousands of the industrious people who through their great numbers seemed secure from any hostile assaults? I shuddered with sadness at this spectacle, at the remembrance of the happiest days of our first journey, which we had enjoyed with the then quite unknown good-natured savages. I turned quite hot with a sense of wrath and internal revolt against the murderous breed of avaricious slave-hunters who had called forth this dreadful devastation.

Among the palms in some banana thickets, which had escaped the destructive hands of the gangs of robbers, my people fortunately found some potato fields covered with grass, where they dug out some huge potatoes, which provided them with most necessary food. Palm nuts, the marrow of palms, sweet potatoes and unripe bananas were to form our only food for some time to

AT KAFUNGOI

come, for during many days' journeys we only found a repetition of what we had obtained at Kafungoi.

I must anticipate in order to tell, what I learned later, how this dreadful fate had come upon countries once so happy. The Arab Tibbu Tibb and Famba, the latter of whom had formerly resided west of the Lomami, intent on trade rather than robbery, had fallen out about the right to these districts. The far more powerful Tibbu Tibb had sent his people, reinforced by hosts of cannibals of the Bena Kalebue tribe, across the Lomami to possess themselves of the countries as far as the Sankurru. Knowing the Arab Hamed bin Mohammed, called Tibbu Tibb, from former times, I am convinced that, had he come here himself, the consequences of the expedition would not have been so terrible as they were; he, however, only sent his subordinates as commanders. Though, his religion permitting it, the Arab is regardless of the natives who are trying to defend their goods and chattels and their liberty with their weapons, yet in general he is not capable of such designing wickedness as those slaves of his, the half-blood brutes from the coast, who, besides the tribute which they have to pay to their master, provide for themselves by stealing slaves wherever they can. They dare not intercept ivory, but they manage to hide slaves, and as long as their master is satisfied with the booty of the expedition, he little cares how his people look after themselves. The Arab generally is more shrewd than the half-blood, who seems to have inherited only the worst qualities of the two tribes to whom he owes his existence.

The former wants to make the native princes tributary to himself, while the latter is only intent on obtaining as many slaves as possible, never caring what will ultimately become of the devastated countries. The fault of originating these outrages lies unquestionably with the Arab, for only his initiative made it possible to advance, to subjugate, and to depopulate more and more. Therefore, if the aim be to benefit and to protect the poor defenceless native, the Arabs in these countries should be extirpated root and branch, before they obtain a force for which we Europeans are no longer a match; as was the case in the south, owing to the distance and the hostile climate. It was high time that, soon after the evil days of which I am speaking here, severe measures should be taken against this African plague. I myself had great satisfaction in being called to suppress the East African rebellion, or to strike the first blow at the coast from whence the above-mentioned outrages chiefly proceed.

Although the English and German fleets lessen the export of slaves, which are chiefly transported from these districts of Central Africa, the future slave trade, and with it the slave hunt, will be cut off only by garrisoning the coasts and the great commercial roads. Now, while I am writing this, much has been done; but the slave traders' centres of operation, Tabora, Ujiji, and Nyangwe in the interior, are still slave markets; Tibbu Tibb is still living: Muini Muharra and other slave-hunters are still raging and destroying the natives, who, armed as they are only with bows and spears, are defenceless against them. Much still needs to be done to protect the liberty and the lives of millions of harmless creatures; it is still possible that the Arabs will be reinforced from the Soudan, south of the Equator. But Germany is already prepared to render further protection, is ready to check a danger threatening from the north; and I may hope that, before this expression of my deepest indignation can be perused by the reader, I shall have again taken up my work, whose goal, the deliverance of Equatorial Africa from the thraldom of the Arabs, has become my life's object.

The progress of this war to the knife has been as follows:

Mona Lupungu had paid tribute to Famba, instead of, as was requested of him, to Tibbu Tibb, and, refusing to pay the latter also, he had been attacked and driven away. He had retreated to his friend Mona Kakesa, and being pursued even here by Tibbu's hordes, those two, after the loss of many lives, emigrated to the south on the boundary of the Belande, leaving many prisoners as slaves in the hands of their assailants. The hosts of Arabs, never minding their enemies, but only eager to obtain slaves and ivory, proceeded to the Benecki, who at every approach of the robbers fled into the forests. The Zappu Zapp of the west had, as we know, fled to the Sankurru, and the Bassange had escaped to the north, where we were now encamping, after many useless attempts to defend themselves, in order to hide, if necessary, in the large, protecting primæval forest.

The Benecki, not wishing to abandon their rich villages and fields, returned every time the rapacious troop turned their backs, and began to cultivate the ground again, but as soon as the fields were ready for harvest the vagabonds reappeared, their expeditions being greatly dependent on the food they found.

In this manner the pacific tribe of the Benecki was attacked several times in succession; many of the bravest, who defended themselves, were killed, many women and children were transported, while the greater number took refuge in the forest. The necessary consequence of the repeated devastation of the fields was a dreadful famine, with small-pox, brought in by the Arabs, following at its heels. War, slave-robbery, famine, and pestilence had actually been able completely to depopulate this densely populated territory, with its towns extending through many days' journeys; and we learned that only a dwindling remnant had taken refuge with Zappu Zapp on the Sankurru.

On January 3 we passed the Lubefu, of 60 metres breadth by a water-level of 0·3 metre; the bed was cut 50 metres deep into reddish sandstone, with almost perpendicular slopes. At the place of crossing deep quicksands became dangerous for our bulls. Whenever we gained a height after leaving the narrow valley of a water-course, we were admitted in the shade of a long-stretched palm forest, where formerly had been a town of the Benecki. We encamped in one of these, once the town of Kifussa. Each member of the caravan had to bring into the camp the food he had found on the way. Bananas, nearly over-ripe, thickets of pineapples, remains of former potato fields, and palm nuts had been found in the arable land and gardens of the Benecki.

Mona Lupungu, patrols of whose camp also were loafing about in the desolate towns in order to get pro-

THE ARABS AMONG THE BENEKI

visions, sent to request me to visit him, which I at first refused, chiefly with the view of preventing my Bashilange from selling their arms in exchange for ivory, and thereby lessening the force of my caravan. During the whole time my mind was busy in trying to ascertain whether it would be possible to punish Tibbu Tibb's troop, which was said to be encamped on this side of the Lomami, and whether this would be judicious and conformable to my commission. If I had had the same number of coasters as Bashilange, who, however, with their guns behaved very well to the savages who were only armed with bows and arrows, the clearing of the districts from the rapacious gangs of Arabs might no doubt have been effected. But with my Bashilange, who, into the bargain, were so much weakened with hunger as to be hardly equal even to the fatigues of the slow march, it would scarcely have been advisable for me to take up the cudgels in a successful combat against the slaves and coasters of the Arabs who had been trained for war. Even if I had succeeded in subduing one of these hordes, I should soon have had to give way to the superior force and the more efficient warriors, and so have lost more than I had gained. Under the prevailing circumstances I could do better with the Arabs in peace than in war. As I was of opinion that the station in the Upper Congo State near Stanley Falls was on good terms with the Arabs, and since I knew nothing of the disorders which had meanwhile broken out there, I was in hopes of intimidating Tibbu Tibb by threatening to take possession of his property in Zanzibar and on the coast. So after due reflection, I may say with a heavy heart,

I had to desist from the plan of immediately supporting the poor natives against their tormentors; but, at any rate, I wanted to be as ready for battle as was possible, considering the unfortunate condition into which my caravan had got through the journey of the last few weeks, and threatened, therefore, to punish them severely for any sale of arms and ammunition. I should have greatly desired to be able to provide each tribe oppressed by the Arabs with a number of arms in order to defend themselves against those robbers.

Le Marinel and I did our utmost to hunt for some game, but in vain; our prolonged and fatiguing hunting expeditions only enabled us to bag some ducks.

On the 4th, twenty men armed with guns approached continually shooting, bringing me a present of seven slaves. These were followed by Mona Lupungu, a Bassonge prince who, in 1882, had received us very hospitably. He had hastened hither to fetch us to his camp, a distance of three days' journey. He was much altered in his outward appearance; he also had been ill with small-pox, which had greatly disfigured him, besides causing the loss of one of his eyes. He was likewise changed from his former modest and amiable deportment: his constant persecution during the last few years had made him restless and savage in a way that he had not been formerly. Being greatly urged by my Bashilange, I yielded to the chief's request to visit him. His companions, with their fine warlike figures, though they had likewise grown barbarous during the wild doings of the last few years, presented as warriors a

MONA LAPUNGU BRINGS A PRESENT OF SLAVES

great contrast to my poor, thin, and ragged Bashilange, who were filled with some anxiety, knowing that we were about to enter a formidable camp, that of Mona Kakesa, who was allied with Lupungo. Another part of the caravan were urging us to visit these two, so that on their return they should have supplies in this district of starvation. Everybody was over-fatigued, weakened, and dissatisfied, which was easily to be accounted for, and in such a humour that most of them would have preferred to return home. In order to prevent this I hastened, as fast as my weak people were able to follow, to the south of Lupungo. On the way we were continually met by armed men, besides a despatch party of Mona Kakesa, bringing us maize and manioc.

On the 6th I halted about a kilometre from the camp of the two chiefs. Many thousands of people, among them a few women, were assembled there; about 300 were armed with guns, while the others carried bows and arrows. The proceedings in this large camp were barbarous and wild, as might be expected under these warlike circumstances, for a troop of Tibbu Tibb's was said to be stationed but two days' journey from here in order to attack this camp. The force was sure to be very strong, and the Bassonge had quite made up their minds not to fight, but to flee at the approach of the enemy.

On my asking the two chiefs whether they, in alliance with me, would attack the warriors of the Arabs, they decidedly declined. Nor did they think that I had been in earnest, for they said they thought the white men were friends of the Arabs, and, at any rate, much weaker than they.

As the ample presents of the chiefs consisted in articles of food, I granted my caravan a few days' halt. We had now reached the southern boundary of the vanished tribe of the Benecki, who were related to the Bassonge. Only a few hours' distant the villages of the Belande, who belong to the Baluba tribe, began; and south of these were the Balungu, under the chief Kassonge Chiniama, whom I had been prevented from visiting a few months ago by the skirmishes with the Baluba. South-west, as far as the Sankurru, the Bilolo, also Baluba, were said to live. The country presented great changes of scenery. The ravines of the rivers were bordered by deep slopes, showing red laterite, and covered with luxuriant vegetation. The summits of the heights, generally pure grass savannahs, were dotted with ruin-like rocks, and along the ridges, like gigantic snakes, extended the dark groves of palm trees we have mentioned before.

The warriors of the Bassonge, crowding the camp, were daily joined by hundreds of Belande, who carried many pedercroes, such as had been brought from the west coast by Bihé caravans; while the weapons of the Bassonge were percussion-guns which, before the breaking out of the war, they had obtained through commissioners of the Arabs. Inferior Arabs, or mongrels from the coast, not so powerful as Tibbu Tibb or Famba, often gave some guns to more influential chiefs, by means of which the latter would hunt slaves for them. This was the point, then, where the fire-arms of the west and the east met. Farther north, however, they have not penetrated, the large primæval forest being a barrier to commerce, whose results we had here ample opportunity of studying.

The only food all these warriors revelled in was the palm wine, and consequently we had often scenes in the camp that led to disputes, several times even to hostilities, between our people and the Bassonge. One evening after dark—not admitting any strangers after this time—I turned out Lupungu, just as he was in the act of taking a saddle-bull (about which we had been negotiating) into his camp, before our bargain was concluded. We soon discovered, as I had apprehended, that a considerable part of the Bashilange had sold not only guns but also powder and percussion caps, so that nearly all the Bashilange were short of ammunition without my knowing it. I was indeed indignant at such indiscretion.

What would have become of us if hostilities had broken out among the mostly drunken hosts of warriors? Before the packed-up ammunition had been distributed, everything would without question have been lost. They had thoughtlessly exchanged percussion caps and powder for victuals. In the presence of the Bassonge chiefs I had the guilty punished by a thrashing, and distributed fresh allowances of forage and new ammunition, which henceforward was inspected several times a day.

I was very glad when the time for starting had come, for the hostilities grew more and more numerous and violent, and my people in their intercourse with the Bassonge warriors became quite intractable.

I imagined I should be able to carry out my commission, which required me to arrange the state of affairs in the southern Congo State as well as possible, only by hindering in some way, or at least restricting, the plundering expeditions from Nyangwe, and therefore resolved to go straight to the camp of the Arabs, and there to decide upon further steps. Considering my former footing with the Arabs, I could not but presume that in Nyangwe I should get canoes and people with whom to go up to the source of the Lualaba and to explore the Kamerondo. We therefore set out towards the north-east, at first conducted by Lupungu's people. We found two more villages inhabited by Belande, before reaching the desolate country of the Benecki.

On the march we found out that the intercourse in the camp had been of bad influence on the discipline of my people. The villages were completely pillaged by the Bashilange and my coasters, and any resistance of the natives soon led to acts of violence, which fortunately never ended fatally. Bugslag and Le Marinel, riding behind, would use a stick, or even a pistol, to drive the pillagers out of the farms, and, if possible, return the belongings of the natives, who were furiously pursuing us. I explained to my people how on my part everything had been done to keep them from starvation, to protect them from hostile assaults, and to avoid hostilities, and how all this had been marred by their behaviour. I further told them that I had in vain used lashes and fetters to punish offences which endangered the safety of the whole caravan and all the lives, for which I was responsible; any robbing from the natives I therefore prohibited upon pain of death. They all agreed to this, quite seeing the necessity of it.

The vast grass prairie, with its long groves of palm trees, here and there showed formations of rivers. Wild ducks and little red moor-hens were found in them in great numbers, and in the evenings the sandy shores were enlivened by hundreds of pigeons which, before choosing their night quarters, would come here to drink. Pelicans, herons, and vultures (*angolensis*) were frequent, while larger game was scarce.

We passed the Mussongai and Tambai, which fall into the Lurimbi, a tributary of the Lomami, and entered the town of our old friends, the Baqua Peshi, called Kintu a Mushimba. This town, five hours' march in length, is now likewise a wilderness, again reminding us of the terrible fate experienced by the childlike, friendly Benecki, who were living so happily but few years ago. In some parts of this once gigantic town attempts at settlements must have been made since, as we found several fields with maize and beans only of a few months old. Since our last sojourn here a territory has been depopulated extending between the 5th and 6th degrees south latitude, and the whole length from the Lomami up to the Sankurru—a country which, on account of its abundance of water and rich soil, was better suited for settlements than any other; a country which, with its prairies, will be some day exceedingly well adapted for breeding cattle.

On the 12th we marched a considerable distance along an outstretched lake, which, framed in by only a few trees of the willow species, presented a lovely picture in the midst of the vast grass prairie. We pitched our camp on the edge of the valley of the Lukassi. On account of the silence reigning now in this district, which had formerly been over-populated, some game had been enticed hither, as was testified by traces of buffaloes and elephants and the large horse

IN THE VALLEY OF THE LUKASSI.

antelope, one of which we chased in vain. Formerly game was an unheard of thing in this country.

We learned that a few kilometres from here eastward, beyond the Lukassi, lay Tibbu Tibb's large camp of robbers, incessantly watched over by Lupungu's spies, who lived in the thickest part of the forest. These spies fearlessly visited us, bringing all the news from the hostile camp. A few men in long white shirts with turbans on their heads were said to be leaders, the principal of whom was called Said. The nucleus of the army was formed by many slaves of Tibbu Tibb's, who were estimated at 500 in number, whilst the troop was completed by a host of Kalebue cannibals, who had formerly been defeated by Tibbu Tibb and were now compelled to join his army. Most of them were without firearms. A few days before, these robbers had left their fortified camp—which, during their absence, always remained garrisoned—and undertaken a pillaging expedition to the south. They had returned the day before, and were said to purpose staying in the camp for the present, the rich fields of this place supplying them with provisions.

CHAPTER VII

THE ARABS—FAMINE AND ILLNESS

Camp of a troop of Tibbu Tibb's Zanzibaris—Said, the leader of the warlike expedition—Said aiming at prisoners in his pistol practice—Cannibalism in the camp of the Arabs—Sad condition of my caravan—A man rising from the dead—Many sick people—On the Lomami—The caravan well-nigh exhausted—The Arabs' form of government—Hungry people eating poisonous fruits — Inundations—Everything gloomy — Amputations — Some people missing — Bridge formed of brushwood—Small-pox—The weakest part of the army left behind—Losses—Reports about hostilities between the Arabs and the Congo State—Bad prospects—At Nyangwe—Hidden threats—Tibbu Tibb's son subjecting me to an examination—Suspicion against me—Famba's aid—My Bashilange sent home uninjured—I remain in the Arabs' power—Separation from Le Marinel and my caravan.

NEXT day we encamped on the Lukassi, called also Lukashi and Lukassia, a river of about forty metres in breadth and two metres in depth, and, making use of an old fish weir and an islet, we, with great difficulty and labour, built a bridge. All the river crossings had naturally been destroyed by the Bassonge. On the 14th we crossed over and pitched a strong camp, since for the present we could not judge on what footing we should be placed with the slave-hunters. I sent Humba and three soldiers down the river, enjoining them to approach the camp with caution and to ascertain whether pacific intercourse with the vagabonds might be effected.

The bridge which we had built with so much trouble was destroyed during the night by the roving natives in our rear.

Anxious about the delay of the patrol, I had waited until midnight, when they returned at last, accompanied by three people—a man from Zanzibar and two slaves

ENTRANCE INTO SAID'S CAMP

of Tibbu Tibb's—bringing a salaam from Said, the second in command, making known to us that this war was an expedition to take vengeance on the Bassonge for having slain and devoured some of their people. Humba told us that on approaching the camp they noticed that they were being finally watched and hemmed in. The natives ran up to them screaming, and brandishing their arms, and only the shouts of Fickerini, my flag-bearer, in Kisuaheli, a language spoken by nearly all the Arab slaves, had saved them from being killed. They had then been seized, dragged into camp, and brought before Said, who after a long conference kept two of my people, sending two of his with them, who were to return the same night and report whether our approach was pacific or not. I was astonished that even the man from Zanzibar did not cease to distrust us till we had been minutely questioned. The reason for this became plain to me much later. Tibbu Tibb, I was told, with two white men, probably Dr. Lenz and his companion, had some time ago set out for the coast; Juma Merikani and the son of my old guest, the Sheik Abed, were at Nyangwe. Many of the Arabs I had known had succumbed to small-pox. Said, the leader of the vagabond troop encamping near us, had formerly made Pogge's and my acquaintance. He was one of Tibbu Tibb's favourite slaves, whom this shrewd Arab had succeeded in making one of his most devoted subjects. We were now in the Kalebue country, and next day passed two little deserted villages, in one of which we came upon seventeen human skulls, grouped in a circle. Said's people drew my attention to this as a proof that the Kalebue of these parts were terrible cannibals, and, therefore, ought to be extirpated. They only pretended this to be a motive for this war, the real cause of which I mentioned above, for the Kalebue, who fought on the side of the Arabs, were cannibals as well as the western members of their tribe. Of this we were soon to have striking proofs.

I halted and encamped 800 paces before Said's camp, whither thousands of savage warriors were running to meet us, full of curiosity, and then, accompanied by four men, I went to Said to ascertain particulars. I was surrounded by Eastern Kalebue, savagely brandishing their arms and uttering wild shrieks; they were tools in the hands of the slave-hunters, who were here in the suite of the Arabs. An Arab mongrel, scarcely twenty years old, accompanied by some people clad in Arab shirts, came to meet me, promising with exquisite politeness —by which the Arab swears until he takes up arms—that he would do all I wished. He regretted that he had not been able to send me a present of meat, as he had not any left for himself. Said was in his manner almost boyish. His companions were equally civil and modest; they did not as yet know my power sufficiently, and wanted to learn what had brought me here.

IN SAID'S CAMP

At Said's invitation we repaired to the camp, which was surrounded by a close barricade of brushwood and thorns. At the entrance they had constructed a gate, a kind of yoke formed of beams; on the horizontal beams were suspended about fifty chopped-off hands, mostly in a state of putrefaction, which smelt terribly; Said, pointing to the hands, merely uttered the word, 'Cannibals!'

We sat down before the house of the former chief of this village, and Said now began to speak in the Suaheli language—somewhat familiar to me—but was frequently interrupted by his companions, who apparently gave him injunctions in a different language as to what he was to communicate to or keep from us. Famba at Nyangwe (Juma Merikani), he said, had formerly transacted business with Lupungu, before whose house we were sitting, though Tibbu Tibb had claimed Lupungu as his subject. Lupungu had repeatedly cut off the heads of Tibbu's messengers and given them to his Kalebue for a treat. Then the powerful Arab had sent Said to punish the rebellious Lupungu as well as the warriors of the tributary chiefs Lussuna, Lagongo, and Dibue. The former had fled, and not as yet reappeared; they did not exactly know his whereabouts, but had received information of his being allied with Mona Kakesa and the Belande, and encamping in the south-west.

The boy Said told me he did not know whether he was powerful enough to attack the Allies; he appeared to me to be irresolute, I may say almost timid, and by no means seemed to deserve the trust put in him by his master. In the valley of the Lukassi, on the opposite side of the river, I had the day before approached the camp, so near that I could distinguish the voices; while he had learned nothing of the building of our bridge or of our approach. He might easily have blocked up the bridge and kept it from being destroyed, but it seemed to me that for the present he wanted to put an end to the war, and to rest satisfied with reaping the fields and chasing the dispersed natives with a small number of troops. Allied with me, he thought he might attack Lupungu; but I made my position clear to him in such a manner that he made no further reference to the subject.

Said returned my visit in the evening, bringing forty loads of manioc and maize and five slaves; several great men and chiefs, his subjects, joined him with similar presents. Since I wanted to allow my people a day's halt, and there was nothing to buy, I requested Said to point out the most southern part of the plantations of Lupungu's former village, so as to abundantly supply my followers with maize, manioc, beans, and pumpkins. Although we had found sufficient food during the last few days to satisfy our craving hunger, my people were still very weak, and suffering from various diseases, principally foot-sores—a consequence of having had scanty food for weeks.

In Said's camp were at least 3,000 people, who were said to have 600 guns. The smell on approaching the camp was pestilential, so great a mass of people being packed into so small a space. Said asked for, and received, different medicines, such as carbolic acid, vaseline, and other simple remedies. In return he promised to supply us with guides on our march to Nyangwe; whence, only, could further explorations be carried out. I could not count upon my Bashilange farther than the Lualaba, they being even now in a condition that scarcely permitted them to drag themselves from place to place. I should then have only a few coast negroes and ransomed Baluba, who would not suffice for a further expedition up the Lualaba. I was, therefore, obliged to try to procure canoes and men at Nyangwe from the Arabs, my former friends, so as to proceed with my commission. On returning to Nyangwe, after exploring the water-courses of the Upper Lualaba, I could, without great expense, go to Stanley Fall Station, and thence by the next steamer to the mouth of the Congo.

In the evening a patrol of about fifty men returned from their hunt after natives who were dispersed and concealed in the woods. They brought a few prisoners bleeding from several wounds. One of Said's people had also got an arrow in the upper part of his thigh, which had been extracted very clumsily. When Le Marinel gave the wound proper treatment, the gallant warrior behaved very stupidly. He screamed and moaned; and even Said made much ado of what, for a warrior, was but a trifling accident. Some of my people who towards evening had taken the wounded man back to Said's camp returned literally livid with fear and loathing, reporting that Said, the apparently irresolute boy, had for a long time practised firing with a revolver, making a target of the prisoners, until they had dropped down after many shots. He had then handed over his

SAID'S PISTOL PRACTICE

dead victims to his auxiliary troops, who had cut them in pieces and dragged them to the fire to serve as their supper. This was the army of an Arab who wanted to punish natives for cannibalism!

I must say in honour of my Bashilange, whose older members had formerly been wont to eat human flesh, that when, on our march next day we passed the camp, decked out with the putrefied remains of slain human beings, they showed disgust and loathing. However, they endeavoured to conceal their abhorrence for fear of Said's savage warriors, who had got morally low in consequence of their bodily sufferings. The pitiful appearance of my people even evoked the scornful laughter and contempt of the fat, well-fed warriors of the Arabs; and in fact the aspect of the withered, long-limbed, bent figures, who were scarcely able to carry their guns and their hemp-pipe, was not adapted to inspire one with awe of their martial worth.

Our onward journey, being on Said's line of march, led through destroyed villages, some of whose former inhabitants had emigrated whilst others were living on the remains of their fields, concealing themselves in the thickets. In the first village we met some people who, evidently taking us for a troop of Said's, fled to a village 500 metres in front of us. Some Bashilange, who likewise went thither to search for victuals, were received with arrow-shots, and soon after the natives themselves burnt down their village and disappeared. At the village where we were encamped we made some interesting discoveries. In the centre stood a war fetish, a man's figure of 0·7 metre height, with points of arrows stuck in like bristles and besmeared with blood, so that our two little terriers showed much ethnographical interest in the fetish. In some houses lay corpses, and near the village, there being want of building materials for our camp, the huts were simply lifted off the corpses and put up in the camp. After being nearly three hours on the spot one of these apparent corpses suddenly raised himself, looking round him wonderingly and asking for food. The man seemed to be dangerously ill and near starvation. The Bashilange brought him food, but as soon as the evening grew dark he disappeared, at which we could not help feeling glad, as it led us to suppose that he would tell the members of his tribe of our not belonging to Tibbu Tibb's rapacious troops.

The daily falls of rain were very tiresome on account of their soaking the heavy clayey roads, and thus causing our weakened people to slip while marching. It was astonishing that, with the constant gloomy weather and cold winds, and in spite of the universal exhaustion and the many diseases, we had so far only to record five deaths in the caravan.

On our march we observed a range of separate mountains between Lubefu and Lukassi, rising precipitously from the prairie, which from a distance appeared quite level. We kept continually along the Lukassi. As soon as we approached the edge of its valley, the generally uninterrupted prairie at first alternated with scanty tree savannahs, which towards the bottom grew thicker and thicker. The country was bare of primæval forests, and was no longer inhabited by the grey parrot, whose habitat is strictly limited to such districts. He prefers, however, small primæval forests and stretches of wood along the river to the vast uninterrupted ones; while his two relatives, the large and the small green parrot, are inhabitants of the savannah. Above on the prairie the dwarf bustard was very plentiful.

At one of the shallow brooks, here often bordered by papyrus jungles, we had to turn, the bridge being torn away, and there being no material far or near with which to replace it; and only after a long circuit could we find a crossing-place. Close thickets and high grass, now dripping with wet, cold winds and clouded skies, made marching exceedingly difficult. Le Marinel had for two hours daily to act as a doctor. Among the 100 invalids, some of whom had to be carried, nearly fifty were footsore; these were in charge of Bugslag and the soldiers of the rear, and generally did not reach the camp till evening.

On January 21 we once more crossed the Lukassi in canoes which we had on the spot. The river, here 100 metres broad and three metres deep, flowed slowly, and its water was of a dark grey colour. Before reaching the canoes we had to cross an overflowed space of two kilometres, the water reaching up to our waists. We now entered the country of those Kalebue who, as subjects of Tibbu Tibb, had taken part in the warlike expedition against the western members of their tribe. At last we succeeded in getting some meat, the chief bringing us four fowls. On the left bank of the Lukassi we had to contend with long grass, thickets, and many bogs, which further weakened the health of the caravan.

On the 23rd, close to the mouth of the Lukassi, we reached the Lomami, near the ferry of the Bena Sala; they, like all the natives here, suffered severely from want of food, the roving troops of Tibbu Tibb

PALMS ON THE LOMAMI.

not even sparing the plantations of a friendly country. The Lomami was here 150 metres broad by three metres deep, and had a speed of eighty metres a minute. The bed consisted of coarse shingle; the brink of the banks was bordered by a thin edge of oil palms and wild dates, besides a kind of willow. The gently sloping banks showed grass savannah. While I was marching, a large-winged spur-goose flew close past me before I could get my rifle ready. 'There goes our breakfast!' I called out to Le Marinel. The bird, however, took pity on us; he turned, and I succeeded in shooting the young goose, which later we greatly enjoyed. The bird was the first warning of the difficulties we should have to encounter, consisting of vast bogs and pools, which afford the wild geese a favourite abode. What our caravan could be living on was a complete puzzle to me. Even the inhabitants of the small, thinly-populated villages that we passed were suffering from hunger. It was impossible, therefore, to allow the dead-tired caravan a rest, for only by a continual and quick change of place could we find the most necessary food for satisfying our hunger. On the way Le Marinel and I often revelled in recollections of the Café Riche in Brussels; Le Marinel especially was a connoisseur of the most refined gastronomy at home, and his descriptions often made my mouth water. The conclusion of such a conversation was generally the tightening of our belts and the hoping for better days.

It made me very sad to observe my poor Bashilange in the morning when starting. But for the strict enforcement of the order to move on, many a one most certainly would have preferred to lie still rather than drag along his sick and weary body. Bugslag complained daily of difficulties with the rear-guard; his lot was not an enviable one. From morning till night he had incessantly to bring on the weary by persuasion or, if necessary, by having them carried, or, when they were ill, by taking them on his bull. He performed his task with an iron calmness and patience. Whenever we halted the people began to scream: 'Kabassu-Babu, give us food, we are dying with hunger!' The complaints of my poor companions cut me to the quick; but where was the remedy? I was not even in a position to show my sympathy, but had to do my utmost to encourage the weary, and urge them onwards. Of any European provisions, preserves, &c., there was of course nothing left; we had distributed everything up to the last tin. The only one of the caravan who did not grow thin was the fat interpreter, Kashawalla. He made use of his cleverness in his intercourse with the natives, which made him a favourite with everyone, and filled his stomach; and whilst so engaged he even lost his good nature, at least as regards sharing his food with others. He was a great adept at concealing food in the baskets of his wives.

On the 23rd commenced the crossing of the Lomami in four canoes; 600 people were brought over. Three hundred more, and the bulls, had to stop till next day, the transport again taking a whole day. The people thought that the Lomami fell into the Lualaba. Farther down the river they knew nothing of either falls or sands; above, the river was supposed to be navigable for canoes for only another five days' journey—as far as the falls which were said to be in the Baluba country.

Here there was not much to live upon either, but I was in hopes that a halt, when I would send my people in all directions to purchase provisions from the natives, would be of advantage to us.

Since my first journey much had changed here to our disadvantage. Formerly we used to make purchases in exchange for cowrie-shells and cheap beads; nobody, however, would take these now: they wanted stuffs and coloured beads which they had seen with Tibbu Tibb's people; and, everything being dear on account of the famine, my goods diminished most alarmingly. However, I could not but pay what they asked, so far as I could afford it, taking my share in alleviating the craving hunger which tormented the people. On the Lualaba I hoped to procure provisions from the Arabs. The governor of the countries on the Lomami which belong to Tibbu Tibb was, at the time, the same Said whom I met as a leader of the army on the Lukassi. He performed administrative duties for his master and for his own pocket—collecting tribute, compelling people to serve under him, and punishing offences. These were often a cause for making war, for even a dispute among the people or the villages will give the Arab's substitute a pretext for interfering in his master's name. If compelled to do so, they obediently follow the army, as we have seen: brothers of the same name fought against each other in the cause of their tyrants. That is the result of the reign of terror with which the Arabs have here established themselves! The collecting of tribute consisted in quite an arbitrary system of pillaging. Each great or petty substitute for his master asked just what suited him, since rules, of course, did not exist. It is astonishing that natives will stay at all in such countries. The cunning Arabs, however, prevent them from leaving the district entirely by flattering some of the greater and more influential chiefs, giving them a certain power, and even bribing them by presents.

Said, as governor of the province, had an old slave or coaster installed as a representative with each of the greater chiefs; then, also, he had his sub-officials and spies at the various villages, so that nothing could happen without its coming to the knowledge of the administrator of the province. If an elephant was killed, one tusk belonged to the master of the country, Tibbu Tibb; the other had likewise to be sold to him at his own price. Each of Said's representatives practised fraud in a gradually increasing degree, and the system of taxation was thus a reckless system of extortion.

During the day's halt we had built a bridge across the Kalui, close by, and next day marched through a plain with tree-savannah and long grass, intersected by shallow and gently curving water-courses. There was great abundance of elephants. These animals evidently at certain times exchange the district of the primæval forest beyond the Lomami for this plain, principally in order to drink the water of the salt lakes, and to enjoy the ripe fruit of the borassus, which has a sweet and pleasant taste. I was indefatigable in pursuing fresh traces of them, so as once more to procure meat for our people. The deep grass, however, not only rendered the shooting expeditions difficult and fatiguing, but it also thwarted every approach to the huge beast, by causing too much noise when trodden on—the elephant

DISTRIBUTION OF PROVISIONS

ELEPHANT ON THE KALUI

being very cautious. I am certain that our people had had no meat since passing the Sankurru, quite six weeks before, except caterpillars, locusts, and the like.

Whenever natives happened to come into the camp with provisions for sale, hundreds of the caravan rushed upon them, and snatched their provisions from them, so that afterwards I posted guards, who had to take the salesmen to a place where Bugslag was ready to buy all the provisions, which he afterwards distributed. During the distribution the stick had to act a chief part; but, in spite of it, there was often no preventing them from tearing away the provisions. On one of these occasions ten of my Bashilange fell dangerously ill. Vomiting and convulsions were the symptoms with all of them.

We found out that, in order to satisfy their craving hunger, they had cooked and eaten bulbs which they knew to be poisonous. Emetics were, however, successfully administered.

Great annoyance was caused by the prickly seeds which fell off the ripe grass at the slightest touch. The seeds, with their many little sharp points, got between the clothes and the skin, and with each movement of the body caused an irritating sensation. In order to remove this torment one had to undress and carefully pick off the seeds.

The country gradually became almost level; only at a far distance, towards the east, we noticed gentle ranges of hills. Everything was dripping with the incessant rain; the tough greyish-white clay of the plain did not allow the water to penetrate, nor did it flow off, so that we had to march half the way in pools over tough and slippery clayey ground. Almost the only tree on the vast grass plain was the fan palm. Swarms of geese and ducks and green pigeons enlivened the endless watery tract; elephants also were plentiful.

On the 27th, when halting at the small villages of the Bena Kapua, I could not bring myself to punish my people for pillaging the fields. They ate even what was not ripe, and especially chewed the green blades of millet, which are rather sugary in taste. Our arrival at the place of encampment was a sorry sight. Grey was the sky, grey did our people look with cold and hunger, and grey was the future. We again had to bury some Bashilange who had succumbed to the effects of hunger. In spite of the suffering, not a word was uttered to reproach me; the unbounded confidence of my sons of the Lulua was carried so far that mothers, who did not know how to feed their children, would hush up their complaints and frettings with the assurance: 'Kabassu Babu will make it all right, he will soon take us to a place where we shall find something to eat!'

It would have been next to impossible to make this journey with other people than my Bashilange. Other tribes might possibly have borne hunger, sickness, fatigues, war, incessant cold and rain, better than my rather weakly people; but discontent, reproaches, and mutiny would have been unavoidable with any other escort.

With one of Le Marinel's patients mortification had set in. The flesh assumed a greyish-black colour and began to waste away. In proportion as the mortification spread, the bone also decayed and fell off the joints. This disease always commenced in the toes, probably in consequence of the continual bogs and damps that we had passed through, and was helped by the sore feet, as well as by the weak and delicate bodily condition, of my people. When the mortification extended to the upper part of the foot, the patient died after violent fever. Le Marinel told the people that the only help would be to take off the joint. At first they all refused, but afterwards they declared themselves ready for the amputation, on condition that I approved of it and that I would be present. It was by no means easy to perform the operation, as we had no surgical instruments with us. While we were cutting into the proud flesh the patients did not feel anything, but had we only gone so far our operating would have been of no avail. So we decided to cut off the joint above the diseased part. Without any practical knowledge, without either surgical instruments or chloroform, Le Marinel, who had great skill in such things, performed the operation, and now had the gratification of stopping the progress of mortification and of saving many lives.

On our march one morning we found that one man with a gun and a load of provisions had not arrived at the camp. I had, therefore, to halt, and send back patrols, who, however, returned without him. I had been made aware of this from the lost gun being a chassepôt carbine; besides, I should have been sure to notice the missing load. To my great consternation I learned that some of the Bashilange had repeatedly lingered behind; very likely they had been overcome by hunger on the way, or they had been kept back on account of bodily pain. As Bugslag always brought on all the weary men who were found on the road, the disappearance of the people could only be accounted for by their having hid in the deep grass, so as to escape encountering new tortures and fatigues.

The involuntary day of rest had, at least, enabled our people to procure sufficient food near the road to satisfy all; but—just as if on this journey everything was to be turned into trouble—the first case of smallpox was now discovered among my Bashilange, and was soon followed by another and others.

The weather did not change for the better; everything came either to a standstill or was spoiled; grey clouds lowered from morning to night, rain was incessant, and the cold was felt even by Europeans.

It often happened that the van of the caravan, wading through a pool, would suddenly sink in to a considerable depth, for below this vast waste of water there proved to be the channel of a brook. In order to cross

BUILDING OF A BRIDGE.

one of these water-courses I invented a new kind of bridge. There was no tree to be seen far and wide, nothing but brushwood, grass, and swamp; the edges of the brooks, some feet under water, were distinguishable by the thicker brushwood. I ordered all the men to disperse, cut down bushes, drag them along and throw them into the water where it was narrowest. The current being scarcely perceptible, the wood remained on the surface until pressed down by a fresh supply; and after 200 men had toiled for two hours, a wall, as it were, arose, which, though unsteady, enabled us safely to cross the brook. As may be seen from the illustration, this kind of bridge can be more easily constructed than one of beams; but naturally it can only be formed in a slow current.

We had, at least, half the distance to wade through water, which increased the number of sore feet. Those ill with small-pox I had tried to leave behind near a small village, after pitching tents for them and supplying them with provisions; but the natives turned them out, and took everything from them.

I had to keep them, therefore, and ordered them to march at least 100 metres behind the rear of the caravan and to build their huts 500 metres off the camp. One day a young Mushilange, ill with small-pox, came contrary to order into the camp, and, as he was not willing to go, I sent him back by force, when his mother, a Mushilange woman, anxious about her son, tried to stab me with a knife, and it was difficult to convince her that the isolation of the patients was for the benefit of all; I could only calm her by giving her some medicine for her son.

All the slaves of the Bashilange, mostly descended from the Baluba tribe, had fled to the natives, so as to be no longer exposed to the hunger and fatigue of the march. Of my ransomed Baluba, however, not one was missing.

In spite of the small number of loads and the large caravan, I was scarcely able to distribute the former. Few people felt strong enough to carry anything, even for high wages.

We were informed daily that two, three, and more people had been left behind dying. As my soldiers, whom I had been in the habit of sending back to look for the missing, grew gradually over-tired, I obliged the Bashilange chiefs to go back even with their best people to look after their subjects. In the evening I made them report how many had not been found. Strange to say, this generally corresponded so well with the number of those who had been missing at first, that one day, on investigating whether the Bashilange were actually looking for their people, I found them concealed in a thicket close to the camp. They intended to wait there till dark and then report in the camp that the invalids had not been found. I could not punish them for this proceeding, convinced as I was that it did not arise from want of feeling, but was simply owing to their inability to march back.

At Kilembue we at last got enough to eat, and the provisions were even fairly cheap, so that, in consequence of their eating such quantities of food, a good many fell ill in the evening. The population increased the nearer we approached the north. We came to the villages of Kawamba Kitenge, the chief of the Bena Nguo, where representatives of Tibbu Tibb were everywhere stationed with some soldiers. The shady villages, with pretty little clay houses, which often have a small verandah and fenced-in gardens, abounded in sheep, goats, pigs, fowls, and there were also fields which produced whatever our delighted Bashilange could desire; even rice, imported by the Arabs, was grown. The natives, notwithstanding, behaved very well; they were rather bold, certainly, but by no means insolent.

On February 1 we reached Kitenge's residence, and pitched our camp in the shadow of the trees which surrounded the tombs of the dead chiefs. An aged Zanzibari, Tibbu Tibb's representative at this place, recognised me, having been with us when, in 1882, I had marched from Tabara to the coast with Tibbu Tibb. He told me why the natives had always been unwilling to accompany me on elephant hunts in these parts; they had been afraid lest I should claim the ivory, half of which belonged to Tibbu Tibb by law, and half had to be sold to him. The old Zanzibari made a good impression on me, though he was exceedingly reserved on being questioned about Nyangwe and the state of affairs at Stanley Falls.

It was a twelve days' march from here to Nyangwe, and as I learned that all the water-courses were greatly swollen, I resolved to leave the greater part of the caravan, with all the sick and weak, behind. I held a review and selected the strongest men for an onward-moving escort. The rest, with Kashawalla, who had made friends with Kitenge and the old Zanzibari, were to stay here, where food was plentiful, and the prices not too high; they were to be picked up again on Le Marinel's return. The review, as might have been anticipated, showed a very bad result; our loss was greater than we had bargained for. Of one family, that had numbered eight when starting, only three were left; of another, a third only survived; and even though we did not succeed in ascertaining the number of the lost—the Bashilange never could be collected together, and the chiefs did not like to state the loss correctly—we estimated it at nearly fifty men. For all that, the chiefs insisted on accompanying me, feeling ashamed, they said, of returning to the Lulua without having seen Nyangwe, the great town of the Arabs. I supplied Kashawalla with another interpreter, some soldiers, and plenty of goods, so that they should not be inconvenienced, and got ready for marching on with the caravan, now numbering 200 persons. Kitenge had brought numerous presents, fifteen goats, six pigs, and large quantities of corn. In return I gave him, at his request, a bull, as he promised to watch over the safety of my people.

After those who were intended to remain behind had pitched their camp near Kitenge's residence, and Tibbu Tibb's representative had been won to our cause, I started on the 5th, but halted an hour later, and in a place where none could hide I reviewed my new caravan, and discovered about 100 people whom I had appointed to stay behind, but who, contrary to my orders, had joined us, and some of whom had to be sent back by force. In order that we should not be followed by stragglers again, I made my outposts wait for an hour at each place, and had another troop carried back to Kashawalla. We received presents from all quarters, but not until the people had heard of my being an old friend of Tibbu Tibb's. Their manner to me was always rather forward, almost insolent; this, considering how they had behaved on former occasions, rather baffled me, since no Europeans had been here meanwhile.

After the Congo had been crossed, where it was twenty metres broad and 1·5 metre deep, with an overflow of two kilometres' breadth, I received news at the village of the Bena Lubowa which enlightened me about much that had so far been unintelligible.

A coast negro, one of Tibbu Tibb's people, was so insolent outside my tent that with my own hands I turned him out of the fence surrounding it. Soon afterwards an old man who had accompanied me from Kitenge appeared, asking for a private interview. He told me that a few months before the Europeans had been at war with the Arabs near Stanley Falls station, and that a cousin of Tibbu Tibb's had taken the station of the white men by storm, when one of these had fallen and three fled, and the station had been burnt down. In expectation of an avenging expedition, thousands of Tibbu Tibb's people had been sent thither, among them many warriors from these parts, who had only lately returned, as the whites, being too small in numbers to fight against Tibbu, had not come back. This was bad news. I arrived here with the same flag [1] against which, as we all knew, Tibbu Tibb's people had fought near the Falls.

To advance in force was not to be thought of, for if there had been a fight none of the Bashilange would have been spared. Three parts of my people had been left behind ill, unable to march or fight; Tibbu Tibb

---

[1] I carried the star-flag of the Congo State beside the black, white, and red.

himself, who was to be trusted most, had gone down to the coast, and my old friend the Sheik Abed had also gone. The only friendly Arab whom I knew, and who was still on the Lualaba, was Famba Juma Merikana, known from Cameron's journey. My prospects, therefore, were very gloomy. Would not the Arabs have blamed me for the fights near Stanley Falls? Would they not keep us as hostages for an avenging expedition from the Lower Congo? Even if such were not the case, would they give me means for a further exploration?

The present representative of Tibbu Tibb was Bwana Zefu, his son, to whom I had been of great service years before, at the residence of the mighty Uniamwesi prince, Mirambo, but whom I had since then discovered to be a passionate, suspicious, and cunning fellow. At present I had to act with caution and prudence, for not only was the progress of my expedition, but also the lives and liberty of my nearly 900 followers were dependent on my bearing. It was a pity that my people also learned the news, which until now had been skilfully concealed from us, and was only now transmitted when we appeared too small in numbers to be in any way formidable to the Arabs. Later I learned that Said, the leader of the vagabonds on the Lukassi, had sent the report of our approach to Nyangwe, and that from thence directions had been despatched to all the chiefs on the road. The people were not to betray the intended war to us, until either we should have reached the territory of the Arabs or be too weak to enter into any hostilities. The behaviour of the natives was now accounted for. At first the only thing to be done was to emphasise the pacific purpose of our expedition and quietly to continue our march. If we had marched back to the bulk of the troop, the surrounding tribes, with Said and his people, and a reinforcement from the Lualaba, would have been brought on our rear at once. Even if, at the best, we had been able to defend ourselves, a return with almost 900 sick and weak into that district of starvation was not to be thought of, least of all in a fighting attitude. This would have been equivalent to the annihilation of the caravan.

Lussana, the chief of the Malela, sent us six loads of manioc, four of bananas, one of sugar, 100 eggs, eight fattened sheep, and one fat pig; in return for which, at his special request, I gave him two small barrels of powder and four handkerchiefs, which he sent back as not sufficient. I soon, however, learned that three insolent young fellows, who had to arrange the exchange of presents, had forged the second demand of the good-natured chief and then intercepted it. The impudence of some people from Nyangwe, who on the way had robbed my people of beads and fowls, made me anxious about the future. Besides, a man with his load was missing again.

We now approached a point where several large tribes meet. North-west of us lived the Batetela of Kassonga Lushia; Kitenge had been the northernmost Bassonge prince, for Lussuma belonged to the Wakussu, who are part of the Wasongora or Bassonga. On the south-east the Baluba extended to this latitude along the Lualaba.

CROSSING THE CONGO-LUALABA

On the Moadi I suddenly met an Arab, or rather a Beloochistan man, who had come on a trading expedition from Nyangwe and offered to accompany me to the Lualaba. He sent me rice and lemons, and told me that Famba was ill, and, in order to allay the excitement that might be caused by my appearance at Nyangwe, he advised me to send messengers to the Arabs there, assuring them of my pacific approach. I did so, and for this mission selected Humba, two soldiers, and the flag-bearer Fickerini.

This arrangement had the advantage of not being conspicuous, if I should need to withdraw the star-flag which Fickerini had carried until now, but which was pursued with threats by many people who knew it from Stanley Falls. As the Beloochistan, Sahorro, cheated me immensely in my bargains with him, he was very amiable and exceedingly useful to me in my precarious situation.

On we marched through the saline country of the Bena Samba, across the ridge of hills west of the Lualaba into the valley of the father of African streams, the Lualaba Congo, which I reached on the evening of February 14, near a settlement of the fishing people, the Wagenic.

In the large beautiful canoes, coming from the northern primæval forests, we next day crossed the Lualaba, which has here a breadth of 1,200 metres, and had a shelter assigned to us at Nyangwe. We Europeans were lodged in a poor and dirty little house, and our Bashilange in a remote part of the town. It was a bad sign that we were not received by any Arab, as was the case last time, and as Arab civility demands. Except the crowds of slaves staring at us, no one seemed to take any notice of us. I soon learned that encroachments had taken place at Nyangwe. My old friend, the Sheik Abed, had been partially compelled to travel to the coast, as they said, by order of the Sultan Said Bargash, in order to pay his debts to Indian traders. His present representative, Halfan, did not come till evening; he behaved civilly, but was most reserved—which, however, did not prevent him from begging continually. The fact of his desires being gratified procured us visits from many inferior Arabs, who all demanded one thing or another. It was almost night when one of them told me at last that, if I were to give him such and such a thing, he would betray any conspiracy on foot against me. They had evidently not made up their minds how to treat me, and I heard that conferences were being incessantly held about this question. Next day came Zefu, Tibbu Tibb's son, in a canoe from Kassonge, accompanied by six insolent young fellows. Zefu's behaviour was shocking. The hot-headed young fellow, made insolent by his sense of superiority, treated me in such a manner that it was only with the utmost effort that I could master myself sufficiently to answer him quietly, as necessity demanded. We were regularly put through a series of questions as to whence we came, in whose commission, how long we had been coming, &c. At our answers, which may have seemed strange to the half-savage Arabs, who are partly negroes (Zefu, too, is quite black)—they would sometimes laugh right into our faces. In quite a nonchalant way they would jeeringly imitate the heavy movements of Bugslag's robust sailor-figure. They criticised Le Marinel's and my looks without hesitation in the Suaheli language, perfectly unintelligible to me. My man-servant Sankurru, who had been given me by Abed, and who had formerly been known here, was called and asked in our presence whether our statements were true or not; in short, to any-one acquainted with Arab civility, their behaviour was rude and provoking. At length, though with great difficulty, I brought myself to assume a stoical tranquillity, which gradually toned down the insolent and noisy behaviour of our inquisitors. The manner in which Zefu told us about the war near Stanley Falls, and the way in which he described the wounds and death of a European, calling them cowards, &c., was most revolting.

This insult, the worst an Arab can utter, made me start and ask him to whom he owed his not having been taken prisoner by Mirambo some years ago; but it was necessary that I should keep my temper, as on the result of this conference might possibly depend the destiny of my whole caravan. This scene had the advantage of making me see plainly that from this point any further undertaking would be impossible, and that my special endeavour must be to send home unhurt the many hundreds of people who had accompanied me. (Zefu pointed out one of his followers to me as being the one who had killed the white man, which the other boastingly corroborated.) That I should not take back the troop myself was decided by Tibbu Tibb's son, who requested me to follow him to Kassongo. It was obvious that they wanted to keep me as a hostage for

Tibbu Tibb, who had gone to Zanzibar, and about whom they felt anxious, in consequence of the skirmishes near Stanley Falls. I prepared myself to remain here as a prisoner for the next twelve months, unless a chance should preserve me from such a fate. A half-bred Arab had from the beginning been commanded to look after my wants, but he was to act as a spy, and was of course not to lose sight of me. He reported my every movement, and was so amiable as to beg incessantly.

Above all it was necessary to remove Zefu's distrust if possible, and the best way was to win him over by presents. Before he left I therefore gave him a beautiful rifle and some silk stuffs which I had taken as presents for the Arabs. Sahorro gradually told me that the Arabs had resolved not to let me go, and so, anticipating the communication on the part of the Arabs, I made known to Zefu my intention of remaining here with Bugslag and some of my people. The Bashilange, however, I would send back first to Kitenge, and from thence to their own country, with those who had remained behind, if they should meanwhile have sufficiently recovered. They were to be conducted by Le Marinel, whom I had introduced here as French and not Belgian, as they entertained a burning hatred against the Belgians since the fight near the Falls. Zefu declared himself to be of the same opinion, and I made it my first endeavour by the purchasing of provisions to prepare for the return of the caravan. These I decided to buy from Juma Merikani, since he, the only Arab formerly known to me, had warned me against his fellow-tribesmen. I was to sail up the Lualaba with Zefu, who was ready to stop with me at Juma's to conclude the bargain.

In the morning, at the hour fixed for embarking, Zefu was rather late, and did not make his appearance at the landing-place. I entered one of the canoes, and, telling the steersman that I wanted to go on to Juma, I made them push off, encouraging the oarsmen, as if for my amusement, to exert themselves, so as to arrive at Juma's as long as possible before Zefu, which would enable me to negotiate with the former undisturbed by Zefu's presence. I noticed two canoes, strongly manned with armed warriors, 'keeping watch' below my house on the Lualaba, in order to prevent me, as I learned later, from taking possession of the canoes of Nyangwe and sailing down the stream. We now went up the river, making the yellow water dash up high above the bow of the canoe, until we reached Juma's place. When I landed, there was no trace of Zefu's canoes. I hurried to the house of my old friend, who again warned me against Zefu, and promised to sell beads and cloth to me, and to do all he could to facilitate my Bashilange's return home as soon as possible. Juma told me that at the rumour of my approach they had conjectured that I intended to seize Nyangwe and Tibbu Tibb's settlement, Kassongo, from the west, and to punish them for the destruction of the station at Stanley Falls.

Afterwards, having learned that I had left the greater part of my caravan at Kitenge, they resolved to keep me as a hostage for Tibbu Tibb, and had taken measures to watch me from every side, as for instance by the canoes on the Lualaba. When Zefu arrived, much annoyed at my having hurried on—though he dared not say so in the presence of old Juma—we entered upon business. I bought beads and stuffs, and, with Juma's vigorous support, we agreed that I should return to Nyangwe, and that, after making my Bashilange start on the 21st, I, with the people who were to remain with me, should go by land to Kassongo, Tibbu Tibb's residence. My people had noticed for some time that something was wrong, that

LIEUTENANT LE MARINEL.

my friendly manners to the Arabs were only pretended, and, for their own safety, they were glad soon to leave Nyangwe and to set out for their beloved Lulua.

On the 21st Le Marinel returned with the caravan across the Lualaba. It was with a heavy heart that I saw the good people, who had suffered so much on my account, depart. I could not requite them for what they had done for me, and could only beg Le Marinel to treat them after their return as well as might be in his power. There was nothing to be feared for the safety of the caravan, except perhaps sickness and hunger; though it was not so bad to have to pass through those desolate districts now, when they knew what to expect and were able to prepare themselves for any cases of emergency.

Le Marinel had quickly learned how to treat the negroes. He had gained the love and confidence of the Bashilange by his truly unselfish surgical assistance and continual kindness. At the same time, he was thoroughly equal to any warlike eventualities, so that I was not anxious about the safety of the Bashilange. They, on their part, felt that I remained behind in a precarious situation; as I read in their eyes and learned from their hearty hand-shake on parting with their 'Moiio Kabassu Babu.'

The ferry on the Lualaba had had repeatedly to witness sad partings. It was here that five years before I bade farewell to my friend Pogge, who was about to return to the western wilderness. Now I was deeply moved at seeing my black sons from the Lulua leave me. Nor did I feel indifferent at having to separate from Le Marinel. This young officer had been a faithful help in sad times.[1]

Only ten of my coasters from Angola remained with me, besides twenty ransomed Baluba slaves, who refused to leave me; and last, not least, Bugslag, good as gold, whose courage and trust were not to be shaken, and whose uniform good temper and devotion have made him my friend for life.

[1] In Appendix I. is added a letter of Le Marinel's, describing the return of the caravan from Nyangwe to their own country.

CHAPTER VIII

AM OBLIGED TO TRAVEL EASTWARD—JOURNEY TO THE TANGANYIKA

Famba's disclosures—Stores of ivory—In the lion's den—'White men are cowards'—Thwarting of my plans—The murderer of a German—The past and present recollections of an old chief—I feel very weak—The places of encampment poisoned by the corpses of slaves—Sad reflections—Apathy of my people—Horrors of the traffic in slaves—On the Tanganyika.

I STARTED from Nyangwe on the 22nd, and next day stayed with Juma bin Salim, who gave me three fatted oxen, a donkey, a red parrot,[1] three sheep, some leopard skins, and many trifling presents; in return for which I gave him my pistol, a musical box, and a bull. Juma advised me to be friendly and unembarrassed in my behaviour to Zefu, to make him presents—and especially to get away from Kassongo as speedily as possible; I was then to march to the Tanganyika, from which point I should find different roads to the coast. I might be sure, he said, that if, during my sojourn at Kassongo, Tibbu Tibb's stations should be attacked by the Congo State, I should be lost; even Tibbu Tibb's son could not protect me from the rage of the coasters and small traders. He also told me that only the fact of my

---

[1] These red parrots are freaks of nature, and occur but rarely. Three or four grey parrots and a red one are now and then found in one nest in the districts between Sankurru and Lomami. These birds fetch a great price on the coast.

JUMA'S ADVICE

JUMA BIN SALIM'S IVORY

having formerly been on friendly terms with many Arabs and also with Tibbu Tibb had saved my caravan from destruction. The excitement in consequence of the fighting at Stanley Falls, the blame for which was entirely ascribed to the hostile bearing of the white men of that place, was, he told me, far greater than was imagined. The reason for the skirmishes, which was known to be quite different from what was reported, he related to me in the following manner: the chief of the station near

Stanley Falls, a certain Lieutenant Dean, had for a long time, and finally by force, withheld the wife of an Arab who had followed him and had assisted slaves in their flight. Afterwards, when the said woman had been seized and beaten by her master, he had fired bomb-shells into Tibbu Tibb's camp, where he had killed and wounded several people. Then the Arabs had attacked him, and after several days' struggle, in which a white man had fallen, they had stormed the station. Two Europeans had saved themselves. and also part of the black troop, Haussa and Bangala. They had then pillaged and destroyed the station. He further told us that at Tabora an Arab had shot a German,[1] who was trading with ivory. This Arab was at present staying at Kassongo, and was, in consequence of his deed, a great man; in short, he said that bad times were at hand, that he was of opinion that a general struggle would soon break out between Europeans and Arabs, when not even the missionaries would be spared. I was, therefore, to caution the missionaries on the Tanganyika. He said he was too clever not to know that the fight might go hard with the members of his tribe; but, being regarded as a friend of the white men, no one listened to his advice; he had not even been admitted to the conferences held about me, though, at the time, he was the oldest Arab at the Lualaba.

Juma himself was ill; he was suffering greatly from elephantiasis, and could only be carried. On account of his illness and the troubles he predicted, I urgently advised him to go with his ivory to Zanzibar, and for

[1] The German merchant, Giesecke.

the purpose of this journey I gave him a quiet bull to ride. He owned great stores of ivory. Once he called his favourite wife—a slight, handsome, large-eyed woman from Uganda—the only one whom he entrusted with the key of his treasures—and made her take me into his camp, where nearly 500 elephants' tusks lay piled up, not counting the small inferior ones. Juma is no bigoted, inveterate Mohammedan, either as regards his faith or his customs. He never hesitated to let his wives, who often brought me fruit and cake, hold intercourse with me. He spoke about religion in a very free manner, and, though this was not a good outcome of his free doctrine, he daily got drunk on a kind of brandy, compounded by himself of bananas and palm wine or millet beer. For me he had preserved a real friendship, and also for the English traveller, Cameron, of whom he always spoke with the greatest affection.

When, in 1889, I came to the East African seaboard, I was very sorry to learn that he had died at Nyangwe shortly after my departure.

On February 26 I left Juma, and on March 2 I arrived at Kassongo, the den of the lion of Manyema, Tibbu Tibb's residence. The Arabs gave us a cold reception and the populace even a hostile one. The crowds of people who had just attended a fair came flocking along to see us, and received us with loud jeers. Again and again we heard them call out, 'White men are cowards!' We took up our abode in a small, dirty, insignificant-looking house, unfit for the abode of a white man, and closed our door against the numerous visits of petty traders, Arab vagabonds, who formerly would not have dared to pay their respects to the friends of the great Arabs. Next day, as is customary, I called on all the gentry of the town, accompanied by Bugslag. Our calm and independent bearing, our emphasising the fact of our being Germans, and the promise

NEIGHBOURHOOD OF KASSONGO

of some presents, called forth greater civility on our leaving than on entering. Any attempt to undertake a journey from this place, be it to the north or south, at once excited the distrust of those on whom we were now depending to such a degree that my conviction of the impossibility of effecting exploring expeditions from this point was more and more confirmed. After giving Zefu more presents, I tried again to get canoes and people, to be selected by the Arab himself, for a journey to Moero Lake and the Kamerondo; but the manner in which he answered me convinced me of the fruitlessness of any further attempt.

My former flag-bearer, Fickerini, from Zanzibar, was of the greatest use to me, reporting as he did everything that went on. He recorded each day the result of conferences held about me; these always ended in their deciding that I should remain at least until they had heard from Tibbu Tibb, though some Arabs, on friendly terms with Juma bin Salim, voted for their letting me go to the coast, since I was a German. The leaving my caravan behind at Kitenge, they said, proved that I had not been aware of the war on Stanley Falls; besides, I had formerly been on friendly terms with the Arabs; and I could not do them any harm, but should rather be of use to them, if, on getting to the coast, I were to tell how they had let me off uninjured.

One day Fickerini came home in great glee and reported that messengers had arrived from the Tanganyika Lake with the news that Tibbu Tibb had arrived at Zanzibar and had not been called to account about the affair on Stanley Falls.

By this time the tide had begun to turn in my favour, especially since nothing happened on Stanley Falls, and I had gradually gained the confidence of the more important Arabs by giving them presents. Once more I made an attempt to avail myself of my commission from H.M. the King of the Belgians. I proposed to

Zefu to send me with some leading Arabs to Stanley Falls, so that, should we happen to meet Europeans there, we might enter upon pacific negotiations. In vain; he was too distrustful in this respect. Therefore, only one road was left to me—that towards the east.

Once more I began to hope, hearing them speak of a European living near a lake north of the Tanganyika, who owned plenty of ivory and soldiers, and who, although a European, was said to be a Mohammedan and an officer of the Sultan of Massr, of Egypt. This could only be Emin Bey, of whom I had heard detailed reports before my last return to Africa. I now thought I might succeed, with the assistance of some Arab friends, in reaching the Albert Lake, if I were to go from Ujiji to the north of the Tanganyika. Although this was only a faint ray of hope, it yet revived me, for it offered the prospect of making the most of my march to the east.

On the 7th, twenty-two days after reaching the Arabs, I was ready to prepare for my start to the east. I had been wavering whether I should stay and wait for a suitable moment to go up or down the Lualaba, but I now abandoned further hesitation, as any day we might hear of new skirmishes on Stanley Falls, which would seal the ruin of my troop and myself. After convincing myself that nothing was to be gained, but everything lost, by delay, I started towards the east on the large caravan road to the Tanganyika, though my heart was heavy at the impossibility of performing the last part of my commission.

Le Marinel, with the Bashilange, would meanwhile have crossed the Lomami, and consequently be beyond

ACROSS THE ILINDI

the power of the Arabs. Had anything happened to him I should surely have learned it through my faithful Fickerini. Besides giving presents to the Arabs, I had been robbed of several loads of goods at Nyangwe and Kassongo, and my attempt to reclaim them from the Arabs had been fruitless. Among the lost loads was one with cartridges for the rifle I had given to Zefu, and, as Bugslag and I carried similar rifles, our ammunition was greatly diminished. I had taken the precaution to give Zefu only fifty cartridges with the rifle, pretending that I was running short, but one day, on going to see him, I noticed that he now possessed a much larger number, which evidently had been taken from the stolen box. Zefu on my departure exhibited a stinginess in making his return presents that one would have thought impossible to a man of rank brought up in Mohammedan customs. He gave me two old goats for the journey, and many salaams, accompanied by ironical gesticulations.

At our first stoppage old Fickerini asked me whether I had known the Arab who shortly before my start had shaken hands with me. On my answer in the negative he told me that it was Mohammed bin Kassim,[1] the murderer of the German merchant at Tabora. Kassim was always present at the meetings of the most important Arabs, and was much respected here.

On passing the Ilindi, which was much swollen and about sixty metres broad. I rode my bull into the water to find a good landing-place for canoes. The bull misunderstood my intention, and with a rush he plunged into the deep water, swimming with me and the heavy saddle on his back over to the opposite side. Once, in the middle of the stream, he had to struggle to keep his balance; but on the whole he swam splendidly.

A few days later we came into the war district. Zefu's soldiers were collecting natives who were to act as oarsmen in transporting some more troops to Stanley Falls. Everyone had taken to flight; only now and then had they stood their ground. Near our camp some natives fled across the Ilindi, and some piercing shrieks that we heard were accounted for next day by the capsizing of a canoe with fugitive Manyema, seven of whom had been drowned.

Marching in this part of Manyema, where the herbage is unusually high, was made specially difficult among

---

[1] In 1890 I sentenced this Arab to be hanged.

the jungle-like marianka-grass, the blades of which are as thick as one's thumb. Some days after, we again passed a scene of hostilities: an Arab who was offering provisions for sale had been shot, and his son, Said bin Habibu, was now avenging his father's death.

On the 12th we crossed the Luamo, winding through piles of clay-slate, which in this latitude we found east of the Lualaba and reaching close to the Tanganyika. My Baluba, who had kept up pretty well until now, began to sicken, and in order to transport my goods, few though they were, I had to hire natives at almost every village, not counting the twenty slaves engaged by Zefu. We daily passed settlements of coasters and Arabs, who told me that the head of the English mission, Captain Horn, had been prevented from carrying out his intention to hoist the English flag at Ujiji, and that the English missionaries were to be turned out from the Tanganyika.

On the 17th I had once more the comfort of pitching a camp in a place far from any villages. A break in the incessant turmoil, the everlasting contest and haggling in buying and selling, and the hanging round and staring on the part of the natives, causes a quiet camp to be a true source of enjoyment to the traveller. The constant strain upon the nerves gradually loosens; one needs not always be ready to interfere with threats or persuasions, but is at liberty to give free course to one's thoughts; in short, one feels like a prisoner who is released for a few hours' relaxation. Never on my former travels had I been so much struck by the change as at present; the uninterrupted succession of all our sufferings and disappointments, and the having continually to ponder and reflect on expedients, had almost exhausted my energy.

On the 18th, after crossing sixteen brooks, we reached Kalambarre, the large establishment of the Arab Rashid, a drunkard, a hemp-smoker, and an insolent beggar. In the evening we had a visit of several Arabs, among them the *amiri*—i.e. officer—of Reichardt and Dr. Boehm on their journey to the source of the Lualaba. We arranged a shooting match, taking for our target the fruits of a melon-tree; in this match I was victorious, though I did not receive the prize—a goat from each of the competitors.

This reminds me of an extraordinary sentence passed by Rashid on being told that one of his men had shot at a native from jealousy. That the culprit should have fifty lashes for having shot so badly as to have only wounded the native, was the punishment for a really murderous attempt on the part of a tipsy slave.

I felt more and more in physical suffering the strain on my nerves of which I made mention above. I suffered from headaches and nervous asthma, which caused the most painful sleeplessness.

And now, on March 21, the rainy season set in again, which enabled me to confirm an observation of meteorological importance which I had made on my first journey. I found out that between the Tanganyika and the Lualaba was the junction of the different courses of thunderstorms; from the west to this point the storms always travelled from the east, and *vice versâ*.

At Ubujive we found the places of encampment

fenced in by trunks of trees and briers to keep off the lions and leopards. I was unable to roam over the game-stocked valleys of Ubujive, being too weak at that time, and on reaching the camp was compelled to lie down.

We found frequent traces of elephants, buffaloes, antelopes, lions, leopards, and hyenas.

One day I had an interesting conversation with an old chief, who spoke to me of former times when as yet the Arabs had not crossed the Tanganyika. He described how the natives had gradually been dispossessed, enslaved, and more and more driven back, so that to-day on this road to Ubujive, which but ten years before had led through a densely populated district, only a single native village was to be found. A number of petty coast traders had settled here, making in every direction inroads into the interior.

Ivory and slave caravans, starting from the settlement of the Arab Kalonda, advance for many months' journeys in a due-easterly direction. I was told that those countries were almost without exception covered with primæval forests, that a great many Batua were to be met with, and that in the course of a few months I should reach rivers, falling neither into the Lualaba nor into the Tanganyika, but into a large lake towards the east. Stanley most likely met such a caravan on his march from the Aruvimi to the Albert Lake.

The villages of the Bena Wasi Malungo, which I had touched on my first journey, had disappeared, nor did I, as then, find a trace of the Batua; the Bena Bussindi were the last remnant of the native population on the caravan road.

R

One day we passed a pool of sixty metres diameter whose waters showed a temperature of 38° Celsius. We were about to encamp near it, in a place often visited by caravans, but such was the pestilential smell caused by eight corpses, which, half devoured by hyenas, were in a state of putrefaction, that we tried to find a more suitable place farther up. A few thousand metres from this point we again reached a camp, and in the huts were some more corpses, one of which was shrivelled up like a mummy. On the road we repeatedly observed skulls and limbs. We had no difficulty in finding the high road of the slave trade, the most frequented line of communication from the settlements of the Arabs on the Lualaba to the Tanganyika.

My health, meanwhile, did not improve at all. I was exceedingly weak, and constantly in low spirits. One day, overcome by melancholy, I gave vent in my diary to complaints at the life in the wilderness which I here repeat, as there is a great deal of truth in them, whilst at the same time they give the reader an idea of the frame of mind in which a European, weakened by fever, may find himself. 'What a strange profession it is that I have chosen! How different is one's idea of the life in the wilderness when at home! Where is the feeling of satisfaction at one's work? where the charm of danger? where the relief at having escaped from it? where, in short, the least poetry of life? How is it that we are so seldom suffered to enjoy the beauty of nature? Never under the scorching rays of the tropical sun have you such a feeling of unconquerable strength as you may have at home; your breast never expands in exultation at your own powers. Not a single one of the many choice enjoyments of our country is to be found here.

'What a miserable existence it is! what privations, disappointments, and anxiety one has to struggle with, in the midst of unpleasant surroundings! Nature mostly offers a dull repetition of the same desolate wilderness, either oppressed by a scorching sun or mouldering with continual damp. We move along like captives, hemmed in by the almost impenetrable vegetation, which does not even suffer our eyes to refresh themselves with a distant view. Who are the companions of our present lives? Poor, naked, stupid children, without trust or faith, without heart or feeling for the sublime, thinking of nothing but the satisfaction of their meanest wants, without any higher thought, any nobler aim. Round about, only misery, wretchedness, and stupidity or barbarism, savageness and want of feeling. A continual struggle with the climate, and everlasting anxiety about the success of plans; while trouble and failure constantly occupy our minds. Is this country, are these people worth labouring for? What results can offer a recompense for such sacrifices? Could we not find a worthier object in our endeavour to be useful?'

Such were the thoughts that tormented me while physically suffering. But no sooner did I gain new strength than hope would return, and aims worth striving for would float before my mind; at such times the difficulties of my present existence became bearable.

I daily met caravans headed by Arabs or Beloochees

bound for the Lualaba or Stanley Falls, here called 'Mitamba.' They generally brought powder and guns with them, scarcely any stuffs and beads. Nearly all the Arabs, as well as most of the leaders of the caravans, had good breech-loaders and plenty of ammunition. We found nearly all the English systems in use.

My ransomed Baluba diminished in numbers daily, either by death or from being lost in the wilderness. The Baluba, mostly big strong-boned fellows, had resisted the effects of our starving marches longer than the Bashilange, but they now began to tell on them. They became apathetic, manageable neither by kindness nor force, and completely idiotic. Neither the numbers of corpses and limbs on the road, nor the shrieks of the hyenas in broad daylight, which I had never heard before, could induce them to keep up on the way and not succumb to fatigue. I believe that many of them who had fallen asleep on the road must have been devoured by beasts of prey, or, as a good find, have been taken back to the west by passing caravans. In this manner I lost several loads together with the Baluba, which was a serious matter for me. The quiet of the night was incessantly disturbed by the horrible howling or baying of the hyena, the hoarse growling of the leopard, and the piercing bark of the jackal. Although the country abounded with game, the beasts of prey found more convenient food in the slaves who had succumbed to exhaustion.

In some small villages near our route we found a new kind of slave-hunters, who set about their work in a less dangerous way than is the case in the attacks

TRANSPORT OF SLAVES

made by the natives. These people lie in wait on the road, seizing straggling slaves, and, offering provisions for sale in the camp, they induce others to run away, so as to sell them at last at Ujiji on the Tanganyika.

Our march on this large caravan road enabled us to make minute studies of the imports to, and exports from, Central Africa. While those coming towards us only carried arms and ammunition into the interior, we met a few days later three caravans who were taking the proceeds of these imports to the coast—some ivory, and hundreds of slaves, fastened together with long chains and neck-yokes in sets of from ten to twenty. The weaker women and children, who were not expected to escape, were only tied with ropes. Those who had to be especially watched were walking by twos in the *mukongua*, the slave-fork, in which the neck is fastened. One would scarcely credit the miserable and lamentable condition the unfortunate human chattels were in. Their arms and legs were almost fleshless, their bodies shrivelled up, their looks heavy and their heads bent, while they were marching along eastward into an unknown future, farther and farther away from their homes, separated from wife and child, from father and mother, who had perhaps escaped into the woods or had been struck down in defending themselves. It was a revolting scene to watch the daily distribution of food in the camp of such a caravan.

The hungry creatures, with dilating eyes, were crowding round the spot where one of the overseers was stationed to distribute victuals, now and then using his stick to drive back the crowds that were pressing close round him. A small pot, about the size of a tumbler, was filled with corn, maize, or millet, and poured into the goat's skin with which they covered their nakedness. Some of them, too tired to rub or pound the corn, simply boiled it in water or roasted it in a saucepan over the fire, and then devoured it in order to satisfy their craving hunger. Before the different sets were allowed to lie down they were once more driven out of the camp, and then they would throw themselves down near one of the large fires to rest their exhausted bodies. The slaves were mostly bound together according to their powers of marching, without the least regard to sex. Scarcely the fourth part of these reach the maritime countries or the plantations of the coasters they are bound for. The large Arab settlements in the interior, chiefly Ujiji and Tabora, absorb great numbers of slaves, especially the former, which is notorious for its bad climate. A working slave—in distinction from the female slaves, who are put into the harem—at Ujiji is said not to stand the climate above a year.

One day, when I was lying in wait for buffaloes near the camp, I was surprised to see, instead of the game, a boy of about eight years of age come out of the thicket, cautiously approaching a place that commanded a view of our camp. When I left my covert he was at first going to take flight, but afterwards followed me into the camp. The boy had escaped from a slave caravan, and he told us that he had always picked up any remnants of food that might have been left in the places of encampment after

FREEING SLAVES

the departure of caravans. He had passed his nights on a tree, in the branches of which he had arranged his bed. He joined us on our march, but died soon after of small-pox, to which disease more people of my small caravan had to succumb.

On April 4 I despatched some men to the Tanganyika to announce my arrival, and beg for admission from the English missionaries, who had formerly been settled on this side of the lake, and had now taken up their abode in the isle of Kawala.

On the 6th we completed our march through the monotonous forests of Ubujive, and the smooth surface of the Tanganyika Lake put us pleasantly in mind of the sea. We halted close to the beach at the part of Mtoa, where there were several dhows which had been brought from Ujiji by Arabs, bound for the Lualaba; these were now to take up a slave caravan that was in waiting. This lake is the cause of many a sacrifice of human life. The small sailing vessels from Ujiji are so crammed with people that in bad weather, which in the rainy season often sets in with thunderstorms, those in charge of them are frequently obliged to throw a number of slaves overboard, so as to save at least part of them. It is a fact that on such an occasion lately an Arab had twelve slaves thrown overboard so as to save his two valuable Maskat donkeys.

On the evening of the 6th, Mr. Larson, from the mission in Kawala, arrived at the port, bringing a kind letter of welcome from Mr. Horn. Mr. Horn's wife and child were ill, and consequently he was prevented from coming himself. On the 7th we sailed in a dhow chartered by an Arab, and after a two hours' sail along the beautifully situated port of Kawala, we reached the missionary station, where we were kindly made welcome and lodged as comfortably as could be managed in a newly-established station.

NEAR MTOA, ON THE TANGANYIKA

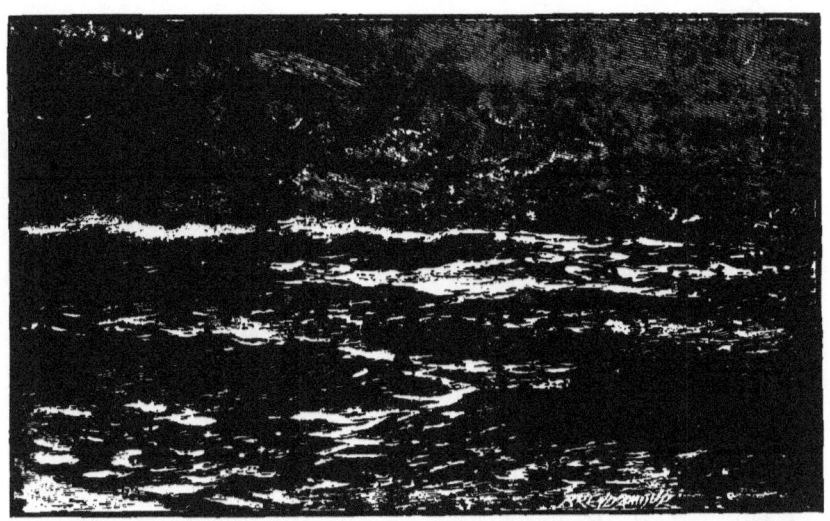

ON THE TANGANYIKA

CHAPTER IX

TO THE NYASSA

Warning against going to the coast—At Ujiji—My going to the south—My exhausted Baluba left with the missionaries—The lake and its discharge—Night journeys—Storm—Mpala—Correct proceeding of the missions—Galula's death—Leopards—Baboons—Progress by land—Water banks—Flight of some carriers—Superstition—Extortions—Wawemba murderers—Scotch mission—Mr. Bain on ethnology—On the Nyassa—Clouds of insects.

THE first thing I learned from Mr. Horn was that disturbances were apprehended on the coast. He ascribed this danger to the advance of the German East African Society, which—a piece of news to me—had recently been formed and had settled on the coast. The Germans were said to be overbearing and domineering over the natives and Arabs, without having the power to impose their superiority. He said that the Arabs were infuriated by the Germans, and that in a short time the discontent would break into open rebellion. They were especially angry that the Sultan (Said Bargash) should have resigned lands to the Germans, and in consequence they threatened to renounce their allegiance to the former. The skirmish on Stanley Falls, too, had aggravated their bad feeling towards the Europeans. He said that at that time Tabora, where not long ago a German had been murdered, was the principal seat of discontent. Mr. Horn warned me, if I were going to the coast, not to take the main road by Tabora; the only open one, which the missionaries also availed themselves of, was across the Nyassa and Shiré.

I did not make any plans for the present, as I wanted to learn particulars at Ujiji as to whether there would be any possibility, if I started north of the Tanganyika, of reaching Albert Lake, and the European (Emin Bey) who had been driven thither with many troops and great stores of ivory.

And now, without any stoppage, and favoured by the wind, I crossed over to Ujiji, which I reached after an hour and a half's sail. I knew the two principal Arabs at Ujiji, named Nasorro bin Zef and Mohammed bin Halfan, as I had travelled with them on former occasions. Their reception of me was civil, but cool. These two, from their point of view, corroborated all I had learned from Mr. Horn. I turned the conversation to Emin Bey, of whom they did not know any particulars; on the other hand, they told me that a German from there had come, some months ago, with plenty of ivory, to Tabora, and reached the coast together with Tibbu Tibb. This was Dr. Junker.

On asking how I could possibly get to Emin from the north of the Tanganyika, I was told that such a thing was out of the question, the tribes north of the Tanganyika, the Wasongora Mino, being numerous and warlike; nor could I avoid Unioro, whose king, Kaba Rega, was at war there with the whites. They could not supply me with any people, having just sent large caravans to the coast; and last, not least, they refused to advance me a large sum of money which I should have needed in order to buy from them arms, ammunition, and stuffs for a new expedition. They considered the understanding with the Europeans so unsatisfactory that a war might possibly break out, in which case they thought they would lose their money.

I found them willing for a heavy sum—knowing how greedy the Arabs are after English gold, I always carried some with me for any cases of emergency—to provide me with a vessel for the journey to the south of the Tanganyika, since even they did not consider it advisable to go to the coast by way of Tabora, where war was raging between the great chief Sicke and the Arabs. It was with great reluctance that I thus gave up any further attempt to be of direct use to the Congo State, and decided upon sailing down the Tanganyika on the side of the Congo State, and going to the coast by way of Nyassa, Shiré, and Zambesi.

On making inquiries about a journey to Emin Bey, I learned that the Arabs had advanced to the north of the Tanganyika and founded settlements on Kiwu Lake, which was said to be five days' journey north of the Tanganyika and to have two discharges, one into Tanganyika and another to the west into the Lualaba. Three days' journey farther north was, as I ascertained, Akaniaru Lake, the country surrounding which was said to be beautiful and rich in abundance of water and grass. The natives were reported to own many valuable kinds of cattle.

Ujiji had lost much of its importance; the greatest attraction at present came from the rich resources of Mitamba, i.e. the countries from Nyangwe down the Lualaba, which Tibbu Tibb had been the first Arab to invade when accompanying Stanley. Everyone was going to Mitamba, there being plenty of ivory, and the natives of those parts still carrying spears and bows, in consequence of which it was easy to conquer them.

Since my last sojourn here, the Tanganyika had fallen above a metre, and consequently the anchorage ground was pushed far out. I chartered a manned dhow, purchased 550 dollars' worth of goods for the journey from the Tanganyika to Nyassa, and on the 11th I crossed over from Ujiji to Kawala, where I had left Bugslag and my people. Our vessel was so old and so full of vermin, that I turned back after an hour's sail, in order to exchange it for another that had just come in. This boat was built after the European fashion and was a good sailer. So I did not set sail till the 12th, in the evening of which day I cast anchor off Cape Kabogo, where I passed the night. Twice we were roused by the near roaring of a lion and by natives approaching our fire; they were probably bent on theft, but, on hearing the clicking of the gun-barrels, they quickly disappeared. Next day I crossed the lake. I was greatly astonished to observe a number of sea-nettles surrounding our boat for about half an hour. They were transparent, of the shape of a disk and like a mark-piece in size; round the edge was a milky circle, hanging down in fibres, by means of which they swam. Though the Malagarassi, the chief tributary of the Tanganyika, contains a good deal of salt, one cannot but call the Tanganyika a fresh-water lake, and in such sea-nettles are very seldom seen. I was sorry not to have any means of preserving some of these rare creatures.

On the 13th I reached Kawala, and at once got ready for continuing my journey. My Baluba were incapable of accompanying me farther. I might have taken some of them with me, but I was unwilling to separate this little band of people. Here, under care of the mission, the Baluba were as safe as possible from any acts of violence on the part of the Arabs. Here they remained, superintended by a white man. Mr. Horn suggested that they might earn something by serving the mission, and with this view I bought a deserted village and a plantation belonging to it, from the chief who introduced himself as the owner of the island. I left the Baluba fourteen guns, the ammunition for which I gave into Mr. Horn's care, twelve goats, a number of fowls, salt, pick-axes, hatchets, pots and pans, and other utensils. I also gave into the keeping of one of the missionaries beads and stuff, so as to supply them with means of obtaining food until their fields should yield all they required. The most intelligent of them, who had distinguished himself as leader of the Baluba, I made chief of this small community, enjoining him always to keep to the Europeans, and to ask their advice in any difficulties; if he found an opportunity of joining a reliable caravan bound for his country he was to do so. As I conjectured that the Congo State would soon build a station at this lake, its eastern boundary, I regarded these Baluba, each of whom had his wife with him, as a select tribe of people standing apart from the rest of the population. Consequently the chief was instructed to offer his services and those of his people, should a station under the star-flag be established anywhere on the lake. The soil at Kawala was apparently good, the lake abounded with fish, the mainland was easy of access in a small canoe, and, the channel between the mainland and the island being well sheltered, there was plenty of game, so that, as regards the future of my people, I continued my journey without any anxiety. Three bulls, which naturally could not be taken in the small vessel, I assigned to the mission, requesting that they might be placed at the disposal of any European.

Now commenced the shipping of the few loads that I still possessed, and general preparations for the journey. I, Bugslag, ten coast negroes with four women and two little dogs, one a terrier and the other a cross-breed of a terrier and African pariah dog, and the boatmen, formed the new suite.

On April 15 we took leave of Mr. Horn, his brave

wife—the first white lady who had ventured so far into the Dark Continent—and the other gentlemen of the mission, to whom we were greatly indebted for their kind reception. We reached Lukuga Bay by the aid of a good breeze; nearly all my people were sea-sick, as we encountered such breakers as rarely occur in an inland sea. This lake, surrounded by high banks, extending nearly eighty German miles from south to north, experiences for almost half the year southerly winds, which are always very high in the daytime, while they calm down in the evening and cease altogether at night. During this time, however, there is an uninterrupted gale from the south, which often proves fatal to small vessels.

The Lukuga, an effluent of the Tanganyika, carries more water out of the lake into the Lualaba than the Malagarassi and the numerous lesser affluents annually supply. The level of the lake consequently sinks about two feet annually. This will last until the water-mark of the lake is on a level with the bottom of the Lukuga bed, when the discharge must cease. Sand-downs, stretching along near the bank of the Lukuga, cause the bed of the river, as soon as it is dry, to be filled up with sand and particles of vegetation carried down by brooks, falling into the Lukuga more quickly than the rising of the Tanganyika. After twenty years' continual rising, the discharge being stopped, the level of the lake has again attained such a height that it overflows the level of the filled-up bed of the Lukuga, and thus forcibly breaks open the old discharging channel. Stanley in 1874 found no effluent, whilst I in 1882 found the Lukuga to be a wide, rapid effluent of the Tanganyika. Thus, between Stanley's and my visit, the lake has swollen so much as to force open its old channel of exit. Now again I found that the constantly falling lake was lower by sixteen feet than the highest water-mark which could be discerned. This periodical rising and falling of the lake naturally causes the banks to change, which is a great detriment to navigation. At a later time, when the civilisation of Africa shall have so progressed that it may have a regular system of navigation, there will be no difficulty in regulating the water-mark of the lake by a flood-gate at the effluence of the Lukuga. My boatmen from Ujiji well knew these peculiar occurrences on the Lukuga, but were not able to find out the cause.

The Wajiji are very skilful sailors; they know all about wind and weather, which is however easy enough, considering the great regularity of meteorological phenomena here. They know every part, every stone; they keep on a good footing with the people on the riverside, and know how to manage sails and oars. After making our boat cut through the surge, which was effected with difficulty, we pitched our camp near the Lukuga under the overhanging wall of a rock.

When bathing I was struck by the great regularity with which the rubble-stones had arranged themselves near the shore. Large stones covered the beach, smaller pebbles were disposed under the shallow water, whilst lower down I discovered gravel, and at last sand. The water of the lake is clear, of a somewhat brackish taste, caused, I suppose, by its saline contents. The banks

A STIFF BREEZE

are covered with many different shells. Sea-gulls were very plentiful, whereas I saw fresh-water birds only near the mouths of rivers and brooks. These were the only spots where we found hippopotami and crocodiles, which are said to venture exceptionally far into the lake. I agreed with the guide of my Wajiji to travel henceforth only in the night-time. During the day we had to encounter high breakers and a smart

CAMP ON THE LUKUGA.

breeze, which made rowing very difficult. To tack against the south wind would have detained us too long. In the evening, as I mentioned above, it generally grew calmer, or a gentle land breeze would set in, enabling us to sail along the coast southward. Towards the morning of the 17th we reached the mouth of the Ruhega river, with a labyrinth of islets and banks, of lagoons and channels. Birds were very plentiful and crocodiles were abundant. The banks reached pretty regularly a height of from 100 to 150 metres. The slopes displayed savannahs of trees and underwood, while the ravines, reaching down into the lake, were thickly wooded. Population seemed to be scanty; while game, chiefly antelopes, were now and then observed near the water.

We always proceeded on our nocturnal journeys until the smart morning breeze set in, when we sought refuge in a sheltering part and rested until the abating of the wind permitted us to continue our journey. Since no bodily exertion was required for the journey, and our people could sleep in the boat, our progress depended only on the weather. Bugslag and I took turns at steering. The setting in of the southern breeze, often very stormy, was repeatedly very strange in appearance. For example, on the morning of the 18th an immense cloud in the shape of a cylinder came rolling towards us. Short showers followed this, accompanied by a whistling wind. Several times we were able to move on in the afternoon and till dawn the next day.

Our Wajiji would sometimes throw beads and pieces of stuff into the water in order to pacify the water-spirit. When the weather was calm, and I forced them to take the oars, they would wheeze like German water-rats. As the thunder-storms during the rainy season often bring violent gales in their train, a vessel used on the Tanganyika should be a thoroughly seaworthy ship. The steamer belonging to the mission, which was being finished in the port of Kawala, was suitable enough in its construction, though I do not approve of the system,

STORMY NIGHT QUARTERS

which was that of a sailing vessel with an auxiliary engine. I should prefer a proper steamer, which at the same time would permit the setting of sails. Within 200 metres off the coast we found the water deep and bare of stones or banks; it was only near the mouths of rivers that we had to keep farther out. The anchorage ground consisted mostly of sand or rubble-stones.

And now I must once more avail myself of the opportunity to point out that for civilisation and the suppression of the slave trade this lake would be of the greatest importance. A steamer carrying a small number of guns and fifty soldiers would be well able to block up the lake and would suffice to support stations on the banks. Such a boat would keep a station from starvation, being able to furnish it with provisions from every part of the lake. If only every Arab vessel putting into any other than one of the few permitted stations were destroyed, there would be no difficulty in limiting the communication on the lake to places easy of control. Any hiding of vessels is out of the question with those open banks.

On the 19th we reached the former station of the Congo State, Mpla, now taken possession of by the Algerian mission; we had shortly before sought shelter close to the land, on account of heavy storms, a rough sea, and waterspouts. On entering the Lufuku, the port of the station, the high surge caused a great deal of water to be washed on board.

We were most kindly received by Pères Landeau and Moinit and Captain Joubert, whom I had known formerly. Through a long village, inhabited by ransomed people belonging to the mission, we passed into the temba, built of very thick clay walls, and capable of being well fortified. Great order and proofs of diligent labour met the eye everywhere; practical good sense and knowledge were noticeable in all the arrangements.

In the afternoon the chapel was filled with 200 people, and the religious worship, the singing and praying, proceeded without a fault. The plantations and gardens of the mission must answer every purpose. Barley and rice were thriving well. The greatest drawback of the station was its position, there being no port; for the beach and the shallow mouth of the Lufuku were constantly under breakers, and the defensible building was too far from the beach to maintain a safe connection with any vessel. The good understanding with the natives was of great advantage for this mission. It had been established by the last chief of the Congo State station, Captain Storms, and by prudence and energy had been kept up ever since. Captain Joubert, the present chief, had of late repeatedly defended the natives against slave-traders, and, supported by natives and fifty armed men of the station, he had vanquished and punished several such hordes. Such success could only have the best results. When a European proves to be not only a missionary but at the same time a defender of the liberty and property of the natives, he cannot fail to be looked up to. Now I greatly regretted not having brought my Baluba here, but such an increase of their *protégés* being very desirable to the heads of the station, I gave them a letter to Mr. Horn, whom I requested to effect the transport of the Baluba from Kawala to this place.

The mission having for the present only taken charge of the station, which was still the property of the Congo State, it was not only desirable, but my duty to instal here the people who had been ransomed by means of the King of the Belgians and who had hitherto been maintained by him.

After having amply supplied ourselves with provisions, we continued our journey on the 21st. After dark we met a vessel in which I recognised a European. We went on board, and I greeted Père Drommeau, whom I had likewise met before, and who was coming from Karema, a station on the eastern bank of the Tanganyika belonging to the same mission.

Next morning, when we dropped anchor on account of the south wind, one of our men suddenly burst into loud lamentations. On going to awake his wife Galula from a deep sleep, he had discovered that she was dead. The poor woman had suffered from sea-sickness throughout our journey; she was so much weakened that for some days she had eaten nothing, and had been lying half asleep in continual apathy. On my suggestion that she should remain at the mission at Mpla, she had replied, 'How am I, then, to meet again my friends on the Lulua, if you want to leave me here?' As we could not detect any cause for her death, I conjectured that gradual weakening through sea-sickness had been the reason. We dug a grave for poor Galula, and marked the spot by a number of large stones.

which we built up in the form of a cross. The loss of our ever cheerful and industrious friend Galula was much lamented by us all.

When we had pitched our camp there arose such a storm on the night of the 23rd that it blew my tent down. The thunderstorms began to be more violent and frequent. When we resumed our journey we sailed for three hours through yellow-tinted water; the colour was owing to small flakes, probably the seeds of a water plant. The banks became more rocky and picturesque; huge boulders forming high precipices caused immense breakers. From the boat we observed a couple of leopards with two cubs basking on one of the rocks. I landed with Bugslag, but we missed the chance of firing at them by trying to creep closer along; the handsome creatures had disappeared in the maze of rocks. Vexed at our failure, we were just about to return, when deep below us among the rubble we distinctly heard the mewing of the young leopards, but could not in any way succeed in getting at them.

The banks grew more and more splendid. Immense pillars projected into the deep green water; passages and caves more than ten metres high opened out below the rocks. The wild scenery, now and again interrupted by luxuriant vegetation in connection with the conformations of the rocks, presented a striking picture. A herd of about 100 baboons suffered us to pass them without showing any more irritation than the short disconnected tones of surprise peculiar to them, which resemble the startled cry of a roebuck. By shooting into the water, not at the monkeys—for

LEOPARDS ON THE TANGANYIKA

ever since I saw a large ape in the agony of death I have entirely lost my taste for such animal hunts—a most ridiculous scene was brought about. Shrieks, barking, and quarrelling proceeded from each throat of this young party. The strange figures, among which we were struck by some species of nearly double the ordinary size, waddled and galloped in grotesque leaps up the precipice, and a shower of rubble and stones, among them boulders of several hundredweight, kept tumbling down to us into the lake. Our people roared with laughter, and would have it that the monkeys had aimed at us. For further observation I shot once more, and again a shower of stones pelted down upon us, so that I felt inclined to agree with

FRIGHTENED BABOONS

the Wajiji; for the number of stones was too great to have rolled down accidentally under the movements of the flying monkeys.

In the splendidly clear waters, in which we could see

stones at about fifteen metres' distance, we noticed great abundance of fish, by which our Wajiji greatly profited.

The more we approached the south end of the lake the more the wind turned to the east. In spite of the area of the breakers getting smaller and smaller, the sea, nearly to the southern extremity of the lake, was very boisterous.

On the 24th, at the mouth of the Lunangua, we met natives with goods and chattels, and numerous canoes, apparently in the act of leaving the neighbourhood. We learned that the rapacious expeditions of an Arab were the cause of their flight, but that they would return to their villages as soon as the banditti should have retreated. Wherever we had happened to come upon natives they had met us kindly and pacifically, selling food, chiefly fish, to us at a low price. The lower we came south, the steeper were the slopes falling into the lake; but we rarely found a position suitable for a camp in narrow places, covered with stones, pebbles, or sand. Any cultivation of these slopes was, of course, not to be thought of; the heavy rains would wash everything away. For this reason, the banks are very thinly populated.

On the 29th, south of the mouth of the Lufuwu, in a sheltered part, we came to the end of our journey, the road from the Nyassa terminating on the Tanganyika. So it had only taken us fifteen days to travel a distance of about 375 kilometres, with the help of the oars and a land breeze, mostly blowing in the night only. According to an arrangement with Mr. Horn, we were here to find one of his boats, whose occupants, familiar with the local state of affairs, were to hire some carriers from me. The boat having left the same morning to buy provisions, we had to wait, and pitched our camp in a spot where there had formerly been a missionary station, which now was only to be recognised by the grave of a European. I sent back the sailing vessel, while we passed our time hunting in this district, which abounded with antelopes and buffaloes.

On May 3 the promised boat arrived with seven carriers and the message that the rest would come by land. Soon after, a troop of five men arrived, then another of ten; they waited for two days, and then left again to fetch the others; in short, we had to furnish ourselves with African patience, until at last I succeeded in assembling the thirty missing carriers on the evening of the 9th. On the eve of our start the Marungu— to which tribe the people belonged—performed their war-dances. They killed some goats to brace themselves for the march, and on the 10th we at length moved on towards the Nyassa.

From Niumkorlo on the lake we ascended the steep and rocky slope; we passed the Nunsua and Manbesi, and encamped in the wilderness in a meadow pleasantly relieved by an immeasurable tree-savannah. The rainy season having set in, many water-courses were rushing down to the lake in magnificent cascades, which, wherever they came to a standstill, formed bogs and pools, and so afforded a favourite resort for buffaloes.

Guinea-fowls were very plentiful, and for the last few days had rarely been wanting on board. I never saw wild grapes so large and sweet as they were here.

On the second day's march we had gained the summit of the plateau, and after a very fatiguing journey encamped near a small lake named Kiila, which, 1,500 metres in length and 1,000 metres in breadth, lay surrounded by rushes in the midst of the forest.

Among the reeds and small grass bunches surround-

BETWEEN TANGANYIKA AND NYASSA

ing the bog we noticed many water-rams. Bugslag and I hit four of them; they were severely wounded, but escaped without our being able to secure them. The terrain being quite open and level, we ascertained that the antelopes did not get away, but remained in the bog; but though half of the carriers searched it they found nothing. The natives said that this antelope, which lives almost exclusively near the water, would dip under if hit; at any rate, the animals knew how to hide in the boggy terrain among the reeds, so that they appeared to be swallowed up. The little lake was about 200 metres above the level of the Tanganyika.

On the 12th we passed the Bississi and Mapensa, two

WATCH-TOWER NEAR BISSISSI

villages strongly fortified with palisades. Near them we noticed small hills covered with a kind of pavilion, lurking-places whence the surrounding country was watched by outposts. These high tomb-like mounds are formed by all the village people carrying their refuse to the same place.

On the morning of the 13th I was surprised by the

disagreeable news that sixteen carriers, who, like the rest, had received half of their wages in advance, had deserted. I succeeded in hiring people from Kitimbue, who engaged to carry our loads to the camp of a Beloochee, Kahunda, which we were to reach that day. But on approaching another village, with whose inhabitants our new carriers were at enmity, they also threw down their loads and fled. The camp of the Beloochee being only a few hours distant, I sent Fickerini with two of my Angola people to Kahunda, requesting him to furnish me with carriers. In the afternoon my messengers returned with thirty savage Ruga-Ruga, i.e. Waniamwesi soldiers. On their approach the inhabitants of the village where I encamped took up arms and opposed this horde of the slave-catcher. I at once rushed among the natives, and promised them that the Ruga-Ruga should not enter their village. I took the latter to my camp, where I at once distributed the loads and started.

In the evening we reached a village where Kahunda had settled. He was a deserted soldier of the Sultan Said Bargash, and was on his way to purchase ivory and slaves west of the Tanganyika. He had settled down here, having got up a quarrel with the natives, from whom, after defeating them, he wanted to extort tribute. Each of the 300 savage Ruga-Ruga, armed with spear and bow, wore ornaments of plumes and a scarlet cloak, a dress which was admirably adapted for enabling them to make an intimidating impression on the natives. Kahunda knew Reichardt, from whom he had learned much about the abundance of gold in the

AFRICAN SUPERSTITION

country of the Katanga under their chief Msiri. After increasing his numbers by allying himself with other Arabs, he proposed going thither to find gold.

Kahunda first promised to let me have carriers next day, but when it came he revoked his promise, as he felt induced to attack a neighbouring village, whence a man in the shape of a lion had carried off one of his people. The belief that human beings can assume the shape of wild beasts is universal in Africa. Whenever anybody is torn by a beast of prey, they find out by some manipulation who has been the sorcerer who had changed him into a wild beast. On a former occasion, in a conversation with Tibbu Tibb, who is on the whole rather enlightened, I was astonished to find him clinging to this superstition. Cases like this are often an occasion of war in Africa.

For some time past I had been suffering from feverish attacks, with excessive shivering. The scanty unvaried food, but chiefly the mental strain during our march west of the Lualuba, had brought my constitution very low.

On my urging a start, an Arab, a business connection of Kahunda's, likewise bound for the Nyassa, offered to supply the desired number of people. I bought a saddle-donkey of Kahunda, as my bodily weakness forbade my walking so long a distance. The donkey was such a wreck that I had to give it back next day, and the Angola people made a hammock for me in case of exhaustion. Kahunda told me of the murder of the German Giesecke at Unianjembe, and maintained that Tibbu Tibb had been in the plot, or at any rate had been aware of it. He said that Tibbu Tibb might have prevented it, which to any one acquainted with African affairs is quite obvious. The reason for this statement against one of his own faith was, that Tibbu Tibb a few months before had forced Kahunda, on one of his expeditions along the coast, to pay him five elephant tusks for having pillaged one of his villages. This shows that even then Tibbu Tibb was powerful enough to extend his plundering raids to coasters, petty Arabs, and Beloochees. In return for high pay, the Arab friend of Kahunda engaged himself to accompany me with his people, so that after all I was able to start on the 15th. We passed the Saise river, which flows down to the Riqua or Ruqua Lake, and marched through an entire plain, covered with short grass, here and there abounding with antelopes, to the village of Munieama.

Since leaving the Tanganyika we had not seen the sun; the sky had always been clouded, a misty rain had fallen incessantly, and the weather had been very cold. Munieama, like all the villages we passed, was built close to the waterside, and had wells inside the solid palisades that surrounded it. Double doors with small openings led into the interior. The round clay houses were surrounded by a circular half-closed verandah, covered with a far-projecting thatched roof. Storehouses, raised high on account of the damp, contained maize, millet, potatoes, and pea-nuts. Manioc is not grown, and the corn, rubbed between hollow stones, is not pounded.

We were now in the Mambue country, the people of which are always in a state of hostility with the rapacious Wawemba, who live farther south. Almost every large village in these parts has forty to fifty cows and nearly 200 goats. During this journey I saw for the first time traces of the rhinoceros, the zebra, and the giraffe.

Now commenced the numerous petty inconveniences which a traveller is exposed to in the border countries, and which were of course avoided when travelling with my Bashilange and my veterans. Premature demands for food and extortions of all kinds on the part of the carriers, begging supported by threats by the chiefs, and —the worst of all—extortions on the part of the Arab who accompanied me—all these were troubles that almost overwhelmed me in my then weak state. The Arab first asked for my revolver and my rifle, and, on my not granting his request, he flatly refused to accompany me any longer with his followers, so that once more I had twenty loads on my hands without carriers. When he actually prepared to carry his intention into effect, nothing was left me but to give what he asked. I sent him my revolver, instructing Fickerini to tell him that I had not before known that an Arab would stoop to beg like a negro chief. He sent back the revolver, and then we started.

After this we entered the river system of the Chambese (river), the largest tributary of the Bangueolo Lake. Thus, in a space of ten hours' march, we had touched the affluents of three lakes, first that of the Tanganyika, then of the Riqua, and finally of the Bangueolo, without having crossed an elevation of only a few metres' height which served as a separation.

After the 18th the results of the nefarious traffic in human beings, in the shape of burnt villages, fields laid waste, and human skulls lying on the road, again began to meet our eyes. The Arabs on Lake Nyassa are the originators of the local slave-hunt. They very seldom come up here themselves, but they have their go-betweens in the savage hordes of Uemba. The inhabitants of this country, the Wawemba, who formerly, under the notorious chief Kitimkuru, were its terror, now continued their doings under his son. The Wawemba convey their goods to the Nyassa, and there sell them in the settlements of the Arabs in exchange for guns and ammunition. According to custom, they only bring women and children; the men are invariably killed and beheaded. Among the Wawemba there exists a perfectly developed rank, determined by the number of heads of the enemies they have killed. This was the reason that we often saw human skeletons, but never skulls. The Arabs bring their slaves across the Nyassa, thence chiefly to the Lindi, Kilwa, and Mikindani, but rarely farther south, so that the slave coast of Africa is the coast of German East Africa from Mikindani up to Tanga. Only a few days before, a horde of Wawemba had passed this road, and we repeatedly found fresh traces of their presence. The consequence was, that my people marched in close formation and would not leave the camp.

On our meeting a caravan bound for the Tanganyika, some of my native carriers again tried to make their escape. Being prepared for this, I had them seized. I then deprived them of their arms, and those not to be depended on I had tied together and watched by some Angola people: for in this district, for the most part laid waste, I should have been unable to hire new carriers, not to speak of those I had having been paid for their services to the Nyassa.

A daily pleasant change of scene was caused by frequent little cupolas of the height of a barrow, displaying huge blocks of Plutonic rocks and massive bits of rubble. Among them, a close growth of trees formed little bowers in the plain, which, however, was chiefly covered only with short grass. The brooks became muddy and the low land round them was covered with dark emerald grass, under whose surface was of course an unfathomable slough. On the 21st, stony hills mantled with wood savannahs interrupted the monotonous prairie. These were the heights forming the partition between the Lualaba, the Congo, and the Zambesi; for on the slopes on this side the network of brooks fell into the Loange, a tributary of the Zambesi. Since setting foot on the African continent this time I had traversed the Congo territory to almost its greatest length.

We were surprised by frequently finding natives encamped before their hidden villages, ready for war or flight; they were expecting an attack of the Wawemba at any moment. Women and children always slept in the wood, and did not return to the village before morning, for the Wawemba rarely attack by day, while the negroes seldom engage in any enterprise by night, but usually choose the morning hour. The poor creatures always took similar measures of precaution when any

T

Wawemba were reported to be near. These villages reminded me of the ostrich, which, when pursued, hides its head that it may not be seen. The villages are built with strong palisades in the closest thickets, where certainly an approach is made difficult; but those approaching cannot be detected, nor can the palisades be defended. I wondered that the inhabitants of these parts did not seek another home, instead of remaining here to be hunted like wild beasts, and not for one moment sure of their freedom or their lives.

The Arab of my suite, whose men were carrying the greater number of the loads, hindered me on the pretence of the over-fatigue of his people, thus forcing me repeatedly to arrange days of rest; so that I did not reach Mwena Wanda, a Scotch missionary station, till the 26th. Mr. Bain, the head of the station, gave me a very kindly welcome, and at once began medical treatment, as I suffered greatly from sciatica and from sleepless nights. Besides, fever set in again with obstinate regularity.

But a few days before the Wawemba had attacked villages only ten kilometres off the station; they had killed thirty men and carried off almost all the women and children.

What good can natives derive from stations that demand enormous sums to convert them to Christianity, when they cannot even defend their lives, their freedom, and their property? How is it possible that savages who are daily, hourly anxious about their lives and property can open their hearts to the doctrines of Christianity? Would it not be a much more useful work, with the means that are spent on the missions, to found stations which, in the first instance, would offer protection to the natives, hunted like beasts of prey? The Africans call all their superiors 'father'; they would show themselves much more docile to the teaching of the European if they felt they were dependent on him for the means of protection. The missionaries here were always ready to escape by flight from a possible attack of the Wawemba; they had even been negotiating with the natives about the direction of their flight.

My opinion on this question was supported by the Scotch missionaries, whose impartial judgment and practical views made me rate them much higher than many English missionaries with whom I had come in contact.

I found Mr. Bain to be a very good observer. He was kind enough to enlighten me from his treasure of ethnological observations about various things which, chiefly referring to the Wawemba, the Wakonde, and the Wawiwa, I will mention here.

The Wakonde burn their corpses three days after death, life having then without any doubt fled from the body; the ashes are collected into small jars and preserved by the family. These tribes often also dissect their dead, especially if the reason for death is not quite clear. They open the stomach with a piece of palm bark, and examine its walls and contents.

The Wawemba bury their dead, but in the course of three days they open the grave, take out the corpse, and completely dissect it; they cut the flesh off the bones, and after having anointed the latter with oil they scatter them in the savannah.

A kind of ordeal, such as I have found to be extensively practised in Inner Angola, is frequently used here for settling disputes. If any offence is to be investigated, all the persons in question are assembled in a circle. The chief takes up a wooden instrument exactly resembling the toy known among our children as a 'Soldatenschere.' While repeating the nature of the offence, this 'Soldatenschere' makes its apparently automatic movements, then suddenly folding up hits the breast of the offender.

In order to search for stolen objects they make use of a board with a handle at each end. Two persons suspected of theft are compelled to take hold of the handle crosswise, and are led by the judge to the place where the stolen article is supposed to be hid. The two, in a bent attitude, are made to move the board close along the ground or the wall of the hut. The evil conscience of one of the two is noticed by the other in his movement when approaching the hidden object, and, in order to be released from suspicion, the former calls the judge's attention to this circumstance.

In accordance with the habit in West Africa, it is customary among these tribes to settle a dispute between two persons by drinking a poisonous draught. There is a certain poisonous bark which, boiled in water and millet beer, rarely causes death, but either instant vomiting or violent swelling of the stomach and great pain. The two persons in question have to drink of this beverage, and the one who vomits is cleared of the suspicion.

THE WAWEMBA ELECTING A CHIEF

The succession to the dignity of chief does not pass to the sons of the chief, but to his eldest sister's eldest son. If this is not possible, a new chief is elected. They assemble, and hold a grand banquet, at which much millet beer is drunk, and discuss who is to be elected. As soon as the greater number of the drinkers are agreed, the whole assembly throw themselves on the one selected, seize and bind him and take him into the common hut, where he is released from his fetters and proclaimed chief. If he shows himself at all timid at the sudden and startling attack, or attempts to flee, they agree upon some one else.

The greatest festival of the year, which here, as with us, consists of twelve months, is the festival of the new fire. Throughout the country the fires are extinguished on the eve of the holiday and the ashes carried to a heap outside the village. Then a great carousing commences, and as soon as the moon has attained a certain height the chief begins to make a new fire for the coming year. Into a small square board of soft dry wood, which in the centre has a little funnel-shaped opening, a span-long peg of wood pointed at the end is inserted and twirled round by the chief until the soft wood begins to glow. The first spark is kindled by vigorous blowing, and taken up with pieces of tinder by the wives of the chiefs, who in their turn distribute them to the women pressing around. This fire has to last for the next twelve months.

Polygamy rarely occurs among the tribes I have mentioned; only rich people indulge in the luxury of a harem, the number of women in which never exceeds three. When a girl has developed into a woman, she is put into a state of intoxication by strong drinks, painted white and red, and laid before the parental hut, so as to show the villagers and fellow-tribesmen that they may now woo the beauty. A suitor first makes himself known to the girl's mother, and in the evening now and again throws small presents for her parents into their house. If they are thrown out again, the suitor is dismissed; if accepted, he has to continue them until the father and mother declare themselves satisfied and consent to the wooer fetching their daughter. If the woman objects, all the presents or their worth have to be returned; if she consents, she is, with the assistance of other young villagers, taken by force from her parents' hut at night, and, according to custom, she is brought, screaming and struggling, into the hut of her lover, where the whole village assembles, singing and drinking.

Thanks to the kind attention of Mr. Bain, I was on the 30th so far recovered from my painful rheumatism as to be able to continue my journey, though, it is true, by means of a litter. Bugslag also suffered from constant attacks of dysentery, and was so much weakened that we were obliged to use the litter in turns. We passed the Lowira or Lowiri, which falls into the Nyassa, and on the 31st encamped near the slope of the plateau which precipitately descends into the lake at Mpata, being part of the Wakondi country. This was the first time that we had found the adansonia in the east of the continent since leaving the Lower Cassai. Next day we descended the steep edge of the plateau and reached the bank of the Nyassa near the station of the

African Lakes Company, close to the village of the chief Karanga.

For the last three days I had been marching on the so-called Stephenson's Road. Only the fact that now and again the higher trees had been cut in straight lines showed that at some time an attempt had been made to build a road. The narrow negroes' path wound through underwood which had grown up to the height of a man. Meanwhile, this attempt at a road, with the English claims to the territory, would have rather amused a connoisseur. By this time not a trace will be left of the 'famous road' in Inner Africa.

The difficulty in the way of an ultimate connection between the two lakes by a railway will be the slopes of the plateaus on the Nyassa and Tanganyika. Both are steep and rocky, and that leading to the Tanganyika is higher by far than the former, having as it has an absolute altitude of 300 metres above that of the Nyassa, whilst the evenly flat land between the two descends very little eastward.

Two Scotchmen, officials of the commercial company I have mentioned, welcomed us, and assigned to us and our people a locality for encampment under the beautiful shady trees, the greatest ornament of the station. Besides being engaged in the sale of ivory, the two gentlemen were busy as missionaries. They kept a small school, where about twenty children were taught, and now and then they held a prayer meeting, attended, although scantily, by the Wakonde of the immediate neighbourhood.

I was delighted to learn that in a very short time

the little steamer of the company, the 'Ilala,' was expected here, and that I was at liberty, with my few West Africans, to continue my journey in it.

I paid off my carriers, but deducted a small part of their wages, since I had found out that they had been aware of the flight of their country people, which had at the time so much embarrassed me.

After several days' fruitless waiting for the Arab who had promised to bring my fifteen loads to Karonga, I learned that he had gone to an Arab settled south of this place, who was here called Mirambo. There he again made an attempt at extortion by retaining my loads until his demands should be satisfied. In order that I might not have to detain the steamer, which might arrive at any moment, I granted his request, and duly received my loads, which I was astonished not to find more diminished.

There was a strange phenomenon here, in the shape of dark, sometimes almost black, clouds which floated close above the lake. They turned out to be swarms of millions of small flies, here called *cungu*; several times these swarms were mistaken for the approaching 'Ilala.' As soon as these flies have settled on land, tired with their flight, the natives collect them, and, after being kneaded into a paste and baked like cakes, they form a favourite dish.

Noting down the route of my journey from the Tanganyika to this place, I came to the conclusion that the Nyassa and the Tanganyika are drawn on the maps too closely together. Since my instruments of observation had become useless, I was unable to take measurements of longitude; thus, my conjectures only rest on careful calculations of the distances I had travelled. I believe the fault is in the Nyassa being placed too far to the west; for the situation of the Tanganyika, through repeated observations on the spot, seems to be more to be depended on than that of the Nyassa.

The natives of Konde may be ranked among the Zulu tribes; their language and their manners and customs suggest this. Of all the natives I ever met, these are the least clothed; a small rag, or even a bunch of leaves, is suspended from their belts in front; now and then I saw quite naked men coming to Karonga from villages lying south-west. The weapons of the Wakonde are a light, prettily worked javelin and a shield made of the skin of the elk antelope. The houses, constructed of bent rods and carefully covered with very soft grass, have a firm, raised floor. They are almost painfully clean. The houses on each side of the road, belted by close banana plantations, form large villages. The principal food is millet and maize, rarely manioc. Bananas and sugar are much cultivated. Nowhere so much as in this neighbourhood did I see the natives side with the Europeans against the Arabs, who were hated everywhere. It was owing to this circumstance that, scarcely a year after my leaving, Karonga station was able to hold out against the attacks of the Arabs.

OUR PARTY

CHAPTER X

TO THE COAST

The Nyassa—The banks abound in game—The Arabs on the lake—Livingstonia—Shiré—Mandala and Blantyre—I am ill—The negroes' deficiency in skill—The journey on the Shiré resumed—Crocodiles and hippopotami—Struggle with a huge heron—Bugslag's true companionship—Portuguese outpost—The Zambesi—Mrs. Livingstone's grave—On the Quaqua—Quilimane—Conclusion.

On July 11th the 'Ilala' arrived. Two days later I went on board with Bugslag and my faithful attendants from the West Coast and left Karanga.

The Nyassa, in its shape and situation and meteorological aspects, greatly resembles the Tanganyika. Here, as there, a strong south-easterly breeze blows continually during the dry season, causing a very rough sea; here, as there, the calm is frequently interrupted by thunder-storms, which, however, are said not to be accompanied by such gales as are met with on the Tanganyika. During the rainy season waterspouts are frequent. Far more rain falls in the peninsulas or promontories projecting into the lake than farther inland. On the whole, more rain falls on the lake than on the coast.

The Nyassa, as ascertained by twelve years' observations of the missionaries, falls 0·9 English foot annually. A periodical rising and falling, as on the Tanganyika, has not, however, been observed. Navigation on this lake is difficult, as the sands reach out to a distance of five English miles from the shore while reefs threaten the navigator for sometimes two English miles off the coast. Huge rocks tower here and there from the sandy shallows, or form a striking contrast to the light-coloured sand beneath the clear water. Contrary to the frequently brackish water of the Tanganyika, that of the Nyassa is clear and sweet, which accounts for the entirely different fauna of the lake. That of the Tanganyika more nearly resembles that of the sea, while the Nyassa is the abode of animals which are observed in every fresh-water lake. The beach of the Tanganyika is covered with many kinds of shells; gulls and sea swallows sport on the banks, while fresh-water birds are only found on the mouths of the rivers. The banks of the Nyassa are destitute of shells; there are no sea-nettles, as on the other lake; and cormorants everywhere perch on the bare trees at the waterside—trees that have died as a result of the noxious excrement of these birds. Where the banks of the Nyassa are uninhabited, they display abundance of game. Buffaloes, wild antelopes, and giraffes are frequent; and from the mainland the sound of the lion's roar, an animal that can live only where there is plenty of game, induced us to undertake frequent hunting expeditions in places where we dropped anchor for cutting wood.

Bugslag once shot an antelope near the bank, and came to the beach to call some people to carry the game to the boat. On returning he found only scanty remains of the animal, which had been torn to pieces; with difficulty he succeeded in driving away some impudent vultures. Traces showed that during his absence some hyenas had possessed themselves of the prey. In similar cases I have spread my handkerchief or part of my clothes on the game, and so caused the beasts of prey to be scared away by scenting the nearness of man.

One evening our men, who had been fetching firewood to the beach, were sitting round the fire they had made, when suddenly a buffalo broke from a thicket and hurried past them. Immediately behind him two lions jumped out, but, frightened by the fire and the presence of men, they abstained from pursuing the buffalo any farther, and after a short pause retreated into the thicket.

At one point of the lake, where lagoons, intersected by jungles and thickets of reeds, stretched for miles landwards, we dropped anchor one evening, but could scarcely get any sleep on account of the incessant roaring and tramping of hundreds of hippopotami which

BANKS OF THE NYASSA

in the evening exchange the lagoons for the banks of the lake.

Next day I landed with Bugslag and entered upon a wilderness, than which a better cannot be imagined for the home of the huge behemoth. Lagoons, creeks, and dried-up watercourses furrowed in inextricable lines an either muddy or sandy flat, covered with jungle-like reeds or marshy plants. Only the splashing of a frightened hippopotamus, or a short, far-sounding bellow, interrupted the deep calm of this pathless wilderness, where only the narrow tunnel-shaped dwellings of the huge pachydermata, running through the jungles, could be traced. Once, when knee-deep in the water in a bent attitude, proceeding under the jungles which closed immediately above our heads, we suddenly met a gigantic hippopotamus. For a moment the animal stopped short, and afterwards, to our great satisfaction, broke away in a side direction. After this startling encounter we preferred giving up the exploration of this wilderness.

In the south the lake scenery is beautiful. High hills advance there close to the bank, tongues of land form harbours, and many islands or high reefs of rocks break the monotony of the flat banks. The traffic on the lake is not so lively as on the Tanganyika.

On the west coast of the Nyassa are two large settlements of slave-traders, Arabs and people of Kilwa and Lindi. These Arabs transact their chief business with the murderous Wawemba. They supply the latter with guns, powder, cloth, and beads, in exchange for slaves. Ivory is, in proportion, rarely brought here, for in these latitudes—I may say from the eighth degree south latitude southward—the gun is found throughout the continent, and this has immensely decreased the number of elephants. Only in large pathless deserts is the elephant still found as stationary game.

Bugslag, in cutting wood for the steamer, came upon a large settlement of slave-catchers, those nefarious vagabonds who depopulate Africa; the same miserable robbers of human flesh and blood, with the same insolence and barbarism usual with men of such an occupation as in the northern centres of the slave-trade. Nay, he was thankful to find himself on board again unscathed, for he had been jeered at and threatened. Among the local slave-hunters, as well as in the north, there seemed to have been a rising which threatened to lead to a catastrophe.

Here I wrote in my journal: 'I believe the safety of the missionaries and European traders will not be of long duration; I cannot imagine how Europeans in such a barbarous country can think of building settlements without fortifying them. It is simply absurd that some English missionaries in building stations give orders to avoid everything that suggests a fortification. This does not make any impression on a native; on the contrary, in this way a white man makes himself unintelligible and ridiculous to him. He cannot conceive why a white man should not look after his own safety; nay, he would only rejoice if a settlement of people who only mean to do him good should become to him a place of refuge and protect him from the merciless man-hunters.'

Those slave-hunters who touch the lake southwards mostly take their goods to Mikindani; those who go across in sailing dhows go to Lindi; while those who go round the Northern Nyassa choose the way to Kilwa.

Besides the station of the Scotch Commercial Company, there are two missionary stations on the lake; of these, Bandawe, where I was kindly received by Dr. Lars, was by far the best. A number of good buildings are here well arranged in the midst of gardens and plantations.

In visiting the schools I counted 130 children, distributed in three classes. Our old 'Ilala' at best not going above four knots an hour, and being often even compelled to seek shelter off the land on account of the stiff breeze and rough sea—the commander of the vessel, moreover, being by no means practical, so that, if it had been possible, I should have preferred taking the command myself—we did not reach the south of the lake till the 25th; we had thus taken fifteen days to go about sixty-five German miles.

In a harbour much sheltered by islands, we dropped anchor off the missionary station Livingstonia. This rather neglected station was inhabited by only one black schoolmaster. The climate is so fatal that the missionary societies have abandoned the idea of sending white men or Europeans to this place. A very large number of graves bore witness to the unhealthy nature of this locality, which in its outer dress has been so much favoured by Nature. From the ever-smooth deep-blue narrow harbour the mainland soon rises to an imposing height, only leaving a short strip of level land on the banks. Fan-palms and huge adansonias surround the banks, and numerous villages peep out of the thickets of bananas. The southern part of the lake is rich in fish, and in the evening the great number of fishing canoes, lighted up with fires, presented a splendid picture.

On the 26th we entered the affluent of the Nyassa, the Shiré. This river varies in breadth from eighty to one hundred metres, and has at its commencement level banks, here and there showing thickets of reeds and papyrus. The coasts are densely populated, and when busy crossing an apparently much-frequented ferry we met a slave caravan with Arabs. This is the most southern point visited by Arabs; farther south and southwest the tribes are too numerous and strongly armed to make slave-hunting profitable. After some little time the Shiré falls into a lake of about two German miles in length. This is the Pamolondo, which has particularly clear water and such an equal depth that we measured everywhere almost exactly ten feet. This little lake greatly abounds in fish, and never have I seen pelicans in such numbers as here. In the same latitude as before the Shiré flows out of the small lake. The banks of the river change, are less populated, and consequently abound in game, as does the river itself, which swarms with hippopotami and crocodiles. We often saw large droves of zebras, and at night frequently heard the mighty thundering voice of the lord of the desert.

On the 28th we reached Mutope, a small station of the Commercial Company, and with it for the present the end of our journey; for some way farther down

BANKS OF THE SHIRÉ

rapids and small falls interrupt the navigation of the river. From Mutope I sent a short note to the chief factory of the said Company to announce my coming, and started on the 29th.

Choosing a broad road with traces of wheels, I rode in advance of my troop on a horse sent to meet me, and in the afternoon reached Blantyre, the large Scotch missionary station, and afterwards Mandala, the station of the African Lakes Company. The broad roads, the avenues of beautiful lofty trees, mostly eucalyptus, the numerous houses, neatly built in European fashion of bricks, with glass windows, and surrounded by pretty gardens, fields of European corn, and similar signs of civilisation, surprising to one coming from the wilderness, awakened within me the same comfortable feeling as if I had been in Europe.

These two settlements are the best and most highly developed I have seen in Inner Africa. A large number of merchants, missionaries, schoolmasters, tradespeople, and five ladies, all Scotch by birth, formed a colony imposing for these parts, and their looks proved the climate to be comparatively healthy. Both stations may be considered prominent test stations for this part of the tropics, for I could scarcely say what has been unattempted in the way of garden and field culture, plantations and cattle breeding. At the missionary station, corn, vegetables, and flowers were cultivated, and cattle bred, solely for the maintenance of the black and white population; but they had at Mandala, after several attempts, fallen back chiefly upon coffee plantations, and had even brought over the necessary apparatus for husking and cleaning the coffee. It would lead me too far were I to enlarge upon the results of the different experiments. But not to give the reader a wrong idea of the results of such undertakings, I must not omit to mention that large sums of money, probably mostly arising from pious legacies, were invested here without the necessity of obtaining corresponding interest. An undertaking meant to pay cannot from the beginning be furnished with such comfort, I might say luxury, as these two stations, one of which, the missionary station, was founded and is maintained by donations, which, practically speaking, *à fond perdu*, have only been given for converting the heathen to Christianity. The African Lakes Company is likewise partly a commercial, partly a missionary association, and in like manner chiefly subsists upon donations.

I lay ill at Mandala for more than a week: my rheumatism had returned, and I suffered from a tedious nervous asthma complicated with attacks of fever. Thanks to the excellent treatment of the doctor at the missionary station and the nursing at Mandala, I recovered so far as to think of resuming my journey, and resolved to wait for the steamer that was expected from the Zambesi. But as day after day passed without its coming I abandoned this idea, and it suited me all the better, as it seemed that the expenses on the boat would be too great for my small caravan. On learning that a Scotch merchant had come up the river in a large rowing boat in order to go farther into the interior on trading business, I despatched Bugslag to the river, and succeeded in obtaining the boat on condition of leaving it on the coast at Quilimane.

On July 22 I started from Mandala, intending to reach the Shiré below the falls near Kattunga and continue my journey by water. Bugslag had marched on with my West Africans, and I followed in a 'jinricksha' (a Japanese conveyance), which was drawn and pushed by two men at either end. We passed through a savannah of trees, here and there relieved by close belts of bamboo, in a rapid down-hill drive towards the river. The negroes found the simple construction of the light vehicle so complicated that they displayed an astonishing lack of skill. It seems almost incredible that they should not have understood so simple a means of conveyance; and yet the fact is so. They always placed themselves in the wrong place, and drew and pushed against each other; at a crossing they would tear off the road into the deep grass or into the thicket; several times they even overturned me; in short, they tormented me with their clumsiness to such a degree that for the most part I preferred walking, although, on account of my rheumatism, this was rendered very painful. On arriving at the Shiré I found the large strong boat that had been lent to me; this saved me about 70*l.*, which the coastward journey in a vessel of the Scotch Company would have cost me.

I resumed my downward journey on the Shiré on the 25th, shortly after the arrival of the expected steamer, which, however, was in such bad repair that for the present my start could not be thought of. Bugslag and I managed the wheel in turns. My eight

West Africans, Fickerini, the Zanzibaris, a native brought as a guide, three wives of my people, and my two little valets, composed the expedition; not to omit the two dogs, one of which was the last of the terriers I took from West Africa into the interior five years ago. Jettchen was the first European animal that had crossed the equatorial latitudes of the African continent. She reached her native country safe and sound, and lived two years longer in Germany.

The first two or three German miles of the river can hardly be called navigable on account of the islands, sands, and narrow channels. The river, which now and then assumes the shape of lagoons, has deep banks, with plain grass savannah relieved by groves of borassus palms. The banks are in some places literally covered with crocodiles, of which Bugslag and I shot a large number. The muscular power of such a reptile is remarkable. The animal, after being hit, would jump up repeatedly more than a metre high, then he would throw himself on his back and lie dead on the spot; others, not mortally wounded, would plunge into the river with extraordinarily vigorous leaps. Being near the coast and so not obliged to save our cartridges, we practised firing at crocodiles throughout the journey. In some places we came upon such numbers of hippopotami that now and then they endangered the safety of the boat. What sounded like the distant rolling of thunder once made us start up in wonder, it being the dry season and the sky being serene; but a violent vibration of the boat afterwards, and the rising of air-bubbles alongside, convinced us that it had been caused by the snorting of a hippopotamus, which strangely resembles the noise of distant thunder.

Having provided ourselves at Mandala with European potatoes, bread, onions, and vegetables, we lived very well; this being the case, the constantly changing scenery and the abundant animal life, continually presenting new and interesting pictures, made the journey a very amusing and enjoyable one. A traveller who for years has had to put up with African food cannot be offered a greater dainty than bread and European potatoes. I quite believe that any African traveller would leave a breakfast of oysters and champagne untouched if he had his choice between it and a dish of potatoes and bread. Good food and pleasant intercourse soon effected the strengthening of my weakened system. No one could have nursed me with greater solicitude than my faithful Bugslag. When, about five in the evening, I halted at a place suitable for encampment, my tent was pitched and arranged within ten minutes, and a simple supper, such as Bugslag well knew how to vary every day, was soon preparing. Since leaving Nyangwe, travelling with my small caravan, there had been no need for me to look after our suite. Bugslag was everywhere, and by his wonderful knack of managing the negroes he saved me many of the little vexations that the life of an African traveller is subject to. I could not have wished for a better travelling companion, a more dauntless and devoted comrade than he proved; and, though only a simple sailor, he showed a rare tact.

A very comical sight, which incited our black

followers to roars of laughter, was a gigantic heron standing in the shallow water, shot through his wing. The bird had attacked with his beak one of my men who went to fetch him, pushed the man on in front until he fell down in the water, and belaboured him, till a shot from Bugslag's gun wounded the heron's wing, and put an end to this unequal struggle.

On the 27th we passed

STRUGGLE WITH A GIGANTIC HERON.

a vast level and monotonous wilderness, where now and then fan-palms towered above the high grass and low brushwood. Elephants are still plentiful in this wilderness, as we learned from their many tracks leading into the water; but though we had been told at Mandala that we should frequently encounter large herds of them, we scarcely caught sight of one. There were, however, large flocks of antelopes, more numerous than I had ever before seen them. Out of a flock of at least 150, Bugslag shot a large ram, which supplied us with meat for three days.

On the 28th I halted at a point from which I could see the Portuguese flag at a village fortified with palisades; this convinced me of its being a military station of the Portuguese Government. Lieutenant Cardoso, the commander of this post, received me kindly. His troop consisted of one man, his servant, called No. 23; for the Portuguese Government arrange their soldiers by numbers, not by names in the rolls. The officer was rather a political agent than the commander of a military post. He assembled the chiefs of his district once a week to transact Government business, and a number of glass bottles filled with *aguardente* ensured the punctual voluntary appearance of his subordinates.

On embarking, No. 23 brought us as a parting present a cask of Portuguese wine, and then we went down the river, which now made frequent sudden turns. Next day we passed, on the right, some enormous lagoons, stretching far into the land, and supplied by a branch of the Shiré. A shot at a crocodile had an extraordinary effect. Clouds of birds, which enlivened the

'OUT OF THE WATER CREPT A LARGE CROCODILE'

sloughs and lagoons, rose with a deafening noise. Ducks, geese, pelicans, herons, storks, rails, snipe, and innumerable other species in many thousands suddenly disturbed the still life of the water-waste.

On the 31st the oarsmen pulled us from the waters of the Shiré into the broad, imposing Father Zambesi. The Shiré, by reason of its uniform depth in its chief arm, was far more navigable than the Zambesi in its lower course, which, in consequence of its breadth, winds along in innumerable channels, mostly shallow, through a labyrinth of sandbanks and islands mantled with grass or mangroves. We ran aground oftener than in the Shiré, and had frequently to drag or push the boat through the water for a long distance. In the afternoon of the next day we were induced by the numerous traces of game, among which were several prints of lions' claws leading to the water, to pitch our camp and go on an evening hunt, though, in spite of the rich abundance of game, we did not succeed in bagging anything. After dark, when we were sitting smoking near a fire, we noticed a crocodile, with incredible insolence, crawling slowly out of the water and approaching us to within a few metres distance; but before we could seize our rifles it had disappeared in the flood, hit with a firebrand by one of our people.

In the afternoon of August 2 I paid a visit to a Portuguese fortress, the Fortalesa Chupanga, built of stone close to the river, where Alferez Machado Leal kindly greeted and entertained me as a German. I say as a German, since the proceedings of the English on the Shiré were regarded with distrust on the part of Portugal. Even then I foresaw what has occurred since, that here the Portuguese would have to give way to the advance of England.

Close to the fortress was the grave of Livingstone's wife, who had here succumbed to the fever—a simple cross, which, strangely enough, had received a singular ornament. Some twelve months before, a huge adansonia, felled by the storm, had fallen across the grave in such a manner that by means of a strong branch and the curve of the stem it formed an arch above the grave without touching the cross.

In the evening of the same day we arrived at the station of the Scotch Company, and thus terminated our navigation of the Zambesi; for to get to Quilimane you have to go across country for one kilometre as far as the Quaqua, and follow it down to the seaboard. The Quaqua is connected with the Zambesi close to the mouth of the Shiré.

On August 4 we put our boat on a strong cart prepared for this purpose, and, through an absolute plain between the Zambesi and the Quaqua, we drew it over to the latter. The Quaqua, which often narrows itself to twenty-five metres, next day carried our boat farther downward.

I shot a crocodile close to the village, the natives of which asked me for it, for the flesh of this disgusting animal is to them a special luxury. On Bugslag's hunting list this was the seventy-fifth crocodile since our navigation of the Nyassa. The crocodiles are greatly feared in the Quaqua. I was told that they would try with their tails to push the occupants of a canoe into the water.

One day, on our journey down the Quaqua, we met forty-seven trading canoes, carrying cloth, beads, iron wire, powder, and guns, all bound for the interior. The banks of the Quaqua, from the frequent appearance of mangroves, assume an entirely new character. This Indian fruit-tree, imported and cultivated by the Arabs and Indians throughout the coast, has quite taken root here, and affords splendid shade. Its dark leaves, of a

THE SEVENTY-FIFTH CROCODILE

black-green colour, are, especially in the dry season, a strong contrast to the general yellow tint of the landscape, caused by drought and a scorching sun.

We had always to stop when the tide was coming in and to go on as it went out, till, on August 8, we reached an expanse of water that gradually forms the harbour of Quilimane. We noticed the masts of a barque from a distance, at the topmast of which was displayed

HARBOUR OF QUILIMANE.

the German flag. Before landing I ran alongside of the vessel, and was not a little surprised to find it to be a ship whose christening I had attended at my garrison at Rostock. The captain of the ship knew me personally, and we renewed our acquaintance with the first glass of German beer I had had since I landed in Africa.

In the town, which is distinguished from all the other border towns of the Portuguese by its pretty gardens,

Bugslag and I took lodgings at an hotel, and with the aid of an Indian tailor we tried to somewhat conform our outward appearance to the civilisation around us.

A few days after, a ship of the Castle Line conveyed us to Mozambique. The Governor-General of the Portuguese possessions in East Africa, Agosto de Castilho, was kind enough to let me make use of a Portuguese man-of-war, which was going from Mozambique to Loanda, to convey my honest West Africans back to Angola. I rewarded the faithful services of my black followers, and then, with Bugslag, my two black boys, who would not leave me, and my old flag-bearer Fickerini, I took the next northward steamer, and in the first place went to Zanzibar. There I found a hospitable reception, just as I had five years before, at the house of business of Mr. Oswald.

It was not till now that I learnt what meanwhile had happened in East Africa: that Germany had here opened a new field for Transatlantic activity. Dr. Peters, just returning from a coastward tour, surprised me by the narration of his work, his success, and his prospects; and, the report he gave setting at rest the apprehensions I had brought with me from the coast, I gave myself up entirely to joy at the successful results of the German spirit of enterprise; not dreaming that I myself should have to act a part in the events which I had foreseen to be necessary forerunners of any work of civilisation in Africa; not dreaming that I should so soon be permitted to deal the first fatal blow against the pestiferous dominion of the Arabs, which was laying waste the African continent.

APPENDIX I

LETTER OF LE MARINEL ON THE RETURN OF THE BASHILANGE TO THEIR COUNTRY

(TRANSLATED FROM THE FRENCH)

Luluaburg: May 10, 1887.

MONSIEUR WISSMANN,—On leaving the Lualaba you told me that our return march might be effected within two months; your prediction has come true—nay, I have great satisfaction in telling you that your caravan reached Luluaburg as early as April 18.

The road we took in marching back differed constantly from the one we marched together.

To put something like order into my narration, I think I had better dissect my journey into stages: (1) From Nyangwe to the Lomami; (2) from the Lomami to Lupungu; (3) from Lupungu to the Lubi; and (4) from the Lubi to Lubuku.

(1) On leaving the Lualaba I reached the left bank of the Lufubu, whose waters were about three metres lower than you found them, in two days' march; the Moadi, which I passed rather below our former camp, was also nearly dry, presenting no difficulties. Leaving Pogge's return road on the left, I went from Goi Capopa in a straight line to Kabamba, where we had left Kashawalla.

The Coango likewise being shallow, some morasses on this march were the only obstacles.

That part of our caravan which you had left at Kabamba I found in a deplorable state. Small-pox had demanded more victims: about ten Bashilange had died, fifteen were seriously ill. Josso and Makenge from Angola died among others, and the chiefs Kajembe, Moina, and Ilunga Mputt. In spite of seeing their countrymen, the people were greatly demoralised.

My first care was to isolate the small-pox patients and those sickening for small-pox.

After two days of rest, or rather halt to buy provisions, I started, and took measures always to prevent the caravan coming into contact with the sick patients.

Owing to this precaution, carried out with restless energy, I succeeded in lessening the deaths. Arrived at Lubuku, I therefore counted only sixty sick people, of whom not above thirty died.

In spite of the strictest measures of M. de Macar, we had, after all, to mourn for many dead, among them our dear old friend Jingenge, brave Katende, and some Ginga soldiers.

Dr. Sommers assured me the epidemic would not spread further. Let us hope that he may be right, for the poor people have suffered enough on this unfortunate expedition. I will not mention the number of victims; it is enormous.

To return to our journey.

On leaving Kabamba I took the road between your route and Cameron's, and crossed the Lomami at our old point, after endless negotiations about the canoes I required.

(2) *From the Lomami to Lupungu.*—Keeping to the right bank of the Lukassi, I found the district rather more populated than we had done on passing through it, and behind Kalambai I even came upon a number of little villages. Beyond the Lukassi, near Milambo, the natives had begun to rebuild their villages opposite to the place where was Said's camp.

At Kalambai we met the last hordes of Arabs, whose guide, a certain Kassia, wanted to ally himself with me for a *coup de main* against the people on the Lukassi. I of course frustrated his design. Said's hordes had laid waste the fields throughout, so that we could not buy anything.

I had intended to take Pogge's route, straight to the Sankurru, not in order to see new countries, but only to push on my caravan as quickly and as well as possible ; my plan was, however, altered in many respects. The guides I had taken from Milambo fled from Baqua Peshi; besides, we were induced to abandon our plan by the Bassonge and Kalebue, who predicted a ten days' march through depopulated districts. So we took our former road to Lupungu.

(3) From Lupungu to the Lubi.—From Lubefu, where I encamped in the same place that you did, I took a south-westerly direction, and reached within four days a group of four or six villages of the Ku-Mapenge ; they formerly belonged to Zappu Zapp, but have since his departure made themselves independent. According to my calculation, Zappu Zapp must have left his old domicile in 1884.

Thence, in a more northern direction, I reached Mona Kialo, the son of Zappu Mutapos ; the latter, likewise dispossessed by the advance of the Arabs, had settled near the Bambue, and had since died of small-pox.

After his death, Mona Kialo made war on the Bambue, and now, as their master, lives among them on the left bank of the Kashimbi, a tributary of the Sankurru.

He must have lived there since 1886. He has about 400 guns, mostly flint-lock rifles. These countries south of your and Pogge's route are mountainous ; from them rise the brooks you passed. Being followed by about 400 Ku-Mapenge bound for Zappu Zapp, I appeared nearly 1,200 strong at Mona Kialo's. But my numbers did not seem to intimidate Mona Kialo's insolent robbers. Just fancy that in broad daylight three guns were stolen from the camp! You may imagine my wrath.

I sent for Mona Kialo, and threatened to cut off his head unless he took care to surrender both the arms and the thieves by sunset. He wanted to excuse himself by alleging the numbers of strangers about him ; but I interrupted him, and swore that he should die unless he did as he was bidden.

I don't believe I should have been strong enough to master him, but I was all the more persistent with my threats. Kashawalla was of course dumb with fear. ' You go too far,' he said ; '' your followers will take flight.'

In a few hours Mona Kialo appeared, bringing with him the stolen guns; the thieves, he said, had been killed and distributed to be eaten.

'You lie,' I said; 'I will see the thieves.'

'But they are dead!'

'Well, then, show me their dead bodies.'

'They are cut to pieces!'

'Let me see them.'

Of course I thought this was all a lie; but fancy my terror and loathing when some Bassonge actually came along with pieces of human flesh, with cut-off arms, legs, &c. Kashawalla had disappeared. Our Bashilange and Angola people freely gave vent to their disgust and horror.

I should have thought that the action of our people would have frightened the natives, but I soon saw that they were all very much excited, most of all Mona Kialo himself.

Towards midnight I was called by the interpreter, as the natives, having arranged a grand banquet for eating human flesh, had drawn all our people out of camp to witness it. I held a 'Moiio,' thereby calling all the lookers-on from this loathsome drama.

Here I felt quite powerless. What could I have done here? Had I taken the terrible prey from those savage brutes by force, this might have become a signal for war, and by this not only the success of the expedition would have been risked—the natives had double our number of guns—but I should have likewise been compelled to obtain food and guides, the provisioning of the caravan presenting the greatest difficulty as it was.

I have been rather circumstantial, but, without wanting to bore you with little casualties of the journey, I could not but tell you about this loathsome spectacle.

I resumed my journey, and after two days' march arrived on the Sankurru, which I crossed just above the Bubila (according to Kiepert, Lubila). I reached Zappu Zapp, who since Dr. Wolf's visit has changed his place of abode, which was formerly on the right bank.

I found Zappu Zapp not nearly so powerful as I had conjectured; his reputation is greatly exaggerated by his people and his enemies. Though he may be called a formidable chief, he is not to be compared to Lupungu, Mona Kakesa, and Mona Kialo. He has subdued many people, but this was not difficult, as they had none of them any firearms.

After a four days' march through a mountainous and densely wooded country, I reached the Lubi.

(4) From the Lubi to Lubuku.—One day's march north of the crossing on your first journey I passed over the Lubi. From thence to the Lubudi I followed our old track, then I went farther south and crossed the Lulua near Luluaburg.

I am anxious to hear about your further adventures since our separation; I hope that you reached the coast safely, and that my letter found you well.

Accept, Monsieur Wissmann, the kindest regards and best wishes from

Yours &c.,
P. LE MARINEL.

APPENDIX II

THE BASHILANGE COUNTRY

My sketch of the population in the Bashilange country, based on my own experience and the reliable inquiries which, in consequence of my long sojourn in those regions, I was able to make, gives a truer picture of one part of Central Africa than maps of a travelling route ever can.

The Bashilange (singular, Mushilange) or, as they are called by the Western tribes, Tushilange (singular, Kashilange). are a mixture of the Baluba who had invaded from the south-west, and the Bashi-Lange, who had been established previously in the district.

Bashi is a term for people, which, as is still the case west of the Cassai with the Bashi-Lele, Bashi-Panga, &c., was also customary with the Bashi-Lange, meaning the same as the term which is now used by the Bakuba and the tribes as far as the Lualaba: Baqua, Bena, or, probably shortened, only Ba (singular, Muqua, Mona, Mu). Baqua means people, Bena. sons; for instance, Baqua-Katana, i.e. people from Katana ; Bena-Lulua, Kasairi, Riamba, i.e. sons of the Lulua, the Kasairi, the Riamba.

The invading Baluba subdued the Bashilange and mixed with them; hence the present Bashilange like to call themselves Baluba, and are called so by people in the north, while the nations bordering on the east, south, and west, call them Ba, or Tushilange.[1]

I have decided upon the appellation 'Bashilange,' this nation being a striking contrast to the pure Baluba on the

---

[1] I am sorry that in my work *Im Innern Afrikas*, the Bashilange have always been called Baluba. This is owing to the circumstance that the work was prepared during my last journey by my followers, who had come back prior to my return, and that its preparation had so far

eastern border—a contrast which is scarcely met with among Bantu negroes throughout the continent.

The present result of the mixture is such that this nation has apparently no characteristic feature of the Baluba left, at least as regards outward appearance. The language certainly is little altered, and this circumstance, as well as the generally well-preserved tradition, gives evidence of the said mixture; the very great differences of colour, skin, and conformation, also are in favour of the sometimes larger addition of Baluba blood.

A BASHILANGE CONCERT.

advanced that a thorough alteration might have delayed the publication of the book. There being, certainly, some justification for the appellation, I did not alter it; but this is the reason why, in these pages, I have called these people by their right name.

The Baluba being bony, muscular, thick-set, and broad-shouldered people, the old Bashi-Lange must have been exceedingly narrow-chested, long-limbed, and less muscular, since the present Bashilange far more resemble the frame of the latter than of the Baluba. The excessive smoking of wild hemp (*riamba*) alone cannot have had this effect, as it is only twenty-five years ago since its use became customary among them; and among the younger generation it is already beginning to decrease. And this reminds me that hemp is smoked, though in small quantities, throughout Africa as it is known to me, from the Atlantic to the Indian Ocean. At Uniamwesi, it was in 1883 greatly on the increase. I even know pure Arabs who are given to this bad habit; though I cannot but add, that the noxious results are much exaggerated.

Other differences influencing the physical development, such as meteorological conditions, food, occupation, care of the body, &c., which might appear to be arguments against the supposed mixture, are not worthy of notice.

The arms of the Bashilange also give evidence of their mixed blood, as they make use of spear, club, bow, and knife. The bow was the weapon of the old Bashi-Lange, and is so still, north and west of this place; the spear is the weapon of the Baluba, who are up to this day seldom seen with a bow. On all my journeys I have never met a tribe armed with the javelin; that always goes with the shield and the bow, though this does not prevent one's finding some spears among bow nations, and *vice versâ*. Between the Cassai and the Tanganyika Lake, in Central Africa Proper, whither the gun has scarcely penetrated as yet, there is a marked limit between the bow-Ubujiwe and the spear-Manyema; the spear-Baluba and the bow-Bassonge; the bow-Bassongo-Mino and the spear nations north of them on the Cassai.

On my own map I marked four classes of Bashilange by means of colours: the Bashilamboa, Bashilambembele, Bashilakassanga, and Bena-Luntu.

The distinction between the three former will soon have disappeared; probably they were a mixture of tribes, formed during the invasion of the Baluba, as new conquerors continued to come from the east, dispossessing their predecessors. Even now it is difficult to ascertain to which of the three a tribe belongs.

1. The Bashilamboa, the largest and most western portion, who only nominally acknowledge Katende, whose ancestors of Baluba blood once governed them as their head. Bashilamboa,

BASHILAMBOA

i.e. Bashilange-imboa (*imboa*, dog), because in war they bit like dogs (allegorically), or because they ate dogs, which habit they had retained from the old Bashi-Lange, while the Baluba despise this food.

The pedigree of the Prince Katende reaches back to Mona

Kanjika, from whom his ancestors obtained the Dikonga dia Difuma, an iron sceptre, of which only one specimen is said to be extant among the Baluba. (The Dikonga, which was surrendered to me after a war with Katende, when I took him prisoner, is, with its far-back pedigree, in the Berlin Museum.) Katende is now powerless, and the mixture of the Bashilamboa is thus only of historical interest. As is the case everywhere, the appearance of firearms has changed everything here.

2. The Bashilambembele, i.e. Bashilange-bembele (*bembele*, mosquito), either because they stung like mosquitoes or because they were as numerous as mosquitoes. They drove the Bashilamboa westward. The family of their former chief is no longer to be ascertained.

3. The Bashilakassanga. Kassanga-sanga, small white ants, which build their hard black cells, resembling dross of iron, in the ground. They burn some of those cells with the insects in them in the houses, so as to drive away the mosquitoes by the smoke; thus the Bashilakassanga drove the Bashilambembele farther to the north-west.

4. The Bena-Luntu, distinct from either of the three former, who from their appearance have most Baluba blood, are perhaps even cannibals, which the others are not. The Bena-Luntu are rarely found to be tattooed, but all the more frequently they paint like the pure Baluba, though they do it much better, and with magnificent colours (black, white, red); and, besides, they are much more barbarous.

The three first classes had either retained or adopted the artistic and tasteful tattooings of the old Bashi-Lange.

In the patterns of the tattooing three distinct motives are easily distinguishable among different ages, which proves that in course of time the fashion has altered. At present—that is, for the last ten years—tattooing has gone out of fashion.

Each of these four tribal associations is subdivided into tribes; these again into communities; the latter into families, each of which sometimes owns several villages. This division, of course, is not one regulated by any authorities, but has in course of time taken its rise from separation in consequence of war, local over-

population, hostilities, &c. Very often I could no longer ascertain which were the tribes, and which communities or families belonged to them; names which are used in connection with many Baqua or Bena, such as Baqua Katana or Bena Meta, or those occurring in different places, as the Baqua-Mulume, may be considered to be names of tribes.

The same names are often found in places far apart, such as the Baqua Mbuju, in the north-east and west. This only proves that members of villages or communities were and are easily induced to leave their abodes to settle down in another neighbourhood. The reasons are, sickness (small-pox), war, oppression by a more powerful neighbour, accidents through lightning (which, contrary to universal belief, are very frequent). The Bashilange never settle among other nations, as is the case with the Kioque, who always press northward.

I have registered 147 names, mostly indicative of tribes, of which fifty-eight fall to the Bashilamboa, fifty-three to the Bashilambembele, twenty-one to the Bashilakassanga, and fifteen to the Bena-Luntu. Several are sure to be missing, chiefly among the Bashilamboa, though this does not signify, since, for the reasons I have mentioned, I am not able to give an exact political map, but only a general picture of the population in this country.

The Bashilange were a warlike people; one tribe with another, one village with another, always lived at daggers drawn. The number of scars which some ancient men display among their tattooings give evidence of this.

Then, about twenty-five years ago, nominally originated by Moamba Mputt, a hemp-smoking worship began to be established, and the narcotic effect of smoking masses of hemp made itself felt. The Bena-Riamba, 'Sons of Hemp,' found more and more followers; they began to have intercourse with each other as they became less barbarous and made laws.

The old people, who had grown up in constant hostility, would not hear of any novelties, and when the adherents of the new worship grew more and more numerous, they retreated to remote districts. These conservatives were called Chipulumba; they were finally pursued by the Sons of Hemp, and many of them killed.

The Bena-Luntu have not as yet adopted the worship of hemp, and are still thorough savages. On the main road between the Cassai and the Luebo one does not notice a higher degree of cultivation among the Bena-Riamba; but, on the contrary, they are insolent, thievish people, though this may be ascribed to the influence of the incessantly passing commercial caravans.

Formerly the country owned a large store of ivory and gum, whose value was then unknown. The Kioque, an itinerant and enterprising nation of commerce and the chase, had repeatedly made futile attempts to make inroads; they first appeared under

TYPES OF THE BASHILANGE

the leadership of Mona Mukanjanga, and, under the influence of hemp-smoking, they cunningly profited by the products of the country.

The first guns were imported. Each man who was fortunate enough to obtain such a weapon, 'chingomma' (*ugomma* is the big kettle-drum), in exchange for an elephant's tusk, was a Mukelenge, i.e. a chief, or at any rate a great man.

The Kioque managed to induce Kassongo, the prince of the Baqua-Kashia, and his brother Mukenge, the present Kalamba-Mukenge, as well as Jingenge and Kabassu-Babu from Jirimba, to follow them into their country, called Jilunga (*Kalunga*, 'great mind'). They returned with guns and many Kioque, and Kassongo was universally acknowledged as the head of all hemp-smokers; when he died, on his second expedition to the Kioques, he was succeeded by Mukenge. Now commenced a pilgrimage of chiefs to the Kioque. They all wished to let themselves be well cheated by them, to buy guns, and to obtain their proper chieftain's commission, mostly by adopting a Kioque name.

Kabassa-Babu had not yet returned from his second journey; Jingenge, however, had, and had brought with him many guns, mostly obtained by extortion. He now renounced Mukenge and became independent, others soon following suit.

The Kioque Mukanjanga was the patron of the new chiefs, and, making a base use of his position, he always enriched himself.

The Bangala, a mixture of Tupende and Kalunda, who had lately released themselves from Portuguese sovereignty, followed the Kioque hither, but only pursued commercial interests. In consequence, great jealousy arose between them and the Kioque, which at first was kept in bounds by the latter, who had to pass through Kassange, the Bangala country, when going with their goods to the sea-board. Soon, however, hostilities broke out among them, and the hatred continued.

The first Portuguese negro at Lubuku (i.e. 'friendship,' as they had called the country of the hemp-smokers) was my present interpreter Kashawalla. He came in 1874, pretended to be a son of the king of the white men, and gave accounts of the latter.

In 1881 Pogge and I arrived, led by Kashawalla. Pogge

was received as Mushangi, i.e. spirit of Kassongo, who had died at Kioque, and I was regarded as that of Kabassu-Babu, which name I have retained to this day.

Gradually the influence of the Kioque disappeared, and ours became paramount. Mukenge followed us as far as Nyangwe. The old Bakelenge—i.e. chief—had had to make room for the hemp-smokers, the latter again for those who had got their licence from the Kioques. Now, after Mukenge had once more accompanied me to explore the Cassai, the acknowledgment of the white man is a sign of being truly entitled to the dignity of chief, and Kalamba-Mukenge, with my support, as well as on account of his great merits, is again raised to be the most powerful prince of the Bashilange. It is to be hoped that this just and comparatively trustworthy negro will long work in this capacity for the benefit of civilisation.

The Bashilange country is more populous in the east than in the west; on an average, I found twenty-six inhabitants to one square kilometre. Thus the sum of the population of the Bashilange is 1,400,000, of whom 560,000 are Bashilamboa, 420,000 Bashilambembele, 280,000 Bashilakassanga, 140,000 Bena-Luntu. While the people formerly used to live in small villages and farms, they now, especially in the Riamba district, live in batches of 1,000 or 1,200; but to this those living in the west and the barbarous Bena-Luntu are an exception.

The country slopes evenly towards the north-west from a height of 880 metres down to 35 metres, and is richly watered. The layer of humus is thicker in the valleys than on the slopes; and on the ridge of the plateau stretching between two watercourses there is found red and sometimes yellow laterite. Towards the north this laterite is spread on horizontally piled soft red sandstone, whose colour is probably caused by the iron which is in it. The northern boundary of the layer of laterite is marked by a range of hills which is especially prominent in the east. The sandstone is laid on Plutonic rocks, granite, and gneiss, which are found on the bottom of many a deep, flowing brook.

Beyond the limit I mentioned, which is wanting in sandstone, the laterite is piled close to the granite or gneiss, as the case may be; the strata of laterite are on the average from 60 to 70 metres thick, which we have proved by repeatedly measuring the slopes near the sources, where they resemble a perpendicularly sloping dark red amphitheatre, ornamented with many crags and pillars.

The northern limit of the sandstone is at a height of between 600 and 700 metres; that of the projecting Plutonic rocks at nearly 500 metres, which naturally forms the line connecting the extreme points of the navigation of the rivers. This line nearly meets the southern limit of the big primæval forests; and, as elephants and buffaloes have retreated into these forests, and the adjoining tribes have no firearms, it has also become a zoological boundary.

If in the Bashilange country all the valleys and ravines of the water-courses could be filled up, it would present one vast plain sloping towards the north-west. The formation of the terrain is exclusively owing to the water; all the peninsulas are thickly wooded, and display a variety of boundary woods, savannahs of grass or trees, &c. The country being so richly watered, a tenth part of the surface at least is covered with primæval forests. From a bird's-eye view, the country would resemble richly-veined marble.

Most tropical plants flourish, chiefly wild, such as sugar, rice, cotton, gum, and palms; so does coffee, which was frequently brought from the forests on the boundaries. Among the still unknown wealth of the flora, I only make mention of some trees which bear excellent oil fruits and dye-wood. The forests abound in timber and trees of splendid colours and perfume.

The Bashilange grow all the African produce of a field that I know of, and since our journey to Nyangwe they also grow rice. Tobacco, if well cultivated, will flourish. Besides pine-apples, bananas, and plantains, the melon tree, pease tree, the fruits of the passion flower, and the lemon tree have been imported and successfully cultivated, as also have onions and tomatoes. Lettuce, radishes, carrots, and kohlrabi will grow excellently, and many other vegetables would be sure to thrive if the seeds were frequently renewed.

All the water-courses flow on white sandy ground, carrying along thin scales of mica. The water is mostly good and cool, on account of constant shade; the rivers are not particularly well stocked with fish, probably owing to their sandy and, in the north, stony beds.

Of huntable game I only mention the *Tragelaphus scriptus* and the Red River pig; elephants and buffaloes have moved to the north; the beasts of prey are represented by leopards, lynxes, and many species of wild cats. The striped wolf and the jackal are rare, while the lion and hyæna are almost entirely absent. The primæval forests house but few monkeys, but abound in many specimens of Rodentia, which play a chief part in the *menu* of the Mushilange.

The rivers are still alive with hippopotami and crocodiles, which, contrary to the often-told fable, live peacefully together. The former are slowly, but surely, going to destruction, for the huge pachydermata must at last succumb to the number of iron shots with which they are pursued by those of their neighbours who are in possession of guns. In the third part of a hippopotamus which I once shot in the Lulua were eight iron balls. The remaining two-thirds were at night dragged into the deep by crocodiles.

The part of Africa known to me does not abound in birds. The extensive fields of millet and maize are often frequented by pigeons, guinea and savannah fowls; for water birds and waders there is no suitable abode here, as all the water-courses run far inland. The grey parrot, the carythaix, and rhinoceros bird, live in the boundary forests; the night raven in open districts; the vulture angolensis, in palm groves near rivers, while the carrion buzzard is found everywhere. Red, yellow, and grey weavers are plentiful; the latter takes here the place of our sparrow.

Venomous snakes are very frequent, especially the puff-adder. Many accidents have been caused by them. In building Luluaburg station twenty-six venomous snakes were encountered in a terrain 300 metres in diameter; six people were bitten, but their lives were saved.

Of the inferior animals. I only mention the termites, which bore through every laterite ground. These insects render house-building very difficult, unless one knows the kind of timber which they leave untouched; while they scarcely ever do any harm to garden and field produce.

The cattle imported, besides the native domestic animals, the European dogs, Turkish ducks, pigeons, and the superior species of fowls, thrive well, and increase most wonderfully. By temporarily scorching the grass, a good pasture-ground may always be procured for cattle. The northern boundary of the primæval forest will here also become a limit to the spreading of cattle, as large buffalo blue-bottles (not the tsetse fly, which is not found here) will soon kill the animals, as the most northern Bashilange have experienced, to their great loss.

The Bashilange, endeavouring as they do to adopt everything connected with civilisation, to imitate, nay to ape, whatever they can, will become civilised sooner than any other African tribe I know. What a change has come about in these people during the last ten years!

Contrary to all surrounding nations, they will travel with white men as convoys or to carry easy loads. They have adopted the cultivation of rice, and enlarged the stock of their domestic animals; they have abandoned many evil habits, as the ordeal drink; they have burnt their idols, and abrogated the penalty of death; they manufacture strong cloths with pretty patterns from the *Raphia vinifera*; they are not only able to improve their guns, but to fabricate every part of them excepting the barrel. They have even commenced to build two-storied clay houses; they try all they can to dress in the European fashion, to construct tables and arm-chairs, to eat with knives and forks off a plate; they ride bulls, and make use of the *tipoia* (a hammock for carrying), though of course only the chiefs are allowed this luxury.

A great drawback is that the Bashilange man is not accustomed to work, and that the woman was, and still is, only a slave who has to do all the work in field and house; while the man will only manufacture cloth or go hunting, but principally smoke hemp and talk with incredible fluency. He is, therefore, not at all inclined to regular work, and thus there is always a difficulty in persuading the people in the village belonging to the station to work half a yard of stuff daily.

When these people first made the acquaintance of black traders, there was still a rich abundance of ivory, and all the necessaries of life were easily procured; afterwards women, and even their own children, were sold; this, however, is fortunately now greatly on the wane, and is even prohibited by some chiefs. Gum was soon produced, though in quite a primitive way, but the yield was good; prices have now been raised, on account of the decrease of the caoutchouc liana.

Want increases, however, in the same degree as the easy mode of satisfying it decreases. Short trading expeditions are undertaken to the north, and in the east the slaves are bought of the Baluba, who suffer from over-population, in order to sell them to the Kioque and Bangala.

But as soon as European houses of business are settled here, with which 'the Dutch house at Banana' will make a start before long; when slaves are no longer sold, when gum is not forthcoming, and when ivory shall have disappeared in the adjoining countries, then real work will be commenced, for, from the progress noted above, one may with some certainty infer a final approach to civilisation.

I hope that I may live to see this last step of a people in the midst of whom and with whom I have worked for six years; this will surely be my greatest reward for a time full of care, privations, frequent disappointments and difficulties, though also of success.

INDEX

Abed, Sheik, 198, 221, 224, 225
Akaniaru Lake, 252
Akauanda, 104
Albert Lake, 236, 241
Anderson, 83
Angola, 66, 74, 91, 129, 136, 145, 229, 273, 276, 300, 302, 304
Aruvimi, 241

Ba-people, 76
Babecki, 55
Babenge, 55
Backashocko, 163
Badinga, 29, 30
Badingo, 163
Bain, Mr., 274, 275
Bajaia, 55
Bakete, 39, 60, 103, 104, 154
Bakuba, 34, 41, 42, 46, 60, 71, 108, 129, 149, 153, 154
Bakundu, 55
Bakutu, 27
Balonda, 169
Baluba, 2, 3, 6, 30, 36, 45, 48, 55, 82, 104–107, 109–115, 117, 121–127, 140–143, 146, 159, 165, 180, 190, 202, 216, 222, 229, 239, 244, 253, 254, 261, 307, 308, 310
Balunbangando, 54
Balungu, 85, 86, 91, 102, 103, 116, 121, 128, 190
Bambue, 303
Banana, 3, 318

Banbangala, 55
Bandawe, 287
Bangala, 55, 135, 232, 313
Bangodi, 27, 28
Bangueolo Lake, 106, 107, 271
Bankutu, 42, 54, 55
Bantu, 176, 307
Baqua-people: Baqua-Kash, *vide* Kash, &c.
Barumbe, 55
Bashi-people: Bashi-Bombo, *vide* Bombo, &c.
Bashilakassanga, 310–312, 314
Bashilambembele, 310–312, 314
Bashilamboa, 96, 97, 310–312, 314
Bashilange, 39, 55, 60, 61, 62, 64, 71, 78, 99, 100, 102–104, 106, 108, 109, 117, 121–123, 127, 130, 133, 135, 139, 140, 146, 149, 150, 154, 158, 165, 168, 170–172, 175, 187, 188, 191, 192, 202–204, 207, 211, 213, 214, 216–220, 223, 226–229, 271, 301, 302, 304, 306–318
Bashobe, 27
Basselle-Kungu, 51
Bassongo, 44, 45, 48, 51, 149, 157, 159, 162, 163, 172, 178, 180, 188–192, 197, 303, 304, 308
Bassongo-Mino, 3, 24, 27, 41, 42, 54, 55, 154, 172, 308
Bateke, 12
Bateman, 6, 39, 60, 61, 74, 101, 129, 137

BAT

Batempa, 162
Batetela, 51, 53, 157, 163, 169, 180, 222
Batondoi, 46
Batua, 55, 73, 157, 159, 163, 165-167, 241
Bayanzi, 43
Bayenga, 55
Belande, 185, 190, 200
Bena—sons : Bena - Luntu, *vide* Luntu, &c.
Benecki, 180, 181, 185, 190, 192, 193
Benguela, 145
Betundu, 163, 168, 169
Bihé People, 116, 145, 148, 190
Bilolo, 190
Bississi, 267
Blantyre, 226
Boehm, Dr., 240
Boma, 4
Bombo, 76
Bondo, 55
Bonshina, 55
Botecka, 55
Bubila (Lubila), 304
Bugslag, shipwright, 3, 7, 36, 39, 55, 61, 63-66, 84, 85, 87, 137, 139, 151, 165, 173-175, 192, 205, 207, 211, 214, 226, 229, 234, 237, 252, 254, 258, 262, 266, 278, 284-286, 291, 292, 294, 295, 298, 300
Bushi-Maji, 112, 114, 115, 123, 127
Bussindi, Bena, 241
Butoto, 42
Bwana Zefu, *vide* Zefu

CAMERON, Lieutenant, 52, 85, 116, 221, 233
Cardoso, Lieutenant, 295
Carvalho, 71, 83
Cassabi, 5
Cassai, 4-6, 10-13, 17, 19, 20, 22,

EQU

24, 28, 30-32, 34, 36, 37-42, 56, 58, 59, 61, 64, 70, 74-76, 85, 97, 100, 107, 136, 137, 147, 155, 156, 308, 312, 314
Castilho, Agosto de, 300
Chambese, 271
Chameta, Baqua, 144
Chia, Baqua, 128
Chikapa, 80
Chikulla, Bena, 148
Chilunga Messo, 90
Chimbao, 99
Chingenge, 39, 86, 95, 113, 138, 142, 144, 302
Chipulumba, 71, 72, 89, 97, 139, 312
Chirilu, 72
Chirimba, 87
Chitari, 87
Chupanga, 298
Coango, 220
Congo, 4, 6, 11, 13, 43, 52, 54, 60, 64, 66, 78, 86, 100, 107, 116, 136, 148, 159, 192, 202, 208, 209, 222, 223, 227, 229, 236, 239-242, 252, 273, 301, 306
Congo Railway, 21
Congo State, 2, 60, 83, 87, 100, 120, 129, 187, 192, 230, 251, 260, 261

DAHOMEY, 36, 57
Dean, Lieutenant, 232
Dibue, 200
Dikonga dia Difuma, 309
Disho (Dishu), Baqua, 112, 124
Dongenfuro, 55
Dongonsoro, 55
Drommeau, Missionary, 261

EMIN BEY, 236, 250
'En Avant,' steamer, 7, 34, 38, 39, 41, 49, 54, 55, 56, 59, 150
Equator station, 6

FAM

FAMBA (Juma bin Salim, Juma Merikani), 46, 116, 183, 185, 190, 200, 221, 223, 227, 228, 230, 232, 233, 235
Felsen, Van der, 39, 59
Fickerini, 198, 223, 235, 268, 271, 292, 300
François, Von, 3, 104, 107, 128
Fumo Nkolle, 153

GALULA, 261, 262
Gapetch, 42
Germano, 85, 86, 91, 99, 126, 129, 131, 135-137
Giesecke, 232, 269
Ginga, 90, 302
Goi Capopa, 301
Grenfell, missionary, 6, 13, 19, 23, 26, 61
Greshoff, 10, 13, 19, 61

HALFAN, 224
Hamed bin Mohammet, vide Tibbu Tibb
Haussa, 232
Horn, missionary, 239, 249, 250, 253, 254, 261, 264
Humba, 113, 115, 136, 137, 150, 196, 223

IKALANGA, 55
Ikongo, Bena, 153
'Ilala,' steamer, 280, 282, 287
Ilindi, 238
Ilunga Mputt, 50, 154, 302

JANSEN, 3
Jettchen, terrier, 292
Jileta, Bena, 153
Jilunga, 313
Jingenge, vide Chingenge

KAN

Jiniama, vide Kassongo Jiniama
Jionga, Bena, 99
Jirimba, 313
Jongolata, 44
Joshomo, 55
Josso, 302
Joubert, 259, 260
Jukissi, 19
Juma Merikani, Juma bin Salim, vide Famba
Junker, Dr., 79, 251

KABA REGA, 251
Kabamba, Kawanba, vide Kitenge
Kabao, 145
Kabassu Babo, 314; the negroes' appellation for Von Wissmann
Kabogo, Cape, 252
Kaffirs, 107
Kafungoi, 181
Kahunda, 269, 270
Kajembe, 302
Kajinga, Baqua, 143
Kakesa, Mona, 162, 180, 185, 189, 200, 305
Kalamba, 36, 38, 39, 58, 62, 84, 86-89, 91, 129, 131-134, 137, 313, 315
Kalamba Moana, 69, 87, 91, 94, 99, 105, 122, 133, 137
Kalambai, 302
Kalambarre, 240
Kalebue, Bena, 183, 195, 198-200, 303
Kalonda (Arabs), 241
Kalosh, 107-109, 111 113, 116 118, 120, 122, 125 127
Kalui, 210, 211
Kalunda, 141, 313
Kambulu, Baqua, 87
Kamerondo, 116, 192, 235
Kangombe, 116
Kangonde Fall, 97
Kanjika, Mona, 116, 309

Y

KAN

Kanjoka, Baqua, 105
Kapua, Bena, 212
Kapussu Chimbundu, 70
Karema, 261
Karonga, 280-282
Kasairi, Bena, 306
Kasairi, Pambu, 106, 109, 111, 124
Kash, Baqua, 72
Kashama, 109, 125, 126
Kashawalla, interpreter, 115, 158, 208, 219, 301, 303, 313
Kashia, Baqua, 61, 107, 313
Kashimbi, 303
Kassanga, 55
Kassango, 85, 313
Kassassu, Baqua, 129
Kassia, 302
Kassonga Lushia, 222
Kassongo, Mona, 180
Kassongo, Tibbu Tibb's residence, 224, 228, 230, 232, 233, 237, 313
Kassongo Chiniama, 85, 86, 91, 103, 115, 126, 129, 190
Kassongo Luaba, 105, 127
Katana, Baqua, 306, 311
Katanga, 106, 116, 269
Kataraija, 113
Katchich, 158, 160
Katende, 70, 97, 146, 155, 302, 309
Kattunga, 291
Kawala, 247, 248, 252-254, 258
Kawamba Kitenge, *vide* Kitenge
Kiagongo, 170
Kialo, Mona, 303-305
Kiepert, 304
Kifussa, 186
Kiila, 266
Kikassa, 79
Kilembue, 217
Kilimane, *vide* Quilimane
Kilunga Mosso, 105
Kilwa, 272, 285, 287
Kintu a Mushinuba, 193

LOK

Kioque, 62, 85, 91, 94, 95, 133, 135, 137, 312-314
Kishi Maji, *vide* Bushi Maji
Kisuaheli, *vide* Suaheli
Kitenge (Kawamba), 217-219, 222, 227, 235, 301, 302
Kitimbue, 268
Kitimkuru, 272
Kiwu, Lake, 252
Koango, *vide* Coango
Kole, 55
Konde, 281
Kongolo Mosh, 89
Kotto, Bena, 45
Krupp, Friedrich, 59
Ku-Mapenge, 303
Kund, 4, 17, 24-26
Kussu, Bena, 87

Laetushu, 51
Lagongo, 200
Lamboa, Bashi, *vide* Bashilamboa
Landeau, missionary, 259
Larson, Mr., 247
Latte, De, 83
Leal, 297
Lebue, 28
Lefini, 11
Le Marinel, *vide* Marinel
Lenz, Dr., 198
Leopold, Lake, 17
Leopoldville, 6, 10, 100
Lindi, 272, 285, 287
Livingstone, 5; grave of his wife, 297
Livingstonia, 287
Loanda, 300
Loange, 31, 273
Lobbo, river, 170
Loka, 5
Lokassu, 99
Loko, 5
Lokodi, 55

INDEX

LOM

Lomami, 17, 51, 52, 54, 55, 79, 116, 157, 162, 168, 169, 183, 187, 193, 206, 208 210, 230, 236, 301, 302
Lors, Dr., 287
Lowira (Lowiri), 278
Lua, 18
Lualaba, *vide* Congo
Luamo, 239
Lubefu, 178, 186, 204, 304
Lubi, 45, 48, 50, 103, 107, 148, 149, 154, 156, 301, 303, 305
Lubila, *vide* Bubila
Lubilanshi (Lubilashi), river, 103
Lubilash, *vide* Sankurru
Lubilasha, 127
Lubiranzi, 115, 125
Lubowa, Bena, 220
Lubudi, 129, 140, 305
Lubuku, 58, 64, 86, 87, 91, 94, 96, 129, 133 135, 144, 301, 302, 305
Luebo, 7, 10, 36, 40, 56, 59, 82, 135, 312
Luebo Station, 7, 37-39, 56, 58, 59, 63, 64, 73, 83, 86, 136, 137, 145
Lufubu, 301
Lufuku, 259
Lufuwu, 264
Luidi, 169
Luilu, 115, 121
Lukalla, 107, 125, 156, 157
Lukassi (Lukashi, Lukassia), 194, 196, 201, 204, 206, 209, 221, 302
Lukenja, 17, 26, 43, 44, 50
Lukoba, Bena, 141
Lukuga, 255, 256
Lulua, 7, 35, 38, 55-61, 70, 71, 73 -75, 82, 83, 89, 91, 97, 99, 101, 103, 134, 138, 145, 154, 219, 305
Lulua, Bena, 306
Luluaburg, 7, 35-37, 39, 56, 58, 61-63, 66, 70, 84-88, 94, 127, 129, 132, 134, 136-138, 145, 301, 305, 316
Lulumba Fall, 96, 97
Lunangua, 264

MIR

Lunda, 85, 86, 104, 106-108, 116
Luntu, Bena, 308, 310, 312, 414
Lupungu, Mona, 162, 180, 185, 186, 188, 189, 191, 192, 200, 201, 301- 303, 305
Luquengo, 71, 130
Lurimbi, 193
Lushiko, 31
Lussabi Baqua, 139
Lussambo, Bena, 50, 148, 154-158
Lussana, 222
Lussuna, 200
Luvo, 77, 80
Luwulla, Bena, 148

Macar, De, Captain, 6, 83, 92, 95, 97, 112, 117, 126, 137, 145, 302
Madeira, 2, 3, 8, 37
Makenge, 302
Malagarassi, 253, 255
Malange, 85
Malela, 222
Mambesi, 265
Mambue, 270
Mandala, 290, 291, 293, 295
Manyema, 233, 308
Mapensa, 267
Marinel, Le, Lieutenant, 6, 53, 83, 94, 130, 135, 137, 151, 158, 159, 171, 173-176, 181, 188, 192, 202, 205, 207, 213, 214, 218, 225, 226, 228, 229, 236, 301, 305
Marungu, 265
Matadi, 4
Mbala, Bena, 71
Mbimbi Mukash, 78
Mbimbi Mulume, 78
Mbuju, Baqua, 311
Meta, Bena, 311
Mfini Lukenja, 17, 43
Mikindani, 272, 287
Milambo, 302, 303
Mirambo, 221, 225

MIR

Mirambo, Arab from the Nyassa, 280
Mitamba, 244, 252
Moadi, 223, 301
Moamba Mputt, 312
Moanga, Bena, 139
Moansangomma, 71, 129, 138
Moero Lake, 235
Mohammed bin Halfan, 250
Mohammed bin Kassim, 238
Moiio, 101
Moina, 302
Mona, singular of Bena — Master; Mona Kakesa, vide Kakesa, &c.
Mona Bena, 170, 172–178, 180
Mozambique, 300
Mpala, 259
Msiri, 269
Mtoa, 246
Mu, singular of Ba
Muata Jamwo, 85, 106, 107, 116
Mubangi, 20
Mudinga, vide Badinga
Muicau, 58, 70, 85, 136
Muini Muharra, 184
Mukamba Lake, 141
Mukanjanga, 94, 312
Mukash, 78
Mukeba, 149
Mukendi, Baqua, 115, 117, 120
Mukenge, vide Kalamba
Mukenge, 128
Mukete, singular of Bakete
Mukubu Forest, 152
Mulenda, Baqua, 128
Müller, 'Forstreferendar,' 3
Mulume, 78
Mulume, Baqua, 311
Municama, 270
Muqua, singular of Baqua
Mushié, 17
Mussongai, 193
Mutomba, 154, 157, 158
Mutope, 289
Mwena Wanda, 274

QUA

Nasorro bin Zef, 250
Ndongo, 55
Ngana Mukanjanga, Mona, 94, 312
Ngongo, Bena, 49, 149 155, 160
Nguo, Bena, 217
Nimptsch, Von, 10, 13, 61
Niumkorlo, 265
Nkole, 55
Nsadi, 5
Nsaire, Nsairi, 5
Nsali Monene, 5
Nshale, Nshale-Mele, 5
Nunsua, 265
Nyangwe, 46, 79, 184, 192, 198, 200, 202, 218, 221–224, 228, 233, 237, 293, 301, 315
Nyassa, 250, 251, 264, 265, 272, 273, 279–285, 287, 288

Oswald, 300
Oto, 54

Pallaballa, 4
Pamolondo, 288
Panga, Bashi, 306
'Paul Pogge,' iron boat, 70, 74, 80
'Peace,' steamer, 6, 10–12, 19, 33, 56, 59, 61
Peshi, Baqua, 193, 303
Peters, Dr., 300
Piari, Kai, 169
Pogge, Dr., 45, 46, 49, 50, 54, 64, 70, 94, 97, 101, 107, 116, 135, 138, 148, 149, 153, 160, 169 181, 198, 229, 301, 302, 313
Pogge, Mount, 21, 24, 26
Pogge Fall, 78–80
Putt, Baqua, 146, 149

Qua, 5, 12
Quamouth, 6, 11, 12
Quango, 19, 20, 25, 32

INDEX

QUA

Quaqua, 298
Quilimane, 291, 298, 299
Quilu, 26
Quitundu, 163

Rashid, 240
Reichardt, 240, 268
Riamba, Bena, 101, 139, 306, 312
Riqua, Lake, 270, 271
Rostock, 299
Rugu Rugu, 268
Ruhega, 257
Ruqua Lake, 270

Sahorro, 223, 226
Said, 194, 196-203, 210, 221, 222, 302
Said Bargash, 224, 250, 268
Said bin Habibu, 239
Saise, 270
Sala, Bena, 206
Sala-Mbi (Quango), 19
Sali Lebue, 28
Sali Temboa, 31
Samba, Bena, 223
Sangula Meta, 39, 64, 69, 87, 137, 144
Sankurru, Von Wissmann's manservant, 113, 225
Sankurru-Lubilash, 4, 5, 17, 34, 36, 37, 39-41, 45, 46, 52, 55, 78, 86, 103, 112, 115, 127, 141, 148, 153-156, 158 160, 162, 163, 168, 183, 185, 186, 190, 193, 211, 230, 303, 304
Saturnino, 58, 65, 71, 83, 127
Schneider, gunsmith, 3, 34, 39, 52, 54, 59, 61
Schweinfurth, 79
Schwerin, Von, Professor, 83
Sekelai, Baqua, 143
Shankolle, 5
Shari, 5

UEM

Shiré, 251, 288, 291, 295-298
Sicke, 251
Simão, 113, 136, 137, 150, 151, 169
Sommers, Dr., 136, 302
Soudan, 185
Stanley, 17, 146, 241, 252, 256
'Stanley,' steamer, 35, 38, 58, 82-85
Stanley Falls, 78, 202, 220, 221, 223, 231, 235, 236, 244, 250
Stanley Pool, 4, 6, 7, 21, 35, 37, 38, 52, 61, 78, 100
Stehlmann, 83
Stephenson's Road, 279
Storms, Captain, 260
Suaheli, 46, 200, 225

Tabora, 184, 218, 232, 238, 246, 250, 251
Tambai, 193
Tanga, 272
Tanganyika, 61, 107, 230, 232, 235, 236, 239-242, 247, 250 253, 255-258, 261, 266-268, 271, 272, 279-283, 285, 308
Tappenbeck, 4, 6, 17, 24, 25
Taylor, Bishop, 136
Temba, 43
Tembo, Baqua, 112
Temboa, 31
Tenda, 105, 106, 111, 122, 126, 127
Tibbu Tibb (Hamed bin Mohammed), 46, 162, 180, 183, 184, 187, 190, 194-198, 200, 205, 209, 210, 217-220, 224 228, 230-233, 235, 251, 252, 269, 270
Togo Country, 36
Tshingenge, *vide* Chingenge
Tubindi (Tubintsh), 104
Tupende, 80, 135, 313
Tushilange, 306

Ubujive, 240, 241, 247, 308
Uemba, 272

UGA

Uganda, 233
Ugogo, 121
Ujiji, 184, 236, 239, 246, 247, 249, 250, 252, 256
Uniamwesi, 221, 308
Unianjembe, 269
Unioro, 251

Vivy, 4

Wabuma, 14, 16
Wagenie, 223
Wajiji, 256-258, 268
Wakonde, 275, 278, 279, 281
Wakussu, 222
Walker, 83
Wanfumu, 12, 14
Wanyamwesi, 46, 268
Wapambue, Bena, 159
Wasi Malungu, Bena, 241
Wasongora, 159, 222
Wasongora Mino, 251
Wassonga, 159
Wawemba, 271–275, 285

ZUL

Wawiwa, 275
Wayanzi, 12
Winton, Sir Francis de, 3
Wissmann Fall, 80, 82
Wissmann Pool, 20, 22
Witanda, Bena, 102
Wolf, Dr., Staff Physician, 3, 6, 22, 34–59, 61, 62, 65, 70, 71, 73, 74, 79, 80, 82–84, 100, 101, 129, 130, 146, 148, 150, 153, 154, 157, 304

Yehka, Bena, 53, 54

Zambesi, 251, 273, 282, 290, 296, 298
Zanzibar, Zanzibaris, 74, 76, 81, 136, 186, 187, 197, 198, 218, 226, 232, 235, 300
Zappu Mutapo, 303
Zappu Zapp, 46–48, 162, 167, 185, 186, 303, 304
Zappu Zapp (Bena Mona), 172
Zefu, 221, 224-227, 230, 235–239
Zulu, 281